Praise for *Bending Toward the Sun*

P9-CDL-704

"Intimately told. . . . Emotionally rich. . . . The book touches on intriguing descriptions of research into how trauma may be passed on, including the theory that fearful memories could be transmitted generationally through biochemistry. *Bending Toward the Sun*, in which the expected push-and-pull of the mother-daughter relationship is warped by brutal history, illuminates both the strength and fragility of that bond and of the human spirit."   —Associated Press

"*Bending Toward the Sun* is a captivating memoir that explores a complicated, loving, and enduring mother-daughter bond, and reveals how doubts, hopes, and dreams are handed down from generation to generation. As both a mother and a daughter, I found it deeply touching."
—Arianna Huffington, author, syndicated columnist,
and founder of *The Huffington Post*

"[An] affecting memoir. . . . Vivid. . . . Riveting. . . . An amazing story of wartime survival."   —*Kirkus Reviews*

"[Rita Lurie and Leslie Gilbert-Lurie's] stories are told, each in her own voice, in this fascinating memoir. The women's personal stories are both compelling; Gilbert-Lurie was behind many of the most popular TV shows of recent years, and she knows how to tell a story."
—*Booklist*

"*Bending Toward the Sun* is like a great episode of *Law & Order*—a riveting story where the stakes are life and death, insoluble moral dilemmas and an ending that is both upsetting and uplifting. Bolstered by writing that is compelling and sensitive, the book transcends the Holocaust genre with its multigenerational point of view on the ultimate effect of fear and evil on young minds."

—Dick Wolf, Emmy Award–winning creator
and executive producer of *Law & Order*;
Law & Order: Special Victims Unit; and *Law & Order: Criminal Intent*

"Here is a memoir that takes us through many worlds, through heartache and noble hopes, through the mysteries of family love and toward a beautiful, light-filled conclusion. Read *Bending Toward the Sun* and enrich your life."

—Rabbi David Wolpe, author of *Why Faith Matters*
and *Making Loss Matter: Creating Meaning in Difficult Times*

"This book is heartbreaking yet inspiring, a story told by three generations—the grandmother, who is a child survivor, the mother, a successful American professional, and the daughter, full of talent, promise, and hope. At its core, this book is a study of how the Holocaust experience wraps itself around each woman—creating extreme fear of separation, setting off depression, filling mind and memory with haunting evil and indefinable ghosts. Yet it also tells us of hardwon wisdom for living distilled from pain and loss, of life force driven by the will to overcome suffering, of Jewishness lost and Jewishness reborn, of unquenchable love—all passed on and shared between the generations through the filter of the Holocaust. Gripping, exhausting, exciting, devastating—this book is at times hard to read but always impossible to put down."

—Rabbi Irving Greenberg, founding president,
Jewish Life Network; former chairman of
the United States Holocaust Memorial Museum

"Powerful. . . . Rita's story is one of inspiration. . . . It does shed light on the toll that the Holocaust had on millions of Jewish families. Rita's story is an important one that must be shared."   —BookLoons.com

About the Author

A writer, lawyer, and former executive at NBC, LESLIE GILBERT-LURIE is a member and former president of the Los Angeles County Board of Education and a teacher of Holocaust studies. A founding board member and past president of the nonprofit Alliance for Children's Rights, she has worked at a major Los Angeles law firm, served as a Ninth Circuit Court of Appeals law clerk, and is a member of the board of directors for several nonprofit organizations, including the Los Angeles Music Center. Leslie is a recipient of the American Jewish Congress's Tzedek Award for Outstanding Commitment to Civil Rights, Civil Liberties, and Justice, and the Alliance for Children's Rights Child Advocate of the Year Award. She is also an honoree of the organization Facing History and Ourselves for her work as an author, educator, and child advocate. She lives in Los Angeles, California, with her husband, two children, and stepson.

Bending Toward the Sun

A Mother and Daughter Memoir

LESLIE GILBERT-LURIE

with Rita Lurie

HARPER PERENNIAL

NEW YORK • LONDON • TORONTO • SYDNEY • NEW DELHI • AUCKLAND

RITA'S DEDICATION

In memory of my mother. Not a day goes by without my remembering her.

In memory of my father, who did the best he could for as long as he could.

In memory of my brother and all those members of my family
who lost their lives during the Holocaust.
My heart goes out to them.

LESLIE'S DEDICATION

For Mom

HARPER ● PERENNIAL

FIRST HARPER PERENNIAL EDITION PUBLISHED 2010.

Designed by Cassandra J. Pappas
Photo editor: Christopher Gilbert

Library of Congress Cataloging-in-Publication Data is available
upon request.

ISBN 978-0-06-177672-4

10 11 12 13 14   ID/RRD   10 9 8 7 6 5 4 3 2 1

Contents

Prologue   1

PART I   IN MOM'S VOICE (1937—1960)
  1   Childhood, Interrupted   11
  2   Stashik Is Coming   27
  3   Safe for the Moment   34
  4   Where Is God?   45
  5   Far from Normal   52
  6   Good-bye Urzejowice   61
  7   *Una Situazione Molto Grave*   72
  8   A Taste of Freedom   80
  9   The Greenhorns   92
  10 But We Just Got Used to It Here   101
  11 Utterly Demoralized   114
  12 I Might Even Marry Him   128
  13 A Wonderful Mother   143

PART II   MY OWN VOICE (1960—1997)
  14 On My Watch   157
  15 Bread Crumbs   163
  16 Magical Distractions   170

17	I Do Understand	175
18	Sunday Inquisitions	179
19	Time to Say "I Love You"	186
20	A Word Game	193
21	Society of Overachieving Offspring of Holocaust Survivors	199
22	Team Leah	207
23	"Just Jump"	216
24	It's Not That Kind of Thing	225
25	Inside NBC	231
26	The Most Beautiful Woman in the Attic	237
27	Water Your Garden	259
28	The Present I Needed to Appreciate	269

PART III   A JOINT VENTURE (1997–2008)

29	Maybe I Should Write It	283
30	Feelings of a Deprived Child	301
31	I Tried My Best	307
32	Ma of the Grand	315
33	A Deluxe Buffet	321
34	Mikaela: Different from Other Kids My Age	328
35	Rita: Lessons to Be Learned	333
36	The Abyss	337
37	Legacy	347

| | Acknowledgments | 353 |

Bending Toward
the Sun

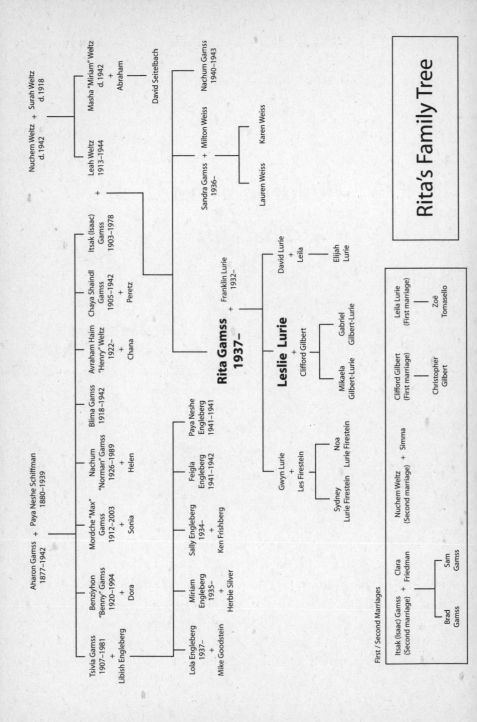

Rita's Family Tree

Prologue

"MOMMY, I WAS afraid that you died."

"I didn't die. Sleeping. I *was* sleeping." Holding my cell phone, I propped myself up on the pillow and regained my bearings. I was in an elegant hotel room in Washington, D.C. Judging from the burning sensation in my eyes, I had not been asleep for long.

"I was so worried when you didn't answer the phone." My daughter's small voice trembled.

"I answered the phone, honey. We're talking."

"Not until the fourth ring."

Her sadness and the demands I knew were soon to follow sent blood rushing to my temples. "Mikaela, I'm fine."

"I can't stay here, Mommy."

I took a deep breath and thought fast. My voice softened. "I just dropped you off a few hours ago. We talked about the fact that the first night might be an adjustment. What did you do this evening?"

"Nothing. I didn't eat. I just cried."

She was in Bethesda, about twenty minutes away. "Honey, it was a big honor to be chosen for this leadership conference. You were so excited about going, you have a good friend there, you'll learn all about government, and—"

"Mommy, please! Take me home! I'm only eleven years old, and I'm not ready for this. *Please*."

"Mikaela, you *are* ready. You'll be so proud of yourself for sticking it out. What do you want to bet you'll love it there by the end of the five days?"

She was sobbing now. "I won't. I hate it! I don't even feel like myself here. I'm hiding in the bathroom so I don't wake up my roommates, worrying that you're going to die!"

"I'm not going to die. Not for fifty more years at least."

"You don't know that for sure."

I was afraid she would say that. "You're right. But I eat healthy foods, I exercise, I wear sunscreen, and I don't drink and drive, so I should live for a very long time, right?"

"Can you at least come over here to give me a hug goodnight?"

It's a trap. She'll never let me leave without her. If I had just flown out of town this afternoon, we would not be having this negotiation. "It won't help, sweetie. You'll just miss me more if you see me." By now my head was aching.

"I won't. I swear."

I was not surprised by her determination, but I held firm. "No."

"You just don't understand," she said angrily.

"Yes, I do." I did understand. She was in pain, a kind with which I was all too familiar, and I could alleviate her anxiety just by jumping into a taxi. But it would be a mistake. Even though she had always been apprehensive about being away from me, she had made significant strides as of late. She'd been nervous about a recent two-night class trip to northern California, but had gone anyway and had ended up having a great time. I was certain that this new adventure would also surprise her, and provide further evidence that she could survive without me. After all, she was a survivor. She came by that honestly.

I GREW UP in 1960s suburban Los Angeles, part of a family that was living the American Dream. My parents raised my siblings and me in a friendly, safe, and well-kept community. Every home on the block and every kid looked more or less the same, with a smattering of ethnic diversity to break the monotony. I loved sports, especially baseball, made friends easily enough, and was a good student. My family ate dinner together nearly every night and took occasional vacations, much like the other families we knew.

Yet some things were different in our family. My mother believed that I could be president of the United States, but she hoped I could make the leap to high office directly from my cozy bedroom, where she knew I was safe. My mother didn't like me to smile at strangers, play outside after dusk, visit friends whose parents weren't nurturing enough, and most importantly, be far away from her. While I occasionally bristled at these restrictions, I lived by them. I knew that my mother's fears were birthed by tragedy. She carried wounds whose power I could never comprehend.

My mother's past bears eerie similarities to Anne Frank's. Both my mother and Anne Frank spent two years in hiding during the Holocaust, from 1942 to 1944, while the Nazis searched for them. Both managed to live in an attic with their families, which was highly unusual. Jewish children were rarely able to hide with their families, and typically, hidden Jews spent only a short time in any one place. My mother and Anne Frank both were kept alive, in large part, because of the courage and kindness of non-Jewish friends. In my mother's case, a Polish farmer and his wife sheltered a bewildered five-year-old girl and fourteen members of her family, including an infant.

Numerous comparisons can be made between my mother's and Anne Frank's experiences. But my mother was fortunate enough to survive. For decades, readers have wondered what Anne Frank might have become, had *she* lived. My mother's coming-of-age story may provide some indirect insight, and shed light on the long-term impact of the Holocaust, and other tragedies, on the children involved.

I've begun this book with my mother's story. Her memories from early childhood are unusually detailed, although surely idealized at times. I've taken some creative liberties in reconstructing dialogue, but always with an eye toward accurately reflecting the spirit of the conversations my mother recalled, and the manner in which she remembered family members speaking to one another. In addition to relying solely on the memory of my mother, I also interviewed six other relatives who hid with her in the attic.

I will never forget the evening my mother and I spent in the living room of her first cousin Sally. Four women, all in their sixties, who had hidden together in an attic as young children, a half century earlier, were sharing recollections. Given how rare it was for children to survive the Holocaust, such a family reunion was remarkable. And then there was my mother's eighty-six-year-old uncle, Max. He had never wanted to share his memories, but that evening, he found himself leading the discussion.

Where most Holocaust narratives conclude, this one gathers momentum. Some of my mother's most unsettling recollections stemmed from the period right after Germany surrendered to Allied forces during World War II. My mother's story illuminates the fallout of the Holocaust as her family wandered throughout Europe for five heartbreaking years before coming to America. Her spirit, deep faith, and endurance against all odds provide powerful—and inspiring—evidence of the resilience of the human spirit.

IN THE SECOND and third parts of this book, my mother's story becomes our joint account, narrated in my voice, and eventually includes my daughter, Mikaela. The stories of three generations merge in these pages, just as our hopes and dreams have so often in my life. Although my mother's and my experiences bear virtually no similarity, it is in the overlapping shadows that we find common ground. My mother's traumas became my nightmares. Not a day went by in balmy Los Angeles that I didn't feel lashed by what she suffered through in Poland during the war. On the other hand, my mother's hopes and aspirations also sowed the seeds for my ambition and my achievements.

Over countless breakfasts as a child I asked my mother the same questions about her past—the few that I knew to ask. What was it like to wake up that morning and see tanks outside your house? What did you eat inside the attic? Did you have meals with your mommy and daddy when you were hiding? If the answers could ever make sense to me, I believed, my world would finally feel safe. It wasn't until some thirty-odd years later, after I traveled back to Poland to meet the family who hid my mother, to sit in the attic where her childhood disappeared like an ice cube on a feverish brow, and then spent nearly a decade writing this book, that I finally began to understand where my mother came from and how her experiences transformed her.

Once I had gotten that far, I felt emboldened to seek more answers. I researched further in hopes of discovering just how the trauma of my mother's past had been transmitted to me, and then to my children. My husband and I had always encouraged our children to be adventurous. I worked vigilantly to prevent my fears from interfering with the messages I communicated to them. Even my daughter, who was more tentative than my son and stepson about separating from me, had always cheerfully rebounded as soon as we were reunited. I was surprised, therefore, when her anxiety did not diminish after she returned home from her trip to Washington, D.C.

There was something particularly persistent about the strain of fear Mikaela seemed to have contracted. I came to see that while scientists had found a way to prevent the virulent AIDS virus from passing, in utero, from mother to daughter, no such barrier had yet been discovered to prevent the effects of trauma from being transmitted across generations. As a result, it was not unusual to find children of Holocaust survivors, or the Second Generation, as we came to be known, weighed down by feelings of loss, guilt, and anxiety, and trapped in a dynamic with our parents of mutual devotion and over-protection. This fallout also clearly extended to a third generation. Like me, Mikaela, too, while strong and resourceful, seemed to be spiraling in the vortex of a tragedy that had taken place a half century before she was born.

As for exactly how such trauma might be transferred from one gen-eration to the next, researchers have proposed a variety of theories. Psychoanalytic approaches suggest that emotions that couldn't be con-sciously dealt with by Holocaust survivors themselves have been passed down to their children. Sociological theories focus on the connection between survivors' beliefs and fears and their child-rearing practices. Other researchers have looked to the family unit as a whole to ascertain the impact of the Holocaust survivors' experiences on their children. They found, for example, that in tightly knit survivor families, attempts by children to establish boundaries are often viewed as a threat to the family's unity.

Finally, some researchers have proposed that memories of fear can actually be carried across generations through biochemistry. Children of severely traumatized Holocaust survivors have been found to have lower than average levels of the stress hormone cortisol, just like their traumatized parents. They also have been found to be more likely than average to suffer from posttraumatic stress disorder when exposed to a traumatic event, and more likely to view a non-life-threatening event, such as illness or separation from a loved one, as traumatic. This bio-logical approach helps explain why children growing up in the same household, but with different combinations of genes, could be affected differently by a parent's trauma—why I was more fearful of leaving home than my sister, why my daughter was more fearful of separa-tion than my son. Hopefully, light shed on stories like ours will further encourage researchers to find new ways to mitigate the most harmful effects of intergenerational transmission of traumatization.

FOR MY MOTHER, at seventy years old, completing this book was bittersweet. Just after she had stoically finished taking me through her life, barely flinching at the most intimate, disturbing details, she plunged into a deep depression. I was left wondering if this project had been a mistake. Thankfully, my mother recovered, and her optimism and hunger for adventure returned. She reminded me that this memoir would help others better understand the Holocaust and its impact, and hopefully would also raise awareness as to the potential long-range complications resulting from other tragedies taking place today, around the world. This book was written with the hope that trauma survivors, their children and grandchildren—as well as others facing less dramatic challenges— might find inspiration in my mother's courageous story.

Last summer, I agreed to teach a course on the Holocaust at my son Gabriel's high school. One of the teachers at the school, a friend who had grown up in Sri Lanka, came to our house for dinner before the semester began. Between margaritas and slices of homemade pizza, he casually asked me, in his perfect English accent, if I knew the Latin root of the word *holocaust*. "Some of my students will be in your course, and they'll quiz you on this right off the bat," he explained.

I searched my memory. In the past decade I had read scores of books and viewed countless documentaries on the Holocaust. I could chronicle the history of anti-Semitism over the past two thousand years, trace the rise and fall of the Third Reich, and expound upon the limits of democratic governments around the world to act morally. I was certain I had come across the origins of the word along the way, but it escaped me. If I confessed ignorance, my erudite Sri Lankan friend, who had left behind a successful investment banking career, would be convinced that his Oxford education was superior to my American one. For the sake of the team, I took a guess. I deduced that *holo* sounded like "whole," and that *caust* had to do with destruction.

"Something like total destruction?" I asked.

"Close."

Yes, I thought.

"But not quite." He told me that *holocaust,* in Latin, means "burned offerings." It stems from the Greek words *holo* (which, as I had guessed, did mean "whole") and *caust* ("burned"). In ancient times, the priests of the Hebrew Temple in Jerusalem would offer animal sacrifices to God. *Holocaustum* referred to those offerings that were burned in their entirety at the altar. Centuries later in the United States, the word *holocaust* became synonymous with the destruction of European Jews by the Germans.

Thinking about that ancient definition, I realized it was not an entirely accurate description of what took place during World War II. The fire of hate that the Nazis lit did not consume everything. The earth was scorched, but from the blackened ground new seeds sprouted. Their genes had been affected by the intensity of the heat, but grow they did, and thrive they would, as my mother would put it, "bending toward the sun."

This book is for those whose hopes have been dashed, or burned beyond recognition. It is for those who may have been born too late to witness the traumatic events that shaped their current experience. And it is for those who are interested in exploring the blurry lines between good and evil, hope and despair, and mothers and daughters. It is my deepest hope to provide you with evidence that despite the depth of pain and horror we may experience, the will of the human spirit is irrepressible, and the blessings of life, of a new day in the sun, will ultimately prevail.

PART I

In Mom's Voice

(1937–1960)

I

Childhood, Interrupted

I was four years old, in 1941, when I saw my first airplane. On a peaceful, sunny day when the sky was clear blue with cotton-puff clouds, I was flying a kite in our wheat fields while my father gardened. Hearing a noise from up above getting louder, I cranked my neck to look up. I couldn't take my eyes off the object floating by.

"What is that? What a strange-looking bird."

"It's a machine that can fly," my father said.

"How does it stay up there?" I asked.

"I'm not sure. It's called an airplane, and it carries people to faraway places."

I was overwhelmed by feelings of joy and freedom. The world was so full of promise.

My home, in Poland's southeast region, was part of a small village called Urzejowice (oo-je-VEET-sih). The house itself was painted a sunny yellow with white trim and surrounded by a white picket fence. Our front yard, brimming with plum trees, sunflowers, and sweet pea vines, seemed like a paradise to me. Poland's winters were harsh, but once spring came, my sister and I loved playing outside in the garden, waiting for our father to return from work. We made houses and pies out of mud, improvised games like tag, and waved to neighbors passing by.

"How old is she again, Sara?" I whispered to my sister one day, as our elderly neighbor floated by on a gurney carried by two of her sons.

"She's one hundred and two," Sara said. My five-year-old sister was wholesome looking, with a heart-shaped face, dark, deep-set eyes, and straight brown hair.

"Wow! That's so old."

"Tatu says we should all live that long," she said. Our father's name was Isaac, but we called him Tatu, which meant "daddy" in Polish.

"Tatu wants us to be old like that?" I asked.

"Ruchel, it's an honor to grow that old." Losing patience with me, Sara looked out into the distance. "There he is!" she shrieked.

"That's not fair. You always get to see him first," I said.

"I'm a year older. I can see farther than you."

Now I, too, saw my father. He was walking proudly, with his shoulders back and his head held high. He and my grandfather and uncles were in business together, selling groceries, clothing, and cows. They bought cows from gentiles and sold them to Jewish slaughterhouses in the big cities, where they would be butchered for kosher meat. As usual, my father was impeccably dressed, in a dark suit and maroon tie that accentuated his straight white teeth and wavy black hair. He was carrying a package wrapped in brown paper. Often, he returned from business trips bearing wonderful surprises. Sara and I raced down the path, vying to be the first to fly into his arms.

"Hi, children," my father said. As his eyes rested on us, they began to dance, and crinkled at the edges. He tucked the package inside his suit jacket and lifted us into the air one at a time. "What are you up to?"

"We're waiting for you, Tatu," I said.

"Where are your mother and brother?"

"They're in the kitchen, and Mama is cooking soup," Sara said. "Is that a present for us?" she added as we approached the front door, pointing to the bulge protruding from my father's jacket.

"Let's see when we get inside," he replied. He always seemed to lead the way. He was the peacock in our home, and the ultimate authority.

Leah and Isaac Gamss with Ruchel Gamss (baby) and
Sara Gamss. Poland, 1937.

In the kitchen, my father greeted my mother, Leah, with a kiss and
hug. Then he took my two-year-old brother, Nachum, and hoisted him
into the air. Nachum squealed with delight. He had pale, Dresden-like
skin, pitch-black eyes, and brownish gold hair.

"Now can we open the surprise, Tatu?" I said.

He handed me the package. My sister and I tore it open, revealing
yellow silk embroidered fabric that looked like rays of sunshine dancing in
our arms. I held it up for my mother to see.

"It's exquisite," she said.

"Can we sew dresses from this?" Sara asked. "Or is it too fancy to cut up?"

"We can make special dresses for Shabbos," my mother said. She was sensitive and kind, and she adored my father. He loved her, too. Isaac Gamss and Leah Weltz had grown up in the same village, and their marriage, in 1935, had been arranged by a matchmaker. He was thirty-two, and she a few years younger.

My mother was attractive and unusual looking, with dark, deep-set eyes, full eyebrows, a patrician nose, long, curly dark brown hair, and beautiful skin. At five foot seven, she was tall for her day. Still, my father was always the bigger, more outgoing personality. The distinguished suit he was wearing that afternoon, alongside my mother's plain cotton house-dress and apron, seemed to accentuate the contrast.

Sometimes my mother would cry for no apparent reason. Her own mother had died when she was a young girl. I often wondered whether she was still grieving over that long-ago separation. Or perhaps she was just tired from working so hard. In addition to cooking and caring for three young children, cleaning our home, and washing our clothes in the nearby river, she also helped my father pick fruits and vegetables and tend to our livestock in fields that we leased from a man named Kapetsky, the aris-tocrat in town. I liked to help milk the cows, although someone first had to lift me onto the milking stool. The only time I saw my mother sitting down during the day was when she shelled peas or snapped green beans.

Back in the kitchen that afternoon, my father had one more surprise. From inside his suit jacket he pulled out another package. With a twinkle in his eye he said, "Hopefully, these will look nice with the dresses."

My sister and I were so excited. We ripped open the brown wrapping, pulling out two pairs of cream-colored patent leather shoes. Sara grinned from ear to ear. When she smiled, her face lit up. Then she handed me the smaller pair.

"They're so beautiful." I sat on the floor to push my bare feet into them.

"Nachum, what are you doing?" I heard my mother ask. I looked over to see my brother pulling apart the brown wrapping paper and scattering pieces all around.

"Playing," my brother said.

Sara and I burst out laughing. My father did, too.

A few days later, the yellow fabric had been transformed into two holiday dresses, by whom I'm not certain. Maybe my maternal stepgrandmother, Simma, who lived next door with Grandpa Nuchem, had sewn them. I used to watch her knit while I threw balls of yarn to her cat. Sometimes she also made me rag dolls out of muslin, with painted faces.

Our home formed the backbone of our spiritual, cozy world. Affixed to the right front doorjamb was a mezuzah—a small, oblong container with verses from the Torah inside—which we kissed whenever we passed through. Also, before bedtime, we said a special prayer and planted a kiss on the mezuzah in the master bedroom. I fell asleep secure in the knowledge that God was watching over us.

In our village, although the Jews worked very hard, they were generally looked down upon by the Christian Poles. On Shabbos, however, the Jews elevated themselves. Shabbos was the highlight of the week for our family. From Friday afternoon to Saturday night, normal life was put on hold. My mother spent Thursdays and Fridays cleaning and cooking in preparation. Dreamy scents of chickens stewing, soup boiling, and cakes baking filled me with a sense of peace and well-being.

The most heavenly aroma was that of challah baking in the oven. My sister and I would stand by our mother's side, enrapt, as she kneaded the dough, formed it into loaves, and slid the loaves into the oven. When they were ready, my mother would announce, "Girls, come and have a nibble." Sara and I would scurry back across the kitchen, past the red enamel pots used for milk products to one side and the blue pots, for cooking meat, to the other. My mother would tear off a piece of soft, piping-hot bread from the tiny extra loaf she baked just for us. I would close my eyes and pop a morsel into my mouth. It practically melted on my tongue. I can't manage to remember ever being kissed or hugged by my mother, although I'm sure that I was, but I do remember feeling her warmth and love whenever her challah was baking.

By sundown each Friday, our home looked beautiful. The wooden table in the kitchen was covered with a white cloth and set with sparkling china and colorful crystal. One Friday, just before Shabbos began, Sara and I were twirling around in our beautiful, newly created yellow dresses when there was a knock at the door. Before my mother answered it, she leaned down and said, "Ruchaleh, bring the package."

I reached up to the kitchen counter, grasped a container of food, and brought it to her. She was standing in the doorway, dressed elegantly in a bright silk blouse, a black skirt, and a pearl necklace, as she greeted a Jewish man in ragged clothing.

"Good Shabbos," my mother said.

"Good Shabbos. Do you have any food to spare, or a few zlotys?"

"We have food," I interjected, pointing to the package in my mother's hands.

"God bless you," he said.

When the man left, my mother looked at me. "Where's your smile, Ruchaleh? You should feel good. Did you know that charity elevates you in heaven?"

"Mushe, that man makes me sad. Why doesn't he have his own food?"

"He is an orphan. Square meals do not come so easily for some people."

My mother led me back to the kitchen table, where my father and sister were waiting. Nachum, my young brother, was already asleep in my parents' room. Shabbos could not begin until sundown, which meant that in the spring and summer months it began quite late. My mother lit candles, one for each member of our family, and said a prayer. Then she sat beside my father on the wooden bench, across from Sara and me. We were expected to listen politely to the adult conversation, and only to speak when granted permission. Over dessert, however, we joined in to sing traditional songs and chant melodies thanking God for our blessings. Everything felt serene and holy.

Our home was newly built, and another bedroom was still being added on for Sara and me. Until that was completed, we shared our parents' bedroom, except on very cold nights, when we slept near the stove in the kitchen. My parents' bedroom was decorated with a huge, gleaming wood armoire, a crib for Nachum, and gorgeous lace curtains hanging from copper rods. A set of exquisite blue ceramic birds sat near a crystal clock upon one of the nightstands. On Saturday mornings I would open my eyes at the first sign of light streaming through the windowpanes and jump right into my parents' bed, giggling. Lounging like this was reserved for holidays, and the Sabbath.

My paternal grandparents, Aharon and Paya Neshe, lived a few miles away in the town of Przeworsk (shev-orsk), along with nine of their twelve children. They seemed like a wonderful couple with a lot of love. My father was their firstborn. Since Grandpa Aharon had a Torah, we walked to his home on Shabbos mornings so that my father could pray there with the other males in the family.

"What was that?" my sister asked, whenever she heard any noise along the way.

"It's not a dog. Don't worry," I remember saying. Ever since a dog chased us one morning, Sara had been wary of unexpected noises.

My grandparents' white clapboard home sat atop a grassy hill, surrounded by wildflowers. As we climbed up the knoll and past the brick well out in front, we anticipated the warm greeting we would receive from our grandmother, Paya Neshe. She was revered in our family, and always seemed to be doing good deeds for needy people.

"Good Shabbos, lalkales [dollies]," she would say when she opened the door to greet us. She was plump, and wore dark, loose-fitting dresses accessorized with jewelry. Her wig, which traditional Jewish women of her generation wore, was dark and curly.

"Good Shabbos, Bubbe," we would respond, using the Yiddish term for "Grandma," pronounced bub-bee. "Come. Come into the kitchen," she always urged. "I baked treats for you."

On the way we would walk through a large, beautiful room with shiny, golden wood floors and a harp off to one corner. There, my father joined Grandpa Aharon and my eight uncles in a semicircle. When they were praying, I wasn't allowed to say a word. Grandpa Aharon, in his early sixties, was always easy to spot. He sported a black suit and white shirt like his sons, but he also wore a big velvet hat, a mustache, a beard, and payis (side locks). My father and his brothers, eager to fit into the gentile world, dressed less traditionally.

On Saturday afternoons, our extended family often took a stroll in the town square, passing by the small grocery store, the pharmacy, the

The Gamss Family. Clockwise from top left, Tsivia, Isaac (Rita's father), Chaya Shaindl*, Paya Neshe (Rita's paternal grandmother), Shia Moshe*, Aharon* (Rita's paternal grandfather), Max, Yosel*. Second row from left, Blima* holding Norman, Ruchel (Rita's great-grandmother/Paya Neshe's mother), Leibish*, Benny, and Henry. *Perished in the Holocaust

Catholic church, and a tiny candy store owned by one of my father's sisters, Chaya Shaindl, and her husband. One Saturday, I held my aunt's hand as we walked past her shop.

"Can we go inside for just a few minutes?" I asked.

"Not on Shabbos," she said, and smiled. "But I have an idea. Why don't you tell me what your favorite candy is, and I'll bring you a piece during the week."

"I like picking them myself," I protested. I loved going into her shop, reaching a serving spoon into the glass bowls, and pulling out turquoise rock candy and the colorful bonbons covered in beautiful, bright wrapping.

In the summer, we played outside until supper was ready. Then our mother would call us in. "Kim en dem hois, Sara and Ruchel."

When we were called to dinner, it meant now. There were a lot of do's and don'ts in our household, and my parents were not afraid to reprimand me when they needed to. Once, I remember, when our kitchen was painted, one of the wet white walls looked so delicious that I walked up and licked it. Immediately, my tongue was afire. "Ow!" I screamed.

"That paint can make you very sick. Don't ever do that again!" my father yelled. He could be short-tempered at times.

"I won't. I promise," I vowed, running from the room in tears.

I felt very secure with these rules. Over warm candlelit suppers, my parents, grandparents, aunts, and uncles had lively conversations about business and family. I listened, taking everything in. Afterward, we gathered around the fireside (priperchik in Yiddish), listening to stories and sipping tea, with sugar cubes in our mouths. The adults often spiced their tea with homemade liqueur. "It helps warm our kishkes [stomachs]," my father would say. On some evenings my parents made up their own stories, and other nights they read to us from books. Even though we lived in a small village, my parents wanted us to be well educated.

"This is one of my favorites," my father would often say, before he began a story.

"Please don't tell one with dybbuks tonight," I always pleaded.

Often, my parents' fables included dybbuks, or evil creatures that took possession of humans if they didn't live according to the Torah, or the highest values. When I misbehaved in some minor way, I was afraid to fall asleep at night for fear the dybbuks would appear.

"Ruchaleh, they won't bother you as long as you're a good girl," my parents would assure me.

In reality, the dybbuks had already appeared. My orderly, loving childhood, where everything had its time and place, was far more precarious than I had been aware. By 1937, the year I was born, anti-Jewish incidents had been taking place throughout eastern Europe. In August of that year, 350 assaults against Jews were recorded in Poland alone. Hitler's Nazi propaganda, casting Jews as the source of all evil, had stirred up jealousies and hatred. Ten percent of the Jewish population in Poland, over 395,000 Jews, had been driven to emigrate by that time. But as a very young child living in a remote village, I was oblivious to any of this tension. I was not even aware that in September 1939, when I was two, Germany had attacked and easily defeated Poland. The German army had torn through town after town, killing every Pole in sight.

Thus it came as a terrible shock to me, that day in 1942, when a sea of gray German tanks invaded our small town, with swastikas or Hakenkreuze molded onto them and their cannons protruding with quiet menace. I could see them out of our large kitchen window, which was lightly coated with frost, as they rumbled by. I can still feel that chill today. Fear rolled through my being like a dark fog.

Although some German soldiers had been in our village for three years already, since the start of the war, until now they had been persuaded by the town's wealthy landowner, Mr. Kapetsky, to leave the Jews alone. But recently Kapetsky had fled, German troops had grown in number, and

Chaya Shaindl (left), Isaac (center), and Tsivia Gamss (right), circa late 1920s, Poland.

the situation was growing progressively more dangerous. For days on end the adults fretted over what to do. My parents, grandparents, aunts, and uncles paced around the kitchen, frantically debating their options.

"The rumors keep getting worse. Every day they're rounding up Jews and deporting them to God knows where," I overheard my father say one day. I stood off to the side, feeling very alone.

"Iche, it's worse than roundups, there's bloodshed everywhere. In Warsaw, they're in ghettos, starving to death. Next thing they'll burn down our homes," Uncle Max said. He was thirty years old and had dark hair and beautiful deep-set eyes, like all the Gamss siblings. I had always thought of him as the funniest of my uncles, and it scared me to see him so serious.

"The Germans don't care about our small village. They're not going to burn down our homes," Grandpa Aharon said.

"They might," Uncle Libish said. He was married to Tsivia, my father's middle sister, and as he spoke, my father furrowed his brow. There seemed to be some sort of tension between the two men, perhaps because Uncle Libish was also in the business of selling cows, which put him in competition with my father. "Mr. Arnold says this is a war unlike any others."

"Mr. Arnold?" Grandpa Aharon asked.

"Yes, Papa. He's the nicest of our soldiers," Aunt Tsivia said. She was short and curvaceous, with curly brown hair and wise dark eyes. She had won a local beauty contest as a teenager, and at thirty-five was still attractive. She was also feisty, and she looked her father confidently in the eye as she referred to Mr. Arnold, one of the three German soldiers who had been living in their home since 1939.

"We play chess after work, and he tells me things," Libish said.

"Now I've heard everything. My sister's husband plays chess with a Nazi," my father said. As the eldest son, he knew he held a place of honor in the family, and that his siblings would support him in almost any dispute.

As each day passed, the world became a scarier place. There was less food, since we could no longer safely go outside to gather produce and care for our livestock. We sensed that anything could be taken away from us at any time. Then a series of incidents hit even closer to home.

One evening, my family was sipping tea in the kitchen when the front door burst open. Three German soldiers in muddy boots stomped in.

"Where is Isaac Gamss?" the shortest one said.

"What do you want?" my father asked.

None of them answered. Instead, they turned over chairs and threw things around. My sister and I covered our ears and clung to our mother.

"Why don't you just tell me what you're looking for," my father said.

"We're in charge of your village now," one of them finally said as they abruptly turned around to leave.

My father came home another day looking confused and disheveled. My mother took one look at him and started crying. She lifted up his shirt and saw bloody welts on his back. Then she led him into the bedroom. Later, we overheard that he had been detained for questioning and beaten by a German soldier. A few days after that, Uncle Max raced into our home. He didn't seem to notice my siblings and me, playing in the kitchen.

"Iche, come quick," Max called to his eldest brother. My parents rushed into the kitchen, serious and pale, as though they had seen one of the dybbuks from their stories.

"What is it, Max?" my father asked.

"It's an order. From the Gestapo. We have to report to the train station, and Papa wants to see all of us right away!"

"We just received our own edict," my father said.

The family gathered in a circle in my grandfather's kitchen. I sat off to the side with my sister, brother, and three cousins—eight-year-old Sally, six-year-old Miriam, and Lola, who was five like me. The adults whispered, trying not to scare us children. But their efforts were in vain. The same room that had once been the hub of lively conversation and sweet aromas now felt cold and frightening. The biggest change of all was that Grandma Paya Neshe, always the heart of the kitchen, had recently passed away. She had been ill, I believe as a complication of her diabetes, but had to be brought home prematurely from the hospital when the doctors fled to escape the Nazis.

"We cannot go to the train station," Grandpa Aharon stated right away. My father nodded his head in agreement. "So I have an escape plan." The room was very quiet as my grandfather described his plan. The family would leave home in the dark of the night and slip into hiding. I didn't know what this meant, but it sounded scary. Then, he explained, we would search for safer hiding places. Everyone just listened until he got to a tricky part. "We'll need to split into groups," he said calmly.

The adults looked at one another with puzzlement, but twenty-two-year-old Uncle Benny was the only one to speak up. He had a dry sense of humor and could be stubborn at times. Uncle Benny thought we should all stick together. He mentioned something about there being strength in numbers. But my grandfather stood his ground.

"No. My plan comes from the biblical story of Jacob," Grandpa Aharon said. "Remember when Jacob returned home with his family after twenty years in exile?"

The adults nodded their heads. I nodded, too, but had never heard the story. Later, I learned that Jacob, fearing his brother's revenge, split the family into two camps so that at least one group would remain safe.

"This way, if any of us are caught, God forbid, at least others will survive." Grandpa Aharon's words hung in the air like December clouds portending cold, stormy days ahead.

My father looked over at his children. When his eyes met mine, he couldn't even force a smile. Grandpa Aharon, meanwhile, was sorting the family into groups. Five of his younger children would stay with him. Three other sons, my uncles Max, Benny, and Henry, would make up a second group. "You're strong enough to go off on your own," Aharon told them. Then he added his youngest son, sixteen-year-old Norman, to that group, believing he would be safer there. I felt sorry for my favorite uncle, with dark hair and beautiful, soulful eyes. He clearly preferred to remain with his father.

Finally, Grandpa Aharon turned to my father and Aunt Tsivia, his two children with children of their own. "Your families will travel as one group so that the children don't endanger the others if they make too much noise." I assumed he meant me because I talked loudly sometimes. But I could keep quiet, too. I wanted to tell him this, but he had moved on. He was saying that we should head toward the farm of a man named

Stashik Grajolski, who might take pity on the children. Grandpa Aharon and Grandma Paya Neshe had looked out for Stashik and his sister after their parents died near the end of World War I. My grandparents had made sure that the teenage orphans had food and clothes, and that they attended school and church.

"Stashik and I were friends in the army," Uncle Max added. "He's a good, smart family man."

Sara and I held hands, frozen. My cousins Sally, Miriam, and Lola looked just as frightened. Three-year-old Nachum kept moving onto and off our laps, trying to get our attention. But for once, we all wanted to listen to the adults.

"How will we sustain the children hiding out in the forest?" my worried mother asked. "Our babies are going to sleep outside like the dogs? Maybe we should just go to the train station. How bad a place could they take us to?"

Aunt Tsivia was concerned, too. "Feigie is only a year old," she said, glancing down at the baby in her arms. "She won't survive the cold nights outside, and I can't bear to lose another child." Feigla's twin sister had died as an infant.

Uncle Libish put his arm around his wife, now in tears, but spoke directly to his father-in-law, Grandpa Aharon. "I've evaluated the edict through Mr. Arnold's eyes. He made it clear we should not go to the train station."

This time my father agreed with Uncle Libish. Apparently everyone did. Only Uncle Henry had refrained from voicing an opinion. He was twenty and the quietest of the siblings. He had remained silent all evening, as the others spoke on top of one another.

"We must leave tonight," Grandpa Aharon finally ruled in a voice filled with resignation, yet loud enough to be heard over the chatter.

Back home, my mother prepared packages of hard-boiled eggs, vegetables, and bread for us to take along. My father came into the kitchen and lifted me up. I wrapped my brown lace-up shoes around his waist and my arms around his neck. "Let's say good-bye," he said. He proceeded to carry me to the doorpost of the master bedroom and then to the front door. We kissed both mezuzahs as my father prayed to God for us to survive. I tried to pray with him, but I was too scared to remember the words. Instead, I hugged him so tightly that I could feel his heart beating through my chest.

We quietly left home, our family and Aunt Tsivia's, dressed in layers, with packs on our shoulders. Walking down our street in complete blackness, I squeezed my mother's hand tightly.

2

Stashik Is Coming

It was the summer of 1942. But in my mind, the trees were already losing their leaves, and the weather was growing colder. At every fork in the road, my father and his brother-in-law, Uncle Libish, assessed the safest direction for us to take.

When we heard gunshots fired, I had to bite hard on the inside of my mouth not to scream out loud. My father would immediately grab my sister's and my shoulders and push us to safety. "Hurry up, girls! Stand quietly behind this tree!"

"A German?" my mother would whisper to my father in a panicky voice.

"Who knows if it's a Nazi or a Pole," my father said. I didn't like their new, tense way of speaking.

The entire group was like one living entity. Everyone's existence depended on everyone else's cooperation. I got the message that I was safe only with people huddled around me. Any sense I had developed of my own borders disappeared. I no longer knew where I stopped and others started. Often, it felt as if we were traveling in circles, which we probably were. Whenever anyone noticed us, we would move on. I developed terrible neck pains from having to hold my head up and walk so much. When I got too tired, one of my parents carried me. Little Nachum, my brother, was usually in the other one's arms.

"I'm so tired, when can we sleep?" I complained.

"Shh!" was always the response.

When I recall those days, my chest begins to ache. We were so scared and exhausted, constantly looking for a safe place to eat or rest, with maybe a tree to cover us so we would be less noticeable. I felt like a piece of furniture, being moved around endlessly.

"Can we stay here for a long time?" I asked when we reached a resting spot in the forest one day. We had been wandering for hours, and I couldn't wait to plop my head down.

"Not for long. But we can stop here for a little while," my father said, slowly easing his way down onto the wet ground.

"I'll cut this delicious apple and we can have a nice snack," my mother said, paring a recent find. She tried to make everything seem somewhat normal as she doled out the slices of the sweet fruit and some crusts of bread between eleven of us. I sat between my parents, where I felt safest, while my young brother put his head in my mother's lap.

"I'm thirsty. I need something to drink," my sister, Sara, said.

"Me, too," I echoed.

"See, we're all thirsty," Sara said.

The adults ignored our complaints. Even my mother didn't seem to hear us. "Nachum feels hot," she said, rubbing my brother's back.

My father felt Nachum's head. "He's fine. He's just tired like all of us," he said.

We were sitting near a field of rich golden wheat, like the ones I had enjoyed playing in back home only a few weeks earlier.

"Can't we sneak back home just to get water? Which direction do we live in?" my cousin Sally asked her mother. At eight, she was the eldest of the children and seemed the most mature. Children were always labeled back then, and Sally was considered "the smart one" in her family.

"We live over there," Aunt Tsivia said, balancing baby Feigla in her arms so she could point toward our village. "But we can't go back there for water."

"Who is in our house now?" Sara asked our mother.

"Hopefully, no one."

"Then why can't we go back there?"

The kids asked the same questions over and over again, because the situation did not make sense to us. After our snack, we began to explore a little.

"Be very careful," Aunt Tsivia warned. "There are land mines out there."

"What's a land mine?" I whispered to Sally.

"I've never seen one, but I know they are extremely dangerous," my cousin said.

"Stop trying to scare us," six-year-old Miriam said to her older sister. "Now look what you've done to Lola!" Miriam added, pointing to little Lola, who had thrown her thin body on the ground and was weeping, her light brown head of hair bobbing up and down.

"Stop crying, Lola," Sally said. "Just be careful, and you won't have to worry."

When one of the children did wander off, an adult brought him or her back immediately, often with a stern reminder that we could be shot at any time.

We pulled hay from the center of newly harvested haystacks, leaving the outside shells intact, to make spaces in which we could sleep or sit quietly when the farmers were in the fields. At night, we would sneak outside again to gather food that nature provided. One afternoon, the children sat inside one of these haystacks to escape from the heat. As the brittle hay pricked through the skin of my arms and legs, I scratched fiercely.

"I really should be in school," Cousin Sally whispered.

"Don't worry, you won't get in trouble," my sister said.

"I know. I'm not allowed to go. Just because I'm Jewish."

"It's good that you're not in school, because the kids called you mean names there," Miriam said. As the sunlight peeked through our dark quarters, I could see flecks of red in her brown hair.

"What names?" I asked.

"Even though they're my friends, when the Catholic kids get mad at me they call me names like 'Christ killer' or 'dirty Jew,' " Sally said.

"And they tell you to go back to Palestine," Miriam added.

"Why do they say those things?" I asked.

Sally just looked at me. "I have no idea."

As we conversed, the voices of other children infiltrated our secret hideout.

"Daddy, my kite is stuck," a Polish boy called.

"I told you not to fly it near the apple trees," a girl, probably his older sister, admonished.

"Let's go play with them," I whispered.

"We're not allowed to," Sara said.

"But they're just little kids, like us." It did not make sense to me. When they began to sing, we peeked out and saw four children holding hands and turning in a circle. Inside, we quietly imitated their dance. I felt very envious.

That evening, when I told my mother how much I had wanted to play with the other children, she put her arms around me. "This is how it is for us right now, Ruchaleh. Try not to pay attention to the gentile children."

Once in a while, a child actually saw us. Early one morning, my sister and I were sneaking out of a ditch where we had spent the night when we noticed a Polish girl walking with her parents. Pointing in our direction, the girl seemed to be asking who we were.

"Don't look," the father said, pulling her away quickly. Since we were supposed to be hidden, I·was relieved that they ignored us.

Each time the adults spotted a farmer in the fields, they debated anew whether to hide or to ask for food.

"What do you think, Leah?" Aunt Tsivia asked my mother one time.

From behind a haystack, she pointed to a farmer with a young boy up ahead in the wheat field.

"He's with his son. Maybe he'll be sympathetic to us," my mother said.

I asked my mother if I could come along, but she told me to wait where we were, by the haystack. I stood still, watching her and my aunt tentatively approach the farmer. He shook his head somberly, genuflected, and walked away quickly with his son. What kind of religion would be so unmerciful as to allow others to starve? I wondered. I was too young to realize that the Catholic farmers were also in fear for their own lives. It actually was miraculous that none of them turned us in. Occasionally, one of them even gave us a bit of food. The sight of seven children apparently softened a heart now and then.

I feared the nights outside most of all. Even now, when I get scared, the feeling—that my body is falling away and I am totally vulnerable, as though I have no skin holding me together—returns. One dark night, we were dozing in the fields when we heard footsteps rustling through the leaves. My heart was pounding so loud that I worried that the intruder would hear the beat. My father sprang up. He hid behind a haystack and stretched his neck around to see who was out there.

"Stashik?!" he exclaimed in a loud whisper, as he stepped out into the open. The excitement in his voice took me by surprise.

It was dark, but I caught a glimpse of a tall man carrying a package.

"Hello, my friend," the man whispered, shaking my father's outstretched hand.

"Mushe, who is that man?" I asked.

My mother was trying to catch her breath. "That must be Stashik Grajolski."

"It is. I recognize him now," Aunt Tsivia said.

I stared at the stranger. I could make out that he was dressed in light-colored pants with suspenders, and a short-sleeved work shirt.

"I heard from your brother, Max, and I've been waiting for a moonless night to come out here," Stashik told my father.

"Do you know of a safe place for us to hide?" my father whispered. "The Nazis know that we didn't report to the train station. Neighbors say they're searching for us."

"We're running out of time. They'll find us out here sooner or later," Uncle Libish added, now standing beside my father.

"This is a terrible situation," Stashik said, looking sympathetically over my father's shoulder at the group of us. "But I don't have good news. In Britain they broadcast that 700,000 Jews have been killed here in Poland. I'm not sure I can do more than bring you newspapers and some food until this craziness ends," he said, and handed my father the package he had brought.

My mother walked over to join the men. "Please hide us," she blurted out.

I was wondering whether someone would ask that.

"You must not ask me this," the farmer said. "I have a wife and children I must think of first."

"It will just be for a short time. God will bless you," my father pleaded.

"It wouldn't work," Stashik whispered. "There's Gestapo around. They come to the farm to buy eggs and butter."

"We'd be as quiet as the mice," my mother said. "No one would know we're there. Look at them." She pointed to the six children huddled underneath the tree. My baby cousin was asleep in Aunt Tsivia's arms. "We have good kids."

I tried to look like I was very good. The man smiled at me. Soon he walked away, his head hanging down. Then, a few nights later, he returned. He continued to sneak out to us, bringing newspapers, food, and suggestions as to which fields were safer for us to hide in. "Stashik is coming," someone would say, as soon as we heard what had become his familiar footsteps in the night. He became our link to the outside world. He treated us like we were of value, worthy of saving. During each encounter, the adults tried to persuade him to take our family in.

"Please stop asking," Stashik would say. "My wife is petrified by the very idea."

This gave our family the impression that Stashik was open to sheltering us, if his wife could be convinced. Perhaps they could bribe her.

"We'll reward you very well," Aunt Tsivia said. "With jewelry and furs."

"It just wouldn't work," Stashik said gently.

We grew increasingly discouraged, until one night, Stashik had a change of heart. "My wife isn't happy about this, but she is willing to chance it for a couple of weeks."

I could feel the surge of relief sweep through the souls of the four adults.

"Provided you give us your jewelry and your furs," he added halfheartedly.

All of the adults thanked him profusely and promised to pray for him.

"My wife thinks I'll be shot by some trigger-happy Pole if I keep violating curfew and sneaking into the fields like this," Stashik said, chuckling for the first time. Then, in a more serious tone, he added, "But she's still very nervous about this."

It was arranged for our family to arrive on the next moonless night.

"You won't be sorry," my father assured our benefactor.

Stashik said nothing.

3

Safe for the Moment

As the sun was just beginning to rise, we walked up to where we could make out Stashik Grajolski's farm. Although we had been wandering for weeks, we were only a few miles away from our home, in a town called Mushanka. We scooted across the lawn quickly, one or two at a time.

"Dzien dobry," Stashik whispered when he met us at the door.

"Good morning," my father said quietly.

"Good morning," I said.

"Shh," my father said right away.

I knew that we had to be quiet, but it was suffocating to stifle every word. Even though it was barely dawn, I saw Stashik more clearly than I had during the dark nights in the forest. He was tall, slender, and nice-looking, with pretty blue eyes and thinning blond hair. As he guided us silently through his home, past religious paintings and statues of angels, I caught my first glimpse of his wife, Maria. Petite, with blond hair, she suddenly appeared by her husband's side, and she seemed to be grimacing at us. Clearly, she was not happy to have us there.

We arrived at a narrow ladder, and Stashik motioned for my father to lead the way up. The rest of us followed him, through a trapdoor at the top, into a dark room. Once we were all inside, our host began whispering instructions to us in rapid order.

"Find places quickly. Don't walk around. Absolutely no talking. Keep the children quiet. I'll bring soup up tonight if I can."

Then he closed the attic door and disappeared. It sounded like he was folding up the ladder behind him. I felt a pain in my chest—the same pain I still experience when I'm left alone somewhere, like a hospital room. After the last visitor of the day closes the door, I feel as if I am marooned on an island or locked up in a prison cell.

That first morning the adults scouted around for a place to settle. They had to walk hunched over because the ceiling was only about four and a half feet high.

"God willing, we won't be in here for long," Aunt Tsivia said.

"It's not so bad. At least we're safe for the moment," my father said.

The adults seemed relieved, so I guess I was relieved, too. But inside, I felt shaky. Exhausted from our predawn sojourn, we lay down on the hard, straw-covered floor, rested our heads on some coats, and covered ourselves with rough horse blankets. I closed my eyes, trying to ignore the sharp straw poking my skin. Nachum cried, and my mother picked him up quickly.

When I awoke later in the day, I saw the attic for the first time. It was narrow and rectangular. Beneath us, covering the entire hard wood floor, hay was spread neatly and evenly. The walls and ceiling were raw wood planks. Above me, I could see sunlight shining through cracks in the roof. The attic also had one small window, but we were not allowed to look out from it, for fear of being seen. We had to peek through the narrow wooden slats in the attic wall.

"Look at that cute piggy running around out there," my eight-year-old cousin, Sally, whispered as she peered out through one of these slats. "Ruchel, Sara, come see."

"Can I see?" Nachum asked.

"No. Stay here," my mother said. My brother always had to be near her.

When I stood up, my father warned, "Careful, Ruchaleh. The Gestapo is right outside, for all we know." I dropped down to my hands and knees and crawled over to the window. By the time I got there, the pig had disappeared.

Toward the end of that first day, we heard a scratching sound that we would come to recognize as the ladder being taken down. Stashik appeared through the trapdoor with a pot of boiled potatoes and beans. He also had two barrels to use as toilets, which he would empty at night. In these first days, we attempted to create a private zone for a bathroom area, affixing a makeshift curtain, but that didn't prevent the sound of our constant diarrhea from being heard.

"I can't take it anymore," my mother cried, unable to obtain any privacy.

"This won't go on for long," my father told her in an effort to calm her down. "God will take care of us."

In our home, cleanliness had been next to godliness. Now, life was turned upside down. Sometimes, when we couldn't bear the stench of the toilets, my father would sneak down at night to rinse them with water from the well. He had to be very quiet so as not to rouse the neighbors' dogs.

A week or two after we arrived, we were awakened in the night by the opening of the attic door. Everyone gasped, and I rolled onto my stomach, covering my ears.

"It's just me," Uncle Max said quietly. "And Norman."

"Oh, thank God," my father said. I sat up and watched him, stooped low, tiptoeing toward his brothers.

My mother momentarily lit a match, and I was very happy to catch a glimpse of my two favorite uncles. They had checked on us a few times out in the fields, but I had never seen them looking so disheveled.

"I cannot believe you are here," Aunt Tsivia whispered, putting her hands up to her youngest brother's cheeks. "Has something terrible happened, God forbid?"

"Norman's not well," Uncle Max said softly. "I've been giving him herbs to drink, but I brought him here to recover."

My sixteen-year-old uncle knelt down to hug me. "I'll be fine," he whispered.

When Stashik brought food up the following evening, he sounded pleased to discover his old friend Max. But he made it clear that there was no room left for my other uncles, Benny and Henry, with whom Uncle Max had been wandering.

"They already have a place to stay," Uncle Max assured Stashik. I believed him. A few evenings later, however, the two brothers crept into the attic.

"I'm not sure this is a good idea," Uncle Libish told my father. "What if Grajolski throws all of us out?"

"As long as we're quiet, he'll let us stay. He's a good man," my father said. But by the way he crinkled his forehead, I could tell that he, too, was worried.

Our attic population had swelled to fifteen. There was my immediate family, Aunt Tsivia's family, and four of my father's single brothers, all together in a very small space. I had not felt much affinity for Uncle Henry up until then, because he rarely talked to me. In fact, even with my uncles he seemed to speak only when necessary. But I heard that he was good with his hands, at building things, and I had always thought he was handsome. At twenty, he had a perfect, beautiful nose, soft, curly hair, and chiseled features. Uncle Benny was twenty-two. He was shorter and stouter than his brothers, and had the curliest hair. I hoped that the stubborn quality I had heard he possessed would not create problems in the attic.

As Uncle Libish predicted, Stashik was furious when he discovered the new refugees. "I don't want to endanger your family or my own," he whispered to Uncle Max. He hunched way over in the attic, since he was tall, and I could still see that his face was red with anger. "Do you know that now the penalty in Poland for hiding a Jew is death?" he added

"I did not know, my friend," Uncle Max said. "I see why you're upset, but we won't be here for long." This seemed to calm Stashik down for the time being, at least. At that point, everyone was still hopeful that our stay was temporary.

In these first few months, Stashik appeared most nights with soup or boiled potatoes and news. One night he was away, and in his place, Mrs. Grajolski came up to bring provisions and empty the toilets. Uncle Norman leaned down through the trapdoor to help her get down the ladder, but instead, he knocked his arm into the barrel, causing the toilet contents to spill. As punishment, there was no food for any of us the next day, which only intensified the mounting tension in the attic.

The two families with children had settled into their separate sleeping spaces, and the single uncles were together in a corner. The adults spent their days worrying and quietly planning. They prayed in the morning and evening, hoping for the best and trying to keep up their spirits. The kids were kept apart from each other as much as possible, so we wouldn't talk. From time to time, we played hushed games together.

"Let's see who can stand on one foot longer," Cousin Sally whispered.

"We played that yesterday," Miriam replied. "Let's do something else."

"Do you have any better ideas?"

"I'll play. I liked that game," my sister said.

We all stood up and tried to balance on one foot. I concentrated hard, wanting to win this time. Then I sneezed and knocked into my sister. We both fell over.

"Shh! Sit down," Uncle Libish said. "You'll get us all killed if you're not careful." I sat down. "Can't you keep your daughters quiet?" he asked my mother.

"They're not making any more noise than your children," my father shot back.

"Please be quiet, girls," my mother pleaded with us.

"Why do we always get in trouble and not them?" I asked my mother, as I pointed to my cousins. "They talk as much as we do."

"It's not easy for anyone right now," she said.

Even my own father expected us to behave like adults. One day we tried to play ring-around-the-rosy. We held hands and carefully tiptoed in a circle, mouthing the words.

"Stop playing that frivolous game," my father said.

"Sorry, Tatu. We'll stop," I said, ashamed. At five years old, I already felt that playing games was foolish.

Aunt Tsivia and Uncle Libish were very concerned about their baby, Feigla. She was sick and cried frequently. They knew that she couldn't survive much longer in the attic, and they worried about her crying after we'd sworn we'd be absolutely quiet. One morning the baby was gone, and Aunt Tsivia lay on the straw, crying. "We've been forsaken by God," she said over and over again.

I summoned up the courage to ask my mother, "Where did Feigla go?"

"To the church. God willing, a kind person will find her and care for her until the war ends."

"Won't she miss her mommy?" I asked.

"This will be better for her. She was too young to be up here."

"But I'm old enough, right?"

My mother sighed, wearily. "Yes, you're old enough."

"And Nachum is old enough too, right?"

My mother didn't answer. Three-year-old Nachum was so quiet now, like a frisky young kitten after ingesting a sedative. My mother held him close against her. She rarely let him out of her arms. When she did, he cried weakly, which alarmed the other adults.

"Shh! Pick him up!" someone would immediately whisper.

There were fourteen of us left in the attic. I slept across from my mother, even though I wanted to sleep beside her, like Nachum did. I was mad at him for monopolizing all of my mother's attention. And I was angry with my mother for neglecting me. I wanted her to soothe or cuddle me. No, you're not angry, I tried to convince myself. Just sad. One of the first things we had been taught was never to get angry with your parents. I slept next to my sister, snuggling close to her, longing for affection.

On Shabbos, my mother still lit matches, and occasionally candles, for the prayers that we had thought of as blessings just months earlier. Now everyone was concerned about fire, since we were surrounded by straw. My mother blew the candles out as soon as the prayers ended.

One evening, my mother looked sad. "We should be home celebrating," she lamented. "I can just imagine the warmth, and the delicious meal I would have prepared if only—"

"Stop that, it makes it worse," Uncle Libish said.

I tried to quietly hum a familiar holiday tune to cheer her up. "Shh!" All of the adults seemed to admonish me simultaneously.

Every day became more monotonous and frightening than the previous one. I felt increasingly lonely and claustrophobic. Crying was forbidden. When I couldn't keep the sadness dammed up, and began to sob, one of the adults rushed over with a pillow.

"I stopped. I'm not crying," I said, gasping for breath. I hated the feeling of a pillow being held over my face.

In the summer, the temperature in the attic reached 100 degrees. The limited amount of water we had to drink never quenched our thirst.

"I'm thirsty," I would whisper. "My tongue is so dry, I can't swallow."

"Tonight Stashik will bring us water," someone would remind me.

"Why can't we get it now?" I asked early on. "The Grajolskis know we're here."

"Their children don't know. And soldiers might be in the house," my father said.

"Can you tell Mr. Grajolski to bring more water next time?" I asked.

"Stashik gets the water from a well. If he takes too much, he will arouse suspicion from the neighbors," Uncle Max explained.

"I want to go home," I said. My father looked at me. "It will be better soon," he said after a long pause.

In September 1942, after we'd been in the attic two months, Stashik came up just before dawn one morning while everyone was dozing. He put his arm on my father's shoulder and led him and Uncle Max to a corner of the attic. I pretended to still be asleep, but I couldn't help overhearing.

"I'm sorry to have to tell you this, but I thought you should know."

"Know what?" My father sounded alarmed.

"Your father and siblings were killed yesterday," Stashik said in a hushed voice.

"*Everyone?*" *Uncle Max whispered. He sounded like a child awakening from a nightmare.*

Stashik nodded sadly.

"*Are you sure?*" *my father asked.*

"*The Nazis murdered them in the forest.*"

"*Oh, my God,*" *my father said, kneeling to catch his breath as silent rivulets of despair streamed down his face. Then he looked over at his youngest brother, sleeping soundly, and said, "I don't want Norman to know yet. He'll be devastated."*

Over the next few days, Stashik got wind of a few more details, which he then passed along to us. We learned that Chaya Shaindl, my aunt who owned the candy shop, had actually made it to the Russian border with her husband, before having a change of heart. She turned back to join her father, Grandpa Aharon, and was murdered with the others. Still, no one told Uncle Norman. Then one morning, days later, he seemed upset.

"*I had a terrible nightmare, Iche,*" *Uncle Norman told my father.*

"*Given our situation, I'm not surprised,*" *my father said.*

Uncle Norman continued. "In the nightmare, Papa [my Grandpa Aharon] came to me wearing a kittel *[a white robe worn by religious men at important rituals, and when they are buried]. He told me, 'I am no longer alive, but you, Norman, will live.'* "

"*Did he say anything about us? Whether we would live?*" *my father asked.*

"*Iche, Papa is dead. I know it.*"

"*I know,*" *my father said quietly, hugging his youngest brother.*

The months wore on. There was no routine or order. No mealtime or wash time. Only praying gave the day any sense whatsoever. We just existed and tried to stay sane, hoping to survive the next hour. Our surroundings came to look increasingly dismal. Where once clean straw had evenly covered our floors, now it grew smelly and was strewn about in clumps. We grew dirtier and weaker. To wash, my father and uncles carried up water from the horses' trough.

"That water is dirtier than me. It's disgusting," my sister complained.

Then I began to focus on the brown water, and I told my mother, "I don't need to wash."

"Yes, you do," she insisted. She would stare at me in all seriousness until I removed the same filthy underwear and rags I had worn when we arrived at the attic. Because I had not grown, they still fit me. As my mother washed me, I felt my bones against her rag. "What is this?" she gasped one day, pulling the washcloth away from my arm. I looked down slowly, afraid of what I might see, and noticed a boil that was the size of an orange.

"What is that, Mushe?"

"It might be some type of infection. Does it hurt?"

I touched the sore spot too hard, and pain radiated throughout my body. "Ouch! Do I have to take medicine?"

"We have no medicine," she sighed, helpless.

"What if it keeps growing bigger?" queried my cousin Lola, who had tiptoed over to inspect the situation.

I burst into tears. But my mother was no longer by my side. She had already crawled over to my crying brother. Days later, the boil burst, oozing white pus all over me. I have no recollection of receiving any treatment. We had no bandages or medicines, but somehow it eventually healed on its own.

When winter arrived, we froze. There was snow on the roof just above us. We huddled together to generate heat. One winter day, Stashik opened the trapdoor to the attic. "Hurry! Look outside!" he urged, pointing to the small window against the far wall where Aunt Tsivia's family slept.

Cousin Sally crawled to the window first. "Is that your cousin?" she asked me after taking a peek outside. By this time, we all were under the window.

"Is it?" I asked. I was afraid to look.

"Oh, my God," my father gasped.

When I dared to steal a glance, I recognized the teenage girl and her *father running in the snow. She was the daughter of my mother's sister, Aunt Masha. Her father was Uncle Abraham. Behind them, a German soldier shouted, "Halt! Halt!"*

"We have to get them inside before they're killed. Maybe they're trying to run to us," my mother whispered. We all were still crouched beneath the window.

"There are too many Germans out there," Stashik replied.

"But it's my sister's husband. And my niece. We have to help them!"

Uncle Abraham and my cousin ran past the window, out of sight. A few seconds later, we heard two shots, and then silence. No one said a word. We were all in shock. As I recall this incident, I feel a pain in my chest and am reminded of a horrible, recurrent dream. I am running for my life when a bullet pierces through me, creating an excruciating sensation; I know the sensation is the cumulative pain of all I was forced to experience in the attic.

One afternoon not long after that, we heard Maria Grajolski's voice down below.

"Shh!" my father said. "Listen to what she is saying." We all stopped what little we were doing to pay attention.

"Yes, that's what I'll do, little chickens. I'll poison your food if you won't leave."

"She's pretending to talk to her animals," my father said. "But the message is intended for us. She wants us out of here."

"We have to bribe her again," Uncle Max said. "Give her the rest of our possessions."

When Stashik returned that evening, he looked resigned but resolute. "It's time for you to leave." He spoke directly to my father and Uncle Max.

"But we can't just walk out of here," my father said.

"My wife is having a breakdown, she can't take it," Stashik said.

Aunt Tsivia neatened her hair with her hands before joining the conversation. "Our children won't survive out there, Stashik. We have nowhere else to go. Please."

Stashik seemed to be caught off guard by Aunt Tsivia. His expression softened as he momentarily regarded her, but then he shifted his attention back to my father and uncle. "It's been over six months. The Nazis are at the farm every day, and it's just by chance that they haven't already posted soldiers in our home. We'll all be killed if you stay. I won't risk my family's life any longer. I'm sorry." With that, he left us alone, in a state of panic.

4

Where Is God?

My father and Uncle Max knew that there were no other viable options. They crept downstairs in the middle of the night to try to persuade Stashik to let us stay. When they returned, discouraged, Aunt Tsivia asked, "Did you warn him that his family will be at greater risk if we leave? That someone will tell the Nazis where we were hiding?"

"Yes. We told him."

"Did you offer him the rest of the jewelry?" my mother pressed.

"He doesn't want our things, he wants us out. His wife wants us out. The Gestapo is constantly stopping by the farm for provisions. Stashik is constantly hammering those nails into the wall to warn us that they are nearby. His family's life is at stake, too," my father said. In the dark attic, he was flapping his arms around in exasperation, as if he were attempting to fly.

The following night, when Stashik came up, the adults pleaded with him again.

"What else do you want from us?" my father asked.

"It's not a matter of you giving me more."

"But Stashik, my friend, we have nowhere to go," Uncle Max said. "Every day, through the cracks, we see Jews being dragged away. You

yourself say that the Jews hiding in the forest are killed by the Poles if the Germans don't find them first. We'll all be slaughtered."

"I am putting my family at mortal risk as well. My wife heard that fifteen Poles were executed by the Germans last week, including a two-year-old girl, for sheltering three Jews! She is terrified," Stashik said.

My father and Uncle Max looked at each other. Then Uncle Max stepped forward. "We have just so much left, but it's yours—jewelry, silver, even money. You can have it all."

"Please let us stay," Aunt Tsivia begged. Then she added, "I have a beautiful leather coat with fur trim, which a neighbor is keeping for us. It can be yours as well."

I hated to watch my parents desperately begging like this. I tried to help, too, staring sweetly at Stashik. He had stopped talking for a few moments, probably considering his options. Finally, he sighed and said, "All right, all right."

At the earliest opportunity, on the next moonless night, Aunt Tsivia and Uncle Libish snuck back to their neighbor's home, several miles away, to retrieve the leather coat. They tapped on her rear window, and when she appeared, they explained their plight. But she did not take pity on them. To their shock, she said no. The war was not over, so they could not have their coat. Thinking on her feet, Aunt Tsivia said that without the coat, our family would be killed and the blood would be on this neighbor's hands. As my aunt had hoped, this troubled the neighbor, a devout Catholic, and she went to talk to her priest the following day. He encouraged her to give up the coat and whatever else she could. When Tsivia and Libish returned a few nights later, the coat was left for them, along with milk and bread.

Although we were given a reprieve, relations with the Grajolskis were increasingly strained. The pot of potato or bean soup and scraps of bread that had often been left for us at night now appeared only on rare occasions. I remember the aroma of mashed potatoes and fried onions wafting up from the kitchen, and feeling so sad that I was choking down a vile-tasting scrap of raw potato instead. My father and uncles began taking turns sneaking out at night in search of food. In the summer they stole plums, apples, and pears from neighbors' gardens. And they went into fields to gather carrots, radishes, tomatoes, and onions—vegetables that could be eaten raw.

Besides what they picked outside, they also gathered food that sympathetic neighbors left out for them on doorsteps. Because they knew that as Jews we kept kosher, neighbors mostly set out potatoes, beans, or bread. From time to time, my father and uncles chanced knocking on the doors of casual acquaintances. Often they were turned away with angry replies, which was not surprising. Even if they were not anti-Semitic, Poles were terrified of being caught helping a Jew.

One night, when Uncle Max was out foraging for food, a friend invited him inside to meet Sonia, a young woman who had sewn for his family before the war and now was hiding there. Sonia turned out to be a distant relative of ours, and she had met Uncle Max once before, years earlier, when my uncle offered a shy schoolgirl a lift on his sled. That night, they spoke for only a few minutes, but I could tell Sonia made an impression on Uncle Max, because he told my father about her the next day.

Another evening, Uncle Max happened upon the home of an acquaintance who gave him a pail of potatoes and a big loaf of bread. Beyond this, she promised to leave more food out for him every Tuesday night. When Uncle Max returned the following week, however, the porch was bare. Maybe he had confused the days. He left quickly and went to the nearby home of another acquaintance. "You're alive!" the surprised man said when he cracked open the door. "You must leave quickly!" Apparently a trap had been laid for Uncle Max at the previous home, and the Gestapo was out looking for him.

When food did arrive, it was the highlight of our day.

"It was a good trip. Maybe this will last two or three days," Uncle Max announced triumphantly early one morning.

"There's bread. Wake up," I whispered to my sister, rousing her from the partial trance in which we existed. There was no clear distinction between the time that we slept and the time we were awake.

We arranged ourselves in a circle to watch Uncle Max divide the bounty. The adults had agreed that whoever went out to forage for the food got to divvy it up. That morning, Uncle Max placed a few crumbs of bread, a piece or two of onion, and a bit of pear before each of us. Although our mouths were watering, we first said a prayer, thanking God for the blessing of food. Then we devoured our few bites, unable to get it into our mouths fast enough.

"Slow down or you'll get a stomachache," my father whispered.

"This pear is delicious. You did a good job, Max," Uncle Norman told his brother. He still had the piece of pear in his mouth, savoring it for as long as possible.

"I would have grabbed more, but a dog started to bark, so I had to run away."

Uncle Libish was staring at my sister's portion, and mine, looking perturbed. "My girls got less food," he announced.

"Everybody is suffering. Nobody has enough food," Uncle Max told his brother-in-law. "Look," he added, pointing to his own ration, "I didn't even take bread for myself so the children could have more."

Coming to his brother's defense, my father added, "Why don't you go out next time and bring back the food if you don't like the way it's divided?"

"Are you saying I don't do my share?" Uncle Libish asked, raising his voice.

"Don't scream. Do you want the Gestapo to take us away?" my father asked.

"It was more amusing to listen to the two of you bicker back home. In here, it's just annoying," Uncle Benny said.

"It doesn't matter. We're going to die of starvation anyway," Uncle Libish said.

"Libish, try not to talk so much about dying. I want to live," Uncle Max said.

These intrafamily struggles were more real to me sometimes than the war itself. To be sure, I had a keen awareness that monsters were out to get us, and I felt a constant sensation that I was being hunted and trapped. But I was too young to understand what war meant, and no one explained any of it to me. I tried to freeze my brain and control the thoughts I allowed in. I pictured my parents' beautiful bedroom, with its comforter and magnificent lace curtains, and the many loving moments that had taken place there. I would imagine the soft pillow and bed where I used to sleep, and then I would relax for a minute or two. I think that's what saved me—thinking about all of the good things back home and believing that we would all go back there someday.

After a year in the attic, depression had descended upon the group. Communication was quieter and less frequent. Everyone withdrew into him- or herself and dozed much of the time. Slowly, I lost the will to talk. This didn't seem to bother anyone, since as soon as one of us children breathed a word, an adult covered our mouth. Each hour was the same as the next. Before the war, my parents had tucked me in at night, but by this point, they didn't seem to notice when I fell asleep or woke up. It was as if I didn't exist. It's a miracle that we stayed sane—or at least mostly sane.

"God, why? Why are you doing this?" Aunt Tsivia asked tearfully in the dark one night. My uncles had asked this same question, but I never heard an answer.

"Tatu, why isn't God helping us?" I managed to ask my father the next morning, after watching him go through his religious ritual of wrapping two small black boxes containing scriptural passages with thin leather straps around his head and forearm while he prayed.

"It is not God who has forsaken us," my father told me.

"So we still believe in God, right?" I asked.

"Of course."

My father never lost faith. His morning and evening prayers probably helped him to keep some sense of order and feel in control of at least the spiritual part of his life. I was still confused about God's role, but I didn't want to ask too many questions.

By early 1944, we had been in the attic for more than a year and a half. My brother, Nachum, then five, became very ill with dehydration, malnutrition, and probably lack of stimulation. He lay helplessly in a corner and weakly cried, "Mama." I don't think he had ever been seen by a doctor. One morning, I awoke to a lot of commotion.

"He can't be dead," my mother sobbed, cradling my brother in her arms. "Nachum, wake up, little baby."

The adults were crying hysterically. My father was trying to comfort my mother. Dead? What did that mean? My brother couldn't be gone. It was incomprehensible to me. As Uncle Max took Nachum's lifeless body out of my mother's trembling arms, I closed my eyes and pretended that what was happening was not real.

Nachum's death left thirteen of us in the attic, at least for the time being.

I don't recall what took place in the days afterward. It's all a blur. Maybe we just slept. A few months later, I do remember watching my mother sitting in the straw, with the rest of us gathered around, preparing to light the candles for Shabbos. My father was by her side, and I was somewhere across from her. Already sick and weak, she lay down for a few moments and cried silently. "I'm dying. It's over," she said quietly.

I was sure I was dreaming. I wanted to ask her what she meant. I wanted to crawl over and sit in her lap. Instead, I sat still, frozen. She sat up in a burst of energy, took a deep breath, pushed her curly dark hair away from her eyes, and looked intently around at each of us, as if she were saying good-bye. Then she laid her head down again and lay very still. I couldn't understand why she wasn't moving.

As they realized what was happening, people became hysterical. "Leah, Leah," everyone whispered, trying to rouse her. Still, she didn't move.

After what seemed like an eternity, my father took her into his arms and helplessly held her limp body. At some point, he hugged my sister and me. Through sobs, with his arms around our shoulders, he whispered, "Your mother is gone. You lost your mother."

I tried to convince myself that what was happening was not real. Then why was Uncle Norman now holding me? I wondered. "Everything will be okay," he was saying.

I felt frozen, totally paralyzed. I leaned against my sister, as my father and his brothers collected themselves to wash my mother's body with water. They prayed as they wrapped her head, torso, legs, and feet in a white cloth, in accordance with the Jewish ritual for purifying a corpse. Then they carried her down to be buried in the garden. It all seemed surreal.

Later that night, I heard terrible, muffled, sobbing sounds all around me.

"Shh! There will be a time to cry. This isn't it," Uncle Max said.

I just watched and listened, in terrible distress, knowing that I was not allowed to say anything. The only way that I could cope at all was to detach myself. That's how I would live a lot of my life afterward—as an observer, plagued with an inability to be fully involved in the present. Suddenly, my mother was gone. In the days that followed, we didn't talk about her death, or the death of my brother. We were all imprisoned in our own private grief, probably feeling that there, but for the grace of God, we went. I was six and a half years old, and felt utterly insignificant. I also felt enormous loss, grief, and emptiness, and clung to that sorrow as a symbol of my mother, because it was better than feeling nothing.

5

Far from Normal

In the summer of 1944, we sensed that the war was almost over. Stashik was appearing more frequently with updates that the Allies were closing in on the Nazis or that the Russians were approaching. The adults continued to pray, but they were afraid to get their hopes up. One morning we were awakened by a commotion outside: people shouting, bombs exploding, and bright flares flying over the attic.

"Could it be over?" Aunt Tsivia asked.

My father crawled over to peek out through the wooden slats. He could see soldiers from the Russian army. "They're running around like crazy out there," he observed. Then we heard more bomb blasts and felt the attic shaking. "Duck down!" he shouted.

"This whole place will be set on fire!" Uncle Libish said.

The noise and rumblings seemed endless. Terrified, I covered my ears. At some point, Stashik appeared, dressed neatly, in clean overalls.

"The war is over," he announced, smiling.

Everyone stared at him, in shock. It was like waking up from a nightmare.

"The Russians won! They chased out the Germans. You're free to go," he said.

"I cannot believe it!" Uncle Norman finally exclaimed. The realization was sinking in. The adults became more animated and had tears in their eyes. They probably wanted to jump for joy, but after two years of immobility, most couldn't even stand up.

"This is the day we've been praying for!" Aunt Tsivia said. She couldn't manage to walk, so she settled for crawling over to hug her daughters.

"It's a miracle! It's over!" said Uncle Benny. He held out his hand to help up his brother Henry. "Let's leave this stench and go into the light."

"I never thought we'd survive," Uncle Libish said.

"Can we get out of here?" Cousin Sally asked. She was the only child who could walk on her own.

"Yes. Let's go home. Live again as free people," my father said. I barely recognized his voice after only hearing him whisper for so long.

The adults, pale and bent over, gathered up their few possessions. My sister and I felt bewildered. We could not imagine what it would be like to be free, or to go home without our mother.

"What's the matter, Sara?" I whispered when I saw tears streaming down her cheeks. I had not used my voice in so long I did not really remember how to speak.

"My legs hurt too much to walk. Look how bent they are." She stood up, and I noticed her bowed legs.

"Don't worry. Someone will carry you down."

"But I don't want to go out there," my sister confessed.

"Why not? You'll see your bed and our beautiful garden."

"I'm afraid to go outside. It's safer in here, as long as we're quiet."

"Oh," I said. Now I was having second thoughts, too.

We were dressed in the same clothes we had worn into the attic two years earlier. They were filthy and reduced to shreds. My shoes didn't fit any longer, so my father wrapped my feet in some sort of fabric to protect them. Somehow, we still managed to look decent. We brushed our hair with a brush Stashik had given us, and the men shaved.

Uncle Max carried me down in his arms. I felt like a piece of baggage that had been warehoused for two years. When we got to the front door, Stashik and Maria Grajolski were waiting.

"May God love you and always be with you," my father told them. The other adults each said their own thank-yous on the way out.

"Go with God," the farmer said. Then Stashik grew serious. "You must get away from here as quickly as possible. Don't forget, no one can ever know I hid you." He opened the door and we tentatively stepped outside, making sure the coast was clear. We would never see him again.

"We have to be careful," my father cautioned the minute the door closed behind us. "We don't know who's out here, or if anyone is searching for us." We left as quickly as possible, in small groups, just as we had arrived. The difference was that many of us, even the adults, had to crawl.

When the Grajolskis' farm was out of sight, Uncle Max set me down and told me to try to walk. Others tried to stand on their own as well. I took a tentative step or two and then fell. Soon, we heard shouting and gunshots from all directions.

"I knew it was too soon," Uncle Libish said. "The Germans are still fighting."

"We have no choice at this point. We're heading home," my father said.

We had assumed that because the war was ending, that was that. But as the German forces withdrew westward and the Red Army advanced from the east, they were still battling. It was a sunny summer day, and as we slowly walked through the cornfields, making our way down to the river, the Germans and Russians fought on either side of us. Flares and bullets flew overhead. Polish farmers stood out in their fields, confused as to what to do.

My father began shouting directions. "Let's move quickly!" he said. "Quick, hide!" he was saying a minute later. "No, keep going."

I took a few steps, in between being carried.

"Be careful where you walk," someone said. We had no idea where land mines might be placed. Soon everyone was exhausted. We were also starving. We had sat down in the reeds along the riverbank to eat some raw corn we had picked when my father bounced up, like a rusty spring.

"Who's there?" he gasped.

"What is it?" Aunt Tsivia shrieked.

I hadn't heard anyone approaching, but I was afraid to open my eyes. When I dared, just a crack, I saw another refugee in the reeds. He was a tall, skinny teenager with straight, sandy brown hair. He looked up at us.

"Uncle Iche?" he said after a couple of seconds.

A look of recognition came to my father's face. "David? Is that you?"

"Yes. I can't believe I found you! I was afraid that none of you had survived."

"Look," my father told all of us, smiling. "It's my nephew David!"

"Of course! Thank God, David," Uncle Max said.

By then, I realized that David was my cousin. His mother, Aunt Masha, was my mother's sister. His father and sister were the pair we had watched run by the attic window, just before they were shot. But nobody mentioned this.

"Where were you hiding?" my father asked.

"First I was in the forest. Then on a farm." David went on to tell us that his mother had been murdered, and confirmed what we had witnessed, that his father and sister had, too.

My father told David to come stay with us. At first, David resisted. He thought it would be safer to remain on his own. Things were still precarious. But my father insisted.

As one group, we slowly resumed our trek home to the background cacophony of gunshots, explosions, dogs barking, and loud Russian soldiers. I was terrified, sensing that at any moment something terrible would happen. Amid the chaos, a Russian soldier in a khaki uniform and triangle-shaped hat approached, his rifle pointed at us.

"I am Jewish!" Uncle Max shouted, lifting his hands into the air.

"I am also Jewish," the Russian said. Then he lowered his rifle. "Where are you headed?"

"Home," my father said.

"I will take you there."

"It's like God would send him," my father said quietly to Uncle Max.

Hours after we had left the attic, we finally arrived home. Once inside, I looked around in shock. The lace curtains had vanished. The brand-new wooden furniture was gone. Apparently it had been burned for fuel, the adults surmised, based on the remnants scattered around. And there was trash everywhere. We were standing in a cold, empty shack. It didn't look or feel anything like the home I remembered. My sister and I started crying.

"We'll just have to make the best of it," my father said sadly, surveying the ruins.

There was a knock on the door. The soldier had returned, with an elderly Russian doctor in tow. "My friend will explain to you how to re-acclimate," he said.

We stood in our empty kitchen listening to the doctor's recommendations.

"You need to slowly expand your lungs. They're congested because you haven't breathed normally for such a long time," he said, pausing to demonstrate with a slow, deep breath. "And be careful to stay out of the sun."

"What's wong with the sun?" I asked. I seemed to have lost the ability to pronounce r's and l's.

"Our skin is so pale that it will burn very easily," Uncle Norman explained.

"We can never go out in the sun again?" I asked.

"No, just for a little while," he said, smiling.

Finally, the doctor advised us to eat only small amounts at first, since we had gone for two years without real food. He wished us luck and left with the Russian soldier.

That evening, we all plopped down on the floor to sleep. The next night my father decided we should sleep down in the basement.

"*The basement? But that's where Mushe stores our crops in the winter!*" I said.

My reference to my mother brought a pained look to my father's face. To my disappointment, however, he skirted any mention of her. "There are no windows down there, so it will be safer," he explained. He had heard rumors of spontaneous pogroms by anti-Semitic Polish neighbors. In nearby towns, as the Germans retreated, local Poles were attacking Jews who returned to reclaim their homes and possessions.

We thought that we would return to normal circumstances and that no one would believe what terrible things we had endured. But we quickly discovered that things were far from normal, and that there was no one around to hear what we had been through. In fact, only one in ten Polish Jews had survived the war. My mother's stepmother, Grandma Simma, who had lived next door, had been killed in one of the Jewish ghettos. Even our Polish neighbors seemed to have vanished. Perhaps they were afraid to be seen with us. Grandpa Aharon's home, where my single uncles had lived before the war, was torn apart, uninhabitable. Uncle Max could not locate even the treasured family Torah that his father had buried behind his home.

Despite the danger, my father and some of my uncles attempted to transact some business. Eager to again earn a living, they took sugar from a bombed-out factory in town and bartered it for unreclaimed clothing and textiles that sympathetic Poles had hidden for Jews. Then they resold the clothing and fabric.

My sister and I stayed home, often with Uncle Norman, when my father was out, trying to work. We were still in hiding. Not only was it unsafe for us to walk around alone, but we were still in shock. We were not remotely ready to socialize or attend school. I was weak and thin as a rail. My legs were bent, and my chest hurt when I took deep breaths. With Uncle Norman, we drew pictures and talked. Sometimes he would braid our hair or help wash our clothes.

Our house never returned to being the warm home I remembered. My father was more preoccupied than before the war. I felt a huge void from my mother's absence, which I longed for my father to fill. Instead, the distance between us expanded as he avoided any discussion of my mother, or of my feelings about her death. Even if my father had been able to talk about those things, it seemed impossible to have a private conversation. There were always other relatives around.

Our lives at least had a daytime and nighttime once again. We brushed our teeth, washed up, and celebrated some semblance of Shabbos. In the evenings, we sat on stools around a makeshift table and ate modest dinners that everyone pitched in to prepare. Over boiled eggs, potatoes, and vegetable soups, my father and uncles discussed business opportunities and the latest rumors.

"Can you believe a Pole asked me today where our family hid during the war?" Uncle Max said at dinner one night.

"You didn't tell him, did you?" my father asked.

"I didn't say a word," Uncle Max said. "But he said to me, 'Never mind, I'll tell you where. The Grajolskis' farm.' I was shocked, but very casually I said, 'Why do you say that?' "

"With a strange, knowing smile, the Polish man said, 'During the winter, all the homes had snow on their roofs—except for the Grajolskis'. And what would explain that? Heat—generated by bodies in the attic.' "

My father's and Uncle Max's eyes met. They looked worried.

"What could I say?" Uncle Max asked, dunking some bread into his bowl of soup.

"You couldn't have lied?" Uncle Benny asked. "You know that Armia Krayova still wants to kill the rest of the Jews here."

"They're not going to touch us. We are five men with guns and grenades," Uncle Henry said. Since he spoke so rarely, when he did, I figured it was important.

"Guns in our house?" I asked.

"No. Neighbors just think we do," my father said gently to me. Then he turned to his brothers and more tersely said, "That's enough in front of the girls."

"*What's Armia Krayova?*" Sara asked. She was absentmindedly pulling her bread apart, sending crumbs cascading onto the table.

"*They're Polish thugs who want to kill the rest of the Jews. During the war, they helped the Germans fight against the partisans,*" my cousin David explained. He told us that he had befriended Jewish partisans in the forest. They had hidden in underground bunkers and strategically struck at the Nazis.

"*I heard that just last month, not far from here, Armia Krayova barged in on a family during Shabbos dinner and killed all of them,*" Uncle Benny added, dramatically.

"*That's enough!*" my father said. He looked at my sister and me and could tell we were scared. "*Every country has good and bad people,*" he said, putting his hand over mine. "*Some Poles helped us, like Stashik. Others did not. We just have to know who to trust.*"

That ended the conversation for the night. But the truth was, we did not know whom to trust. Poland had been a center of Jewish life for nearly a thousand years. Now, it seemed, we were despised in our own country. Soon the situation grew more precarious.

One morning, a few months after we had left the attic, my sister and I were sitting on our front porch when Uncle Max raced over, looking pale. We followed him inside.

"*Everybody! Come quick!*" he yelled.

"*What's going on?*" my father asked.

"*You won't believe,*" Uncle Max said. "*Thank God they were alive.*" He told us that early that morning, when he had gone over to Aunt Tsivia's home, he found the entire family lying facedown, crying hysterically, with rags pushed into their mouths. As he worked quickly to untie them, one by one, he pieced together what had happened.

"*Masked men came with rifles,*" Tsivia said, trying to catch her breath. "*They were screaming about not wanting Jews in Poland. That we should go to Palestine. Then they fired a shot right past my head.*" At the mention of the gunshot, all three girls, Sally, Miriam, and Lola, burst into tears again.

"*They shot at you?*" *Uncle Max asked his sister.*

"*Yes, Max, honest to God. To prove that they were serious about killing us if we didn't leave Poland.*"

"*They called us 'Christ killers' and said they would kill all of us,*" *ten-year-old Sally said as she sobbed.* "*But they didn't.*"

"*Thank God,*" *Uncle Max said, looking to his sister to explain.*

"*God was good. There was one man who showed mercy and convinced his partners to rob us but not kill us,*" *Aunt Tsivia said.*

Standing in our kitchen, Uncle Max breathlessly retold the story and then raced ahead to his conclusion. "*We can't stay here any longer. It's absolutely not safe. You should have seen the looks on their—*" *He was interrupted by a knock on the door. When my father opened it, a young Polish man around the age of twenty stood there with a machine gun. No one moved. My heart was pounding so hard it hurt my ears. Then our cousin David broke the silence.*

"*Don't worry. This is an old friend of mine.*"

David turned to his friend. "*Don't tell me you belong to Armia Krayova.*"

The man ignored the question. Instead, he looked directly at David. "*I promised when I saw you last that I would do you a favor if I could. Well, this is the favor of your life.*"

"*I'm listening,*" *David said calmly.*

"*Whoever sleeps in your uncle Isaac's home tonight will not be alive tomorrow morning. I'm sorry to tell you this.*"

By evening, my father had made arrangements for us to leave home once again.

6

Good-bye Urzejowice

"We have to go quickly, Ruchel," my father called.

I raced into the kitchen where my family was gathered, clutching small bundles. I noticed that Uncle Max's new friend Sonia was also there, along with her brother and two cousins. Apparently my uncle had convinced her that she would be safer if she joined us.

"Let's get going. Quickly," my father said, leading the way. Everything was always rushed.

"Where are we going?" I asked.

"To Rzechow."

I had heard of Rzechow because it was the largest city near us, in the southeast of Poland. In the dark of night, we climbed into the horse-drawn wagon to begin our hundred-mile journey. I felt like a suitcase that was being transported.

"Are you as scared as I am?" I whispered to my sister.

"Not quite."

"Then why are you shivering?"

"Shh!" my father whispered.

I looked back one last time through squinted eyes. My home seemed like an apparition. I concentrated on inhaling the aroma of the lilacs in the air, pretending our exodus wasn't real.

"Good-bye Urzejowice," I said, bidding a final farewell to our village, as our horses trotted over stones, past the familiar farmhouses and trees I could only sense in the darkness. Around each corner, I closed my eyes in fear of who was lurking. It felt as though someone was chasing us and we had to get away quickly—a sensation that would remain with me throughout my life.

"Do you hear anything?" I asked my sister, snuggling as close to her as possible.

"No. Just your voice." Sara had changed since the war. My favorite playmate was now as serious as Yom Kippur, the day of atonement. She hardly ever smiled.

We arrived in Rzechow in the early morning. The city, its gray buildings taller than I had imagined, was in ruins from the war. It was now packed with refugees, and there were few apartments to rent. But we managed to find two large rooms that resembled banquet halls upstairs in a cold, damaged, rat-infested concrete building. My uncles, cousins, and Aunt Tsivia stayed with us in one room, while Uncle Max's friend Sonia moved into the other room with her group.

At the first opportunity, we went downstairs to check a list of survivors. I held my father's hand as we maneuvered through a crowd that had congregated around sheets of white paper posted on one of the concrete walls of our building. I felt so small, I was sure someone would step on me. My father stared at the names on the list for a long while. His eyes grew watery and his jaw tensed. Then, silently, he led us over to a spot away from the crowd.

"They're all gone," he said, shaking his head from side to side. It was now official that all of our other relatives in Poland had perished—my grandparents, aunts, uncles, and cousins. Again, no one said anything directly to the children. They believed that this way, we would get over our losses more quickly.

"I kept praying that there would be another miracle," Uncle Max said, with tears rolling down his cheeks. "That someone else had survived."

My father and his siblings cried and hugged each other. I hoped that somebody would pick me up and comfort me. No one did. I felt dead. Later, when I watched Aunt Tsivia hold her own daughters and brush their hair, I felt even more deprived.

"I wish I had a doll like that," I said to one of my cousins, eyeing a shmatte *(rag) doll she had been carrying around with her.*

No one responded. My cousins now seemed more aloof. Maybe they feared that being motherless was contagious. Meanwhile, their father, Uncle Libish, so gentle and funny with them, called me "a bratty runt." When I cried about it, he said, "You should be ashamed." I felt bad enough about myself without being denigrated by a member of my own family. My father tried his best to take care of Sara and me. He took walks with us and tucked us in at night. But he treated us more like his younger siblings than his children.

We ate our meals at makeshift tables in a large hall. The food was probably provided by the United Nations, which had established a relief agency to assist survivors. I preferred to have meals with just my family because I was unaccustomed to conversing with strangers. There were children all around, but like me, many of them were very sick. I coughed a lot and felt constant pains in my chest and back. Weak and terribly underweight, I rarely ate. When we lined up for dinner, even the smells made me sick to my stomach.

"At least have some dessert," my father would urge. "You have to eat," he pleaded. I couldn't refuse, because my father worried that I was so unhealthy. Once, he spooned Jell-O from his plate into my mouth. Immediately after it touched my lips, I vomited. I wouldn't touch Jell-O again for years.

Eventually, my stomach began to accept small amounts of food. In the street, my father bought a strange round fruit and divided it into sections. "It's a pomerants," *he said, invoking the Yiddish name for an orange. "Taste it."*

"It's delicious," Sara said, squeezing the juice from a section onto her tongue.

I tentatively put a small piece in my mouth.

"I like it."

"Eat, eat," my father said, relieved to see me getting some nourishment.

Another afternoon, we were in front of our building when a vendor passed by, pushing a cart on wheels.

My father stopped him and bought a waferlike cone filled with a creamy-looking substance. He gave it to me.

"Try it, Ruchaleh. You'll like it. It's called lody," he said, using the Polish word for ice cream.

I hesitantly took a tiny lick. To my delight, the sweet cream melted in my mouth.

"It's good," I proclaimed. "Can I have more?"

My father looked surprised. "Yes. It will help you gain weight." As he dug into his pocket for a coin, he added, "If I earn money today, we can buy more tomorrow."

My father aspired to make a better life for us. He dressed up in slacks and a jacket, and tried to do some "hondling," which meant wheeling and dealing. He would buy whatever he could and resell it. In the dining hall, he sought out new acquaintances to drum up business. There was one woman there to whom my father paid particular attention. Instead of talking about business with her, he made small talk.

"Where are you from?" he asked.

"Kraków."

"Ah, Kraków," he said. I noticed some lightness in him for the first time. "I was very fond of that city. Who are you here with?"

"I'm by myself, I'm sorry to say." I thought she sounded very intelligent and sincere. She would look over at my sister and me with her warm brown eyes and include us in the conversation. "Your daughters are very beautiful," she would tell my father.

Sara and I smiled back. We liked her. But she would not be in our lives for long. After two months in Rzechow, the Russian army ordered the Jews into the marketplace first thing one cold morning. It was early spring, and I stood shivering in the square. I nervously clutched my father's hand as we awaited the news.

"Our army cannot protect you any longer," an officer announced. He was referring to the Russian army's inability to protect the Jews from the Poles. "At this time tomorrow, military trucks will arrive and transport you to a new location. If you're asked questions along the route, play mute."

"Where will they take us?" I asked my father, as the officer continued with a litany of directions.

"God willing, somewhere better."

The following day, armed soldiers escorted us onto a large, canvas-covered military truck packed with refugees. Like us, most of them were sick, nervous, and confused, with no idea where they were heading. My family still did not understand why the nightmare was continuing. While anti-Semitism had long existed in eastern Europe, in our village, at least, we had been seen as good people and liked by our Christian neighbors. Now a whole country didn't want us. I looked around, hopefully.

"Who are you looking for?" my father asked.

"The nice lady you talked to in the dining hall. Will we see her again?"

"I'm afraid not."

I put my head down on my father's lap and closed my eyes. Others stood up and lifted the truck's canvas top to catch glimpses of the sights—the beautiful countryside and bombed-out factories along the way—but I was carsick and in no condition to sightsee.

After several hours, the truck came to a halt. "It's time to get out," a soldier ordered. Our family got off the truck and huddled together, unsure of what to do next.

"Where are we?" I asked.

"We're at the border of Czechoslovakia, in a city called Humenné," someone told me.

"Why are they leaving us here?"

My father knelt down and put his arms around my sister and me. *"Someone will come and explain,"* he said.

A short while later we noticed a few soldiers approaching, female as well as male. *"They're Jewish!"* Uncle Max exclaimed. *"Like angels sent from heaven."*

As it turned out, the soldiers, known as chayalim in Hebrew, had been sent by the Zionists in Palestine, who were working to create a Jewish state. For many Holocaust survivors, Palestine symbolized life in a country free of anti-Semitism. But it was not so easy for Jews to emigrate there. The British, concerned about conflict between the Arabs and the Jews, restricted the visas they issued into Palestine. To thwart these restrictions, underground Zionist groups organized border crossings for Jewish survivors to immigrate illegally. That afternoon, these soldiers sorted us into large groups and led us into a building with a kitchen and sleeping areas. This would be our first displaced persons (DP) camp. These camps were set up by the Allied armies after the war to assist those of us who had been rendered homeless.

We remained in Czechoslovakia for only a short time, and then were moved to Romania. There, we encountered a strange new sight— emaciated Jews dressed in striped black-and-white uniforms, with turbans wrapped around their heads.

"Why are they wearing uniforms?" Sara asked.

"They are former concentration camp prisoners," my father said.

"Why are the women staring at you?" I asked Uncle Max's friend Sonia.

"They're probably surprised to see a Jewish woman who still has long hair." I learned that women in concentration camps had been forced to shave their heads.

On the afternoon of May 8, 1945, ten months after making our way down from the attic, my family was in a beautiful Romanian park in Satu Mare when an announcement came over a loudspeaker: *"The war in Europe is officially over." We jumped up and down and hugged one another, momentarily feeling a sense of freedom that had thus far eluded us.*

After three months in Romania, we were transferred again, this time to Budapest, Hungary. In the DP camp there, we slept on cots in military barracks, with curtains separating each family. Over the next half a year, our lives took on more of a routine. The men tried to conduct some business, and Sonia found a sewing job in the city. At this camp, I attended a version of school for the first time, although it was extremely unstructured. I also took my first shower there. The warm water running down my face, into my eyes, felt uncomfortable. So did bathing in public with naked women. In the religious culture I had known, women were modest, often even avoiding wearing short sleeves.

This strange environment did not intimidate feisty Aunt Tsivia, however. One day, she heard some men bothering Uncle Libish on the opposite side of her own makeshift shower stall. She grabbed a broom and started poking it over, yelling at the men to leave her husband alone. Lo and behold, both my aunt and uncle emerged unscathed.

In addition to Aunt Tsivia, I would soon acquire a new aunt as well. I was sitting on my small cot one night, talking to my father and sister, when Uncle Max, by then thirty-three, and Sonia, in her late twenties, came in giggling.

"We have some good news," Uncle Max said with a smile.

"You're getting married?" my father asked, springing up from his cot.

"Yes, we're engaged!" Sonia shrieked. After weeks in Budapest, going on dates to kosher restaurants and spending time getting to know each other, she and Uncle Max had fallen in love.

"Mazel tov! Mazel tov!" we all said, taking turns hugging them.

Despite Uncle Max and Sonia's exciting news, we were still in a zombielike state. Huge clouds of unresolved loss and pain continued to hover overhead, when the Jewish soldiers escorted us by train to Austria after six months in Hungary. In 1945 Austria had been divided up into four zones—British, Russian, French, and American. My family had wanted to avoid the British zone because the British, unhappy with the Zionist situation in Palestine, were less kind to the Jewish refugees. In their zone, Jews lived in separate blocks within larger camps. In the American zone, on the other hand, Jews were provided separate DP camps and given a preferential status for emigration.

Despite our intentions, we somehow initially wound up in an ugly DP camp in the British zone. If the wind blew in a certain direction, we could detect the scent of burning flesh emanating from the mass graves at what had been a nearby death camp. When we arrived, we were directed into a tent where stern-looking women were armed with scissors.

"Quickly, come over here," a heavyset woman said.

"What is she going to do to us?" I asked my soon-to-be aunt, Sonia. My legs were shaking, I was so scared.

"Don't worry. She won't hurt you," Sonia said soothingly.

"Come stand right here," the woman interrupted. When I walked over, she sprayed disinfectant all over me.

"Yuck! It smells terrible," I protested. Then she whipped out her scissors and began chopping off my hair. "Ouch! Stop!" I cried.

She continued hacking away before shaving off what was left. "Now the scabs from the lice have light and air to heal," she said.

We moved from camp to camp in Austria, until we made our way to the Linz Bindermichl camp in the American zone. There, the adults continued to do a little business and some socializing as well. Uncle Benny got engaged to a refugee named Dora, and we were thrilled to congratulate another hopeful couple. One afternoon my sister and I were walking around our camp when we noticed Dora talking to a short, stocky woman with high cheekbones and straight brown hair. They kept looking over at us.

"Who is she?" I asked.

"I don't know. She probably wants to meet Uncle Henry," Sara said, with a knowing laugh. "She's too old for Uncle Norman."

We had noticed that the female survivors always wanted to get to know our handsome single uncles. With Uncle Max and Uncle Benny engaged, only the younger Henry and Norman remained available.

A few days later, Sara and I were playing in the camp with some of the other children when we heard our father calling us. We ran inside to find the same woman we had noticed a few days before with Dora. She and my father were smiling.

"Sara, Ruchel, this is Clara Friedman," he said.

"We saw you in the street with Dora," my sister said. "She's almost our aunt."

"Exactly," Clara said. "That was me! Such bright girls, I can tell," she said. When we didn't say anything else, she said, "Do you know Czechoslovakia? That's where I come from."

"Yes," I said. "We've been there."

"I can see this one is an alte kop," *she said, referring to me in Yiddish as an "old head." "Do you girls like music?" she then asked.*

We didn't say anything. My father jumped in. "Sure, the girls like music."

"Well, later, I will come and play the violin for you," she said with a big smile.

Afterward, my sister and I assessed our father's new companion.

"I don't like her," I said, as soon as they got out the door.

"Me neither," my sister agreed.

"The other lady was nicer," I said.

"What other lady?"

"The one in Rzechow who used to eat dinner with us."

"But this one looks younger. That's probably why Tatu likes her better," my sister said. To us, choosing a wife was like buying a chicken.

"Do you think she knows that Tatu is old?" My sister and I were laughing about this when my father returned. Fortunately, so eager was he to tell us more about Clara, he never asked what was so funny.

"She survived the war in Auschwitz," he said.

We were familiar with Auschwitz because refugees had described their experiences there. "Was she there with her family?" Sara asked.

"Not really," my father said, probably not wanting to frighten us.

"Tatu, how old is Clara?" I asked.

"I think she's twenty-nine, why?"

"I was just wondering." I glanced over at my sister, and we smiled.

From then on, Clara was always around. In the evenings she played the violin for us. Her only relative in the camp, a nephew named Wolf in his early twenties, accompanied her on the accordion. My father would watch with pride. Then he and my uncles would dance. I loved to fox-trot, tango, and waltz with them, especially with Uncle Norman, even though I had to take a lot of breaks. I kept coughing and grew weaker because I was often too nauseous to eat.

My sister and I were inside drawing pictures one evening, a few weeks after Clara arrived on the scene, when our father walked in with a serious look on his face. We waited for his words to come, but he seemed at a loss. This made me nervous. Finally, he gave us each a hug and announced, "Girls, Clara is going to be your new mother."

Neither of us knew what to say.

"We're going to get married," my father said, more slowly this time. Again, we just stared back.

"But we don't need a new mother," I said. Sara and I were both under the delusion that our real mother might come back.

"Just give her a chance, and everything will be fine," my father said.

Not long after, Clara came to talk to my sister and me. I barely looked up at her when she walked into the room, pretending that she didn't exist. But she did. "I'm happy to be marrying your father," she said. "And I like you both very much."

I forced myself to smile. Filling the uncomfortable silence, Clara said, "I hope you will like me. If you're nice to me, then I'll be very good to you."

Clara tried to act sweet after that. But I was sure that she didn't really want my sister and me. Because I lived mostly inside of myself, I had become very intuitive about people——even before they realized I was old enough to think. Clara never asked me what I needed or told me that she loved me. She didn't fill an ounce of that empty vessel I carried around inside me. Although her sheep's clothing remained intact, it was clear that she expected me to simply do as she told me and not to have my own feelings.

When we left Austria, our family split up. Since Aunt Tsivia's group of five had learned that their immigration might be sponsored by Uncle Libish's brother in the United States, they went to Germany to await visas. Cousin David remained behind to await a visa of his own. My father hired a guide to take the rest of us across the Alps into Italy. With a tiny knapsack each, my sister and I bundled up for the journey in peacoats, hats, scarves, and underneath it all, heavy blue felt pants that Sonia sewed for us.

The steep mountainous route was particularly difficult because we were traveling at night to avoid detection. Not only were vigilantes still out to murder the Jews, but we were entering Italy without visas. Through much of the ten-hour march, my aunts-to-be cried that they would not make it. One of them fell and injured her ankle. I also was carried a lot of the way. I remember my father tossing me across a stream into Uncle Max's arms. Every time I tried to walk, my legs collapsed. None of us were aware how sick I had become.

7

Una Situazione Molto Grave

I was eight years old when we arrived in Italy in late 1945. It had been nearly a year and a half since we had left the attic. We first stayed briefly in DP camps in Trani, Barletta, and Bari before settling in a large camp in Cremona, in the hills surrounding Milan. Because this camp was near the Austrian border, many of the hundreds of refugees had arrived as we had, by crossing over the Alps, in hopes of arranging for emigration from Italy.

We moved into a long one-story schoolhouse that had been used by soldiers during the war. At first our family had our own small room. We cooked meals there on a hot plate. Although we shared a common bathroom down a long hallway, this was luxury to us.

In the winter of 1946, just two weeks after Sonia and Uncle Max's wedding, my father married Clara in the Cremona camp. Clara wore a royal blue dress with gold buttons, and my sister and I wore matching navy blue wool dresses with white lace appliqué collars. The color scheme matched my mood. At the reception, Clara played the violin while guests sang and danced. I sat in a chair, feeling deprived, confused, misunderstood, and lonelier than ever. I thought of myself as an orphan, which was the worst thing you could be in Europe at that time.

Wedding photo of Isaac and Clara Gamss. Italy, 1946.

"Come join the celebration, Ruchaleh," my father urged.

What is this woman doing in my life? I wondered. *How can I treat her like my mother?*

I grew more rebellious. When my new stepmother would comb my hair, which wasn't long enough to braid after it had been shaved off, I said, "You don't have to comb it." I didn't want to be beholden to her, and in my fantasy, she was going to be temporary. My attitude did not go over well.

"You ungrateful brat. You would still have crust on your scalp from lice if it weren't for me."

"*You're not my mother. Leave me alone,*" I shot back.

"*I'll tell your father that you don't appreciate anything I do for you.*"

"*Good. Tell him,*" I shouted, before storming off in a corner to cry. Yes, I didn't want anyone taking my mother's place, but Clara gave up trying to win me over very quickly.

"*You're spoiled rotten. You want to keep your father to yourself,*" she told me.

"*No, I don't.*" It seemed odd that she was competing with me for my father's attention.

"*Why can't you be more like your sister?*"

"*Stop asking me that!*" Wasn't it obvious that my sister was fourteen months older, and she wasn't sick? I felt as though a pillow was being stuffed over my face once again; no one allowed me to talk about what I was feeling.

I was coughing more and more, in pain when I breathed, fatigued, and not eating. When Clara looked at me, she would say, "*Yuck! You look so sickly. I don't even want to touch you.*" My father eventually took me to an Italian doctor, who told us that in addition to being malnourished, I had tuberculosis and rickets. He explained that tuberculosis was a bacterial infection that probably had spread to my lungs, joints, and bones. Rickets was a disease caused by a lack of sunlight and vitamin D that had softened my bones. This explained why I was now bowlegged and slightly stooped. When the doctor added that I needed to be treated in a sanatorium for seriously ill children requiring long-term care, I burst into tears.

"*I'm not going to go!*" I told my father the following day. He was forcing socks and shoes on me in preparation for taking me to the Catholic hospital in Cremona.

"*You have to get dressed. You heard the doctor say how sick you are.*"

"*Please don't make me go!*"

Feeling terrified and desperate, I screamed and cried as my father pulled me down the street by the arm.

"You're very sick. The doctors are going to help you," he kept saying.

"I'm not going to stay."

After walking for forty-five minutes or so, we arrived at a big black wrought-iron gate, surrounded by beautiful gardens. Two nuns were waiting for us.

"Good morning," they said solemnly.

"Good morning," my father said.

"What is your name?" one of them asked me.

"Ruchel."

"Ah, Rachele," she said, pronouncing my name in Italian. "Come inside."

She led us down an antiseptic-smelling corridor into a long, austere-looking room. The walls, the floors, the bed linens—everything was white. She guided me over to an empty bed, and told me to change into a hospital gown and climb in. I dragged myself onto the bed, and a nurse took my temperature and pulse. My father pulled up a chair and sat next to me for a while. But when the time came for him to leave, I panicked.

"Don't leave me," I pleaded, grabbing his shirt. "I'll die if you leave me here."

"I'll be back tomorrow." He loosened my arms from around his neck and left. I felt abandoned.

As promised, my father returned the next day. Again, I cried hysterically, "Please, please, please take me home. I can't stay here another night," I begged. I was so upset I could barely catch my breath. Eventually, my father and the nurse left the room. When they returned, the nurse said, "Get dressed. You're going home."

My father was so upset with me that he barely spoke on the long walk back. Clara was furious when she saw me. "I can't believe you are so weak as to allow an eight-year-old brat to manipulate you," she told my father. Then she turned to me and said, "You are going right back."

Over the next few days, I grew sicker and my father took me back to the hospital. An impeccably dressed elderly doctor named Dr. Del Vecchio came in. He marked red ink on my chest to indicate where my lungs were affected.

"La situazione e molto grave," I overheard him telling his colleague.

"Poverina," the colleague said, as he gave me a shot.

I agreed. Poor me! I was very frightened of death. I was also terrified that my father would vanish, as my mother had. Each day when he left, I felt abandoned. I feared that if I fell asleep, I would die. At night, a tall, older nurse with curly steel gray hair took care of all the children. She wore a blue-and-white-striped uniform and a white cap on her head. As she walked around taking temperatures, she stopped at my bed and whispered, "You must go to sleep." I closed my eyes. But as soon as she walked away, I opened them again. I spent the long, dark nights concentrating on staying awake.

I learned Italian quickly, which wasn't necessarily a good thing, because the nurses said things to one another, assuming I didn't understand.

"She's on the critical list," I heard one nurse tell another.

"What's a critical list?" I asked, surprising the nurse. She told me that it was something for doctors and nurses to worry about, not little girls.

In a bed not far from mine lay a boy about my age who looked gravely ill.

"Can you speak to him?" one of the nuns asked me.

"I really don't speak Polish well."

"Just ask him his parents' names. And tell him not to be afraid," she said.

To me, this boy symbolized death, maybe my brother's death. Ultimately, I summoned up the courage to walk over to him. Keeping my distance, I asked, "What's your name?" He responded so softly I could barely hear him. The following day, his bed was empty, and I heard the nurses say, "Morto," which means "dead" in Italian. Once again, nothing was explained to me. I began to feel that I had this evil effect on people; they were always dying around me. I was convinced that I, too, would experience an untimely demise.

My father visited me every day. Often, he brought me chicken soup in a glass jar. "Clara made this for you," he never failed to remind me.

"She hates me."

"She doesn't hate you. Just be nice to her when you come home."

Standing beside my bed, my father would feed me small spoonfuls of the soup. I pretended to enjoy it. But I couldn't really swallow much of anything in the beginning. When he wasn't looking, I spit it onto the floor. Once, I got into a spasmodic coughing fit, which produced a terrible pain in my chest and back. "Something got caught in my throat," I said, willing myself to sound relaxed.

"Are you okay?"

"I'm fine." I was determined not to upset him. Also, I didn't want anything to interfere with my going home.

The nuns wore black headpieces and walked around with their hands in their sleeves, half in prayer. They were extremely disciplined and somber, always whispering. But they took care of me and never yelled or swore. It was the first time in years that I felt safe and accepted—even pampered a little.

Sorella (Sister) Jacomina and Sorella Theresa were my favorite nuns. The attention I received from them was wonderful.

"Eat," Sorella Jacomina urged. She was tall, with dark eyes and eyebrows. Although she was very serious, I felt warmth emanating from her. "I can count your ribs and wrap my fingers around your thighs."

I smiled but didn't open my mouth.

"It's delicious. Minestrone with pastina," Sorella Theresa pleaded, holding the bowl of soup with little bow-tie noodles up to my mouth. Short and chubby with piercing blue eyes, she smiled a lot. She was older than Sister Jacomina, but seemed to have more fun with the children.

"I can't," I said.

"God will bless you," Sorella Theresa responded. As she leaned forward, the prominent cross she wore on a long beaded chain around her neck dangled before my eyes.

As I grew healthier and could get up out of bed, the nuns encouraged me to mingle with the other patients. I knew little about playing with other children, but I was like a chameleon, just wanting to adapt and blend in. "Was your temperature normal today?" the kids would ask each other. We couldn't go on the outings to the velvety, fragrant rose garden or for ice cream in the park if we had a fever.

When the nuns put my hair in braids, the girls told me that I looked cute. Sometimes one of the kids would ask me what happened to my mother. I hated this question and would quickly try to change the subject. If they persisted, I would say, "She's at home."

Of all the patients, I liked the Italians best. It was in my nature to try to fit in wherever I was. An Italian girl named Angelina became my closest friend. I don't remember what her illness was, or whether I ever knew. Most vividly I recall that she brought me home from the hospital with her one weekend, and I felt sad there, seeing her surrounded by her family. And I was beginning to feel very strange in the midst of all the Catholicism that everyone around me took for granted.

The children dressed as angels in the hospital Christmas show. "This is for you, angel," Sorella Theresa said, presenting me with a white choir dress, a gold halo, and wings. She thought of me as a miracle child because I had not been expected to survive. Although I was still so weak I could barely stand up, I walked to the gorgeous rose garden to take photos and then to the church for the performance. I couldn't even bring myself to mention to my father the next day that I had been in a Christmas show.

On another occasion, the nuns carried me down to the hospital chapel. I had an uncomfortable feeling, which I was right to have. They intended to convert me. I sat in the front row and watched them prepare to place the host on my tongue. Then three of them walked over to me, smiling.

"Stick your tongue out, Rachele. God will take care of you," a nun instructed.

"Today you're going to receive communion," another proclaimed.

"You'll be one of us. In God's good graces."

Knowing I had to get out of there, I slipped down from my chair, pretending to faint.

"Oh, poverina," *one of the nuns said, sighing.*

"Poor little girl! She must be sick!"

They lifted me off the floor and carried me back to bed. They didn't ever try that again, but there was a lot of talk about Christ the Savior. They urged me to go live with an Italian family, and I think my friend Angelina's family wanted to adopt me. It wouldn't have taken much for me to agree, except that I couldn't hurt my father, and I didn't want to give up my religion. I was proud of being Jewish.

After nine months, I was healthy enough to leave the hospital.

"Look what I made you for this special occasion," *Aunt Sonia said proudly, standing beside my bed. She had accompanied my father, and was holding up a long-sleeved maroon dress with tiny flowers.*

"It's beautiful," *I said, putting it on. Just before we left, the doctors, nuns, and children gathered in my room to say good-bye.*

"Take care of yourself," *Sorella Jacomina said, hugging me.*

"Come back and visit," *Sorella Theresa added before giving me her own big hug.*

"We'll miss you," *Dr. Del Vecchio added.* "And make sure to eat plenty of fatty meats and cheeses."

"Good-bye, Rachele," *they all said, waving.*

"Good-bye. I'll visit," *I promised.*

I walked home between Aunt Sonia and my father, holding their hands. Tears rolled down my cheeks.

"We're going to fatten you up," *my aunt vowed. I was still underweight.*

"Clara bought butter and raw eggs especially for you," *my father said enthusiastically. Raw eggs were thought to be good for the lungs. Then he looked down at me.* "Don't look so sad. You're going home. You'll be with your family."

I made no reply.

8

A Taste of Freedom

Back at the DP camp I discovered that my family had been moved into a large, crowded room with beds all around and a wooden table in the middle. All the loud noises of everyday life there scared me. I longed to return to the peaceful hospital.

We were living in a beautiful country, and yet we couldn't advance ourselves because we were not citizens. The few items of clothing we had were made ourselves, or occasionally sent from relatives in the United States. One day, a large cardboard container arrived in our room.

"I wonder what's in it," I said excitedly, as my father opened the box.

"Ugh. There's that smell again," my sister said.

"Mothballs," Clara said. Then she looked inside. "Oy. Thank God. Beautiful things they sent," she told my father. She unloaded the used clothes into coordinated piles. There were jackets, sweaters, long skirts, and stylish floral-patterned dresses made out of stretchy nylon tricot and wool.

"Look at this," Sara said, holding up a fuchsia-colored round-necked wool sweater. "I think it will fit me."

"Why do you get it?" I asked, sorry to see my sister claim the prettiest sweater.

"This will look nice on you," Clara said, handing me a white shirt and

Ruchel (front, far right) and family members, playing cards and reading in Cremona displaced person's camp. The blankets (behind the family) separate the family's room from the others.

blue cardigan. The skirts were all too big for me. I vowed to gain weight so I could fit into prettier clothes.

The camp was a self-contained world of displaced people. There was a makeshift school organized by Zionists who had come from Palestine to help us prepare to immigrate there. Our classes were conducted primarily in Hebrew. We celebrated Shabbos, learned a little math and geography, and performed in plays. The teachers who came from Palestine, like the drama instructor, were upbeat and happy. Others were East European refugees, recruited within the camp; by contrast they seemed subdued and preoccupied with their own tales of woe.

"Tell me the answer to this equation," my East European math teacher would ask me, after scribbling some subtraction or multiplication problem on a chalkboard. He appeared to be in his midthirties and had pale, pocked skin and thin light brown hair.

"I don't know." I would shrug. I hadn't even learned addition yet.

"I just showed you how to do it," he inevitably said. "You need to focus."

I was constantly told that I was lucky to be a child because the adults had suffered so much more. Clara also told us how much harder her situation had been, as a concentration camp prisoner, than ours. She often reminded us that her sister and twelve nieces and nephews had been killed and put in the ovens at Auschwitz. How could I be angry with someone who had been in a concentration camp? And I couldn't be angry with my father either. In the attic, I had been jealous of my young brother for getting my mother's attention, and then he had died. I had been angry at my mother for not giving me enough affection, and then she was gone. Now I was terrified of even acknowledging any feelings that I feared could harm my father's health. He was my last prayer.

Over time, I made a few friends in the camp. I walked around holding hands with two girls my age named Raya and Shoshana. Raya was from Russia and Shoshana was from Poland. Together, we played hopscotch and hide-and-seek, and we embroidered. One day I was in the courtyard with my friends, picking sunflowers, when a handsome man named Alex walked over. He and his wife had briefly shared a room with us at the camp.

"Ruchel, do you want to go on a bike ride?" he asked.

I was surprised by the invitation, since I barely knew him, but I shrugged and said, "Okay." For me, any attention was flattering. Besides, I had seen other kids riding with grown-ups on bikes, and it looked exciting.

I sat in front of Alex on his bicycle, and he rode me through beautiful fields. As I was enjoying the feeling of freedom, he leaned closer and told me that I was cute.

He pedaled on, holding me tighter. By the time he stopped in an isolated grassy field, I sensed that something was wrong. "Let's have a picnic," he suggested. Suddenly his dark eyes and olive complexion looked sleazy rather than handsome. I was afraid.

"I want to go home," I said.

He sat down on the grass. "Come sit next to me," he coaxed.

"Please take me home," I repeated, as tears welled up in my eyes.

I felt like I couldn't breathe as he guided me by the hand to sit beside him. He reached his arm around my waist and held me tightly. I looked around, praying someone would be there to save me. I wanted to run, but instead I froze in place.

"You're such a pretty girl," he whispered into my ear. I was afraid that if I cried out, he wouldn't take me home. My heart pounded as he pulled down my pants and started to reach his fingers between my legs. I tried to

Ruchel (left) and her sister, Sara, 1946, Italy.

squirm away, but I couldn't. He unzipped his pants and rubbed his hard penis against my back. Finally, he let go of me. I began to run away.

"Okay, I'll take you home," he yelled.

I wasn't sure whether to believe him, but I didn't know how else I would get back. I kept my eyes focused on the grass as I walked back to the bike.

"It's okay. You're a nice girl, and this happens to nice, pretty girls," he said.

I don't remember the ride back. I never mentioned the incident to anybody for fear that I had done something wrong. It just confirmed my feeling that I was not safe anywhere.

When the camp grew too crowded, a children's dormitory was built, with cots for girls in one room and boys in another. I was devastated when Clara insisted that my sister and I sleep in the dorm. I felt like I was being pulled away from my father.

"I'm afraid to be without you, Tatu," I said. He was sitting at the wooden table in our room, looking distressed.

Before he responded, Clara said, "Stop being so spoiled. We need privacy." They probably did. By then we were living in a one-room bungalow, where they shared one bed, Uncle Henry and Uncle Norman slept in one pair of bunk beds, and Sara and I in another.

"Your sister will protect you," my father said. "Sara, you make sure to take care of Ruchaleh."

"But I'm just a kid. How can I protect her?" my sister said.

"You're the older sister. You need to make sure that Ruchel is safe."

"What if something happens to her?"

"Sara, you are very responsible. You won't let anything happen."

"Okay." My sister sighed. She was popular with the children in the camp and was bigger, stronger, and prettier than me, with healthy apple cheeks. I looked up to her with pride. I hoped that if I latched on to her, she could help ease the pain of missing my mother. But the more I pursued her, the more she tried to distance herself.

From left to right: Norman Gamss, Sonia Gamss, Max Gamss, Sara Gamss, Isaac Gamss, Clara Gamss, and Henry Gamss, circa 1946, Italy.

I slept in the dormitory on some nights and with my family on others.

I still particularly loved being with Uncle Norman. Sometimes he sat with me in our room and we drew pictures at the big wooden dining table. I loved to draw women wearing fashionable clothing, even though I had never seen a fashion magazine.

"What's on her scarf?" Uncle Norman asked me one afternoon, examining a drawing I had made of a woman with a scarf around her neck.

"It's a bird. I don't know how to draw them very well," I said.

"This is how you draw a bird," he said, as he drew one on a piece of paper.

"Like this?" I asked, trying to follow his directions.

"Exactly." He looked up at me and smiled. "You have talent."

"Really?" I loved to receive compliments from Uncle Norman. He was a good person, and I wanted to model myself after him.

On Shabbos, we tried to put our worries away and maintain the traditions we had enjoyed in Poland. We dressed up, lit candles, and ate festive dishes that Clara had cooked. On Saturdays, after my father attended shul, or synagogue, in the camp, we took walks together through the farms and wheat fields of Cremona. While these times together were enjoyable, I was often struck with the existential sense that I was living in a superficial, fake world, and that the people around me were acting. I kept confusing the happy feelings I had had years earlier, on my walks in Poland, with my present situation. I was always conscious of what Clara was thinking. Her mood either brightened or ruined my day.

It was 1947. Our family was taking a walk one Shabbos afternoon, my father and his brothers speculating when their visas would arrive, when I heard Aunt Sonia talking to Clara about babies. They kept placing their hands on Clara's belly. I looked more closely and noticed that it had expanded.

"Is Clara going to have a baby?" I asked my sister.

"I think so," Sara said.

"It will be fun to have a baby around," I said. My sister shrugged her shoulders.

Not long after, in November of that year, Sara and I walked into our room to find Clara lying on the bed, a midwife by her side. Uncle Max, Aunt Sonia, Uncle Henry, and Uncle Norman were there. My father shooed us out of the room.

"Wait outside, girls. This isn't for children's eyes."

We sat on a stoop, listening to strange groans and screams coming from inside.

"I hate loud noises," I said.

"It's better than the noises the men make at night."

"I try not to listen." I shrugged. Actually, I did notice the sounds, but I was embarrassed to talk about sex, even with my sister.

After what felt like a long time, my father came out to get us. "Come see your baby brother," he said, smiling.

Sara (left), Ruchel, and baby Sam, 1947, Italy.

Inside, Clara was in bed with the baby. I moved closer and stared in awe. "He's beautiful," I said, unable to take my eyes off of him.

"His hands are so tiny," Sara said. "Oh, look at his fingers."

"We're going to call him Aron Shmuel," my father told us. Aron was for my grandfather Aharon, and Shmuel, for Clara's father.

I was suddenly overcome with worries. I worried about the baby's health, confusing him with memories of my baby brother, Nachum. I also wondered whether my father had forgotten his first son. I feared that the baby would take away what little attention I got from my father. And I worried that expectations would be placed on me to take care of him. And then I became angry at myself for thinking these things, so I just repeated, "He's so beautiful."

Over the next few weeks, I enjoyed pushing the baby stroller into town with my sister and Clara. In the park, we would see the Italian kids jumping rope and eating ice cream. I longed to be one of those joyful children who so obviously belonged, rather than an outsider, weighed down with secret shadows and pain. I quickly came to adore the baby, but I insisted on thinking of him as only my half brother. Besides the ten-year gap in our ages, from day one there was a great difference in the amount of love we each got from Clara. From my perspective, he was constantly kissed and called beautiful, while I was criticized and called names.

We were still living in Cremona in May 1948 when Israel became a state. I wore blue and white and carried a flag as I excitedly marched down the street with a group of children. We had heard a lot of talk about "Eretz Israel" (the state of Israel) and the "land of milk and honey," where Jews would always be safe. Just knowing that such a place existed was encouraging. Some nights, Israeli soldiers would take us in trucks into the hills to learn survival skills in preparation for the war going on in their country.

Ruchel (second from the front), marching through the streets of Cremona, Italy, when Israel became a state, 1948.

"Hide behind a tree. . . . Run across to the next hill . . . ," they shouted at us.

I was terrified, racing across rocks from tree to tree and hill to hill, as flares soared overhead.

"Faster. Like you're running for your lives!" they drilled us.

On the rides back to camp, we sang "Shalom Chalutzim," which meant "welcome pioneers." The song gave me such a feeling of optimism.

My most wonderful memories of Italy are connected with a beautiful mountain resort in the Alpine town of Selvino. There my family spent a few weeks for two summers in a row, because the air quality was conducive to my recuperation. To get up to Selvino, my family traveled for many hours in a rickety truck over narrow, rocky, and windy roads. Everywhere we looked along the way, we saw crosses marking deaths from fatal automobile accidents. We thanked our lucky stars that we had arrived in one piece.

The resort was housed in a former Fascist children's home and run by members of a Palestinian Jewish unit of the British Army. Many of the children there had been orphaned by the Holocaust. Here they could recover emotionally, physically, and spiritually. Although it was a simple camp, through my ten-year-old eyes it was luxurious. My father rented a room for our family in the tiny house of an old lady who wore long black dresses and a black kerchief on her head. I loved rolling down the grassy hill covered with forget-me-nots in front of the house. As I gulped in the fresh air, I felt a little sense of freedom and well-being for the first time in years.

There was a welcome routine to the days in Selvino. In the early morning, I joined the fifteen or so other kids for calisthenics. "It's very important to exercise," the leader said. He demonstrated how to touch our toes, do knee bends and jumping jacks. Breathe deep. Take it all in. Breathe out. I did. We were receiving training to be young soldiers or pioneers in the likely event that we relocated to Israel. "In Israel, the soldiers exercise like this every day. Now it's time for side bends."

I stretched to the side, reaching my arms down one leg, and then the other.

"Ruchel. Bring your shoulders back. It's good for your lungs," the leader said gently. I tried to press my shoulders back, but I quickly grew tired and out of breath. Although I had walked everywhere, I was still weak. Also, this was the first time I had exercised in an organized setting. Some Hebrew and math were also taught, but the main point was to help us socialize and have fun. We sang songs, played cards and board games, embroidered, and danced. There was a cute boy with dark, curly hair and huge eyes. I don't remember his name, but I liked when he held my hand while we were dancing.

In between activities, my family took long mountain climbs and picnicked along the way. The mountains were like mossy forests, with beautiful flowers, mushrooms, nuts, and other edible delicacies.

"Isn't this air beautiful?" Clara would exclaim on our hikes.

We took deep breaths, inhaling the aromatic scents from the flowers and spruce trees. All around us blackberries and blueberries grew wild.

"Can we pick the berries?" I asked.

"Go ahead, Ruchaleh," Clara said, laughing. "I love the mountains," she told us. "They remind me of my beautiful childhood in the Carpathian Mountains. Do you know my family would stand me up on a table to play the violin when I was three years old, and everyone applauded?"

"Yes," my sister and I said. We had heard.

"I was a child prodigy."

Clara still wasn't my mother, but when she was in a good mood I felt hopeful and unafraid of her.

"My sister and I walked all the time like this," she reminisced.

"I wish we could stay here longer," I replied.

"If only you behaved yourself like this more often, everything would be so nice," Clara told me. I was thinking the same thing about her.

All of the little villas in Selvino had blue or green shutters. The residents would open their windows and energetically inhale the fresh air. Next door to our rental house was a beautiful villa. One day, my sister and I looked over the fence and spotted a pretty Italian teenage girl in the garden. She looked up at us and said, "Hi."

"Is this your house?" I asked.

"It's my family's vacation house. Do you want to come over?"

"Sure," my sister said.

The girl led us through a ballroom with crystal chandeliers and gorgeous fabrics draped over narrow couches against the walls. When we arrived at the sunroom, she introduced us to her parents, brother, and grandmother. They were Jewish, as it turned out, and I noted how gentle they were with the grandmother. Their obvious affection for each other in the few moments I observed them became an ideal for me.

"Where are you from?" our hostess asked when we finished the tour.

"Cremona." We never shared our past. We just wanted to be normal.

Selvino was a big help on the long road to my recovery. Not only did I rediscover friendly, contented people, but in these surroundings, I became aware again of sunshine and beauty. I learned that there was another way to live. I saw a possibility that I could grow healthy and strong and that my family could actually enjoy each other's company. Perhaps, most importantly, hiking in the mountains and interacting with the other kids gave me a taste of the freedom I had briefly experienced years earlier. I left there motivated to strive for a better life.

9

The Greenhorns

Our family had wanted to go to Israel, but we had been advised that the fighting there might prove too stressful, given all we had suffered. Consequently, we applied for entry to every other country we could. In 1948, Uncle Norman and Uncle Henry received visas to go to the United States. I remember being in our bungalow at the DP camp in Cremona, watching my uncles gather up their possessions. For the journey, my father had taken them shopping for the good suits, coats, and hats they now were wearing.

"Why are they leaving without us?" I asked my father.

"It's better this way. They'll get to America and look over the land for us," he answered. All I could think about was how I wouldn't see them again for a long time. I knew I would miss them, especially Uncle Norman.

"I'll see you soon in America," he said when it came time for our goodbyes.

"I'll miss you," I said quietly, with tears in my eyes.

"God willing, we'll be together before you know it," he said. He set his cardboard suitcase down and gave me a big hug.

Uncle Max, Aunt Sonia, and their young son, Leonardo, received their American visas nine months later, in July 1949. They were sponsored by a cousin of my father's who had left Poland before the war. Then, in October of that year, our visas arrived, too.

"We got the visas! We're going to America!" my father walked into our room and exclaimed. One of his uncles in New York, Grandma Paya Neshe's brother, had agreed to sponsor us.

"Oh, my God. When are we leaving?" Clara asked.

"When are we leaving? Early November."

"But that's in two weeks!"

"Yes. We have a lot to prepare."

I wanted to share in their joy, but I don't remember feeling any. I had come to love the sounds, smells, and feel of Italy over the past four years. America was another unknown.

"We have to pass a medical examination tomorrow," my father mentioned right away. He and Clara exchanged glances. I knew they were concerned about me.

"Maybe the doctors could be paid under the table. I still have a few gold coins," my father said.

The following day we all went to the doctor. The middle-aged man listened to my heart and lungs. I was shaking with fear that I would be left behind. But to our great relief, the doctor brushed his hands together and declared, "Everything is clear."

Two weeks later, we were boarding a huge cargo ship in Naples, en route to the golden land where opportunities abounded. Passengers were strewn all over the ship. There were no staterooms, just makeshift dividers. We shared one area with several other families. From the moment we embarked, I was seasick. I stayed rolled up in a fetal position on my cot for days.

Even as I lay still as possible, I found myself captivated by one couple. They had two young children and appeared too healthy and intact to be Holocaust survivors. The man was dark and handsome, and the woman *gorgeous and fashionable. Unlike most of the passengers, she spoke Polish, not Yiddish. Maybe only he was Jewish. She had silvery blond hair and wore sophisticated makeup, jewelry, and high heels. I don't know how she did it. It's not as if there were hairdressers or separate quarters. Seasick as I was, I felt uplifted when I stared at this woman. I realized how nice she looked being thin, and I felt better about my own figure. I vowed that when I grew up I was not going to stay with the lowest of the low and be sick. I was going to make the most of my brains and my looks and stand out—assuming I could just survive this excruciating journey.*

When the ship finally arrived in New York Harbor after two weeks at sea, all I could think of was, How do I let go of this cot? As we disembarked, following the crowds down a ramp off the ship like sheep in a herd, I was careful not to lose sight of my father. Strangers were all around me, excitedly kissing the ground or being greeted by relatives. Finally my father spotted his brothers. Uncle Norman and Uncle Henry were standing behind a roped-off area in the midst of a crowd, jumping up and down and waving as they tried to make themselves visible to us.

"There they are!" he pointed excitedly. "Norman, Henry!"

It was so thrilling to see their familiar faces as we ran toward them with open arms. Soon we were reunited, hugging, kissing, and crying. As my uncles helped us navigate our way through immigration, I could not wait to see the bright new world I had heard about.

"Where is the beauty, and the gold in the streets?" I asked my father. Everything looked run-down and depressing as we exited the subway station in Brooklyn.

"Be patient," he counseled.

We arrived at an apartment building where Uncle Max and Aunt Sonia greeted us at their front door. My cousins Sally, Miriam, and Lola came running down the building staircase. Everyone hugged and kissed. I had pictured my three cousins just as they had been when we parted company in Austria, but of course, four years had elapsed, and they looked more grown up.

"You're finally here!" Miriam said in Yiddish. She was now fourteen. Then Sally said something to her. I was surprised they spoke to each other in English. "I just meant that we were worried you would never get here," Miriam said.

I realized that I now felt shy around my cousins. I just smiled, hoping my sister would speak for us. But she just smiled, too.

"Wait until you meet the kids in America," Lola said. She had always been very small, but now she was taller than me.

"Come inside. I want to show you around," Aunt Sonia said.

We stepped inside. Aunt Sonia was already explaining that she, Uncle Max, and their young son, Leonardo, who now was called Lenny, lived in the apartment. My father's sister, Tsivia, lived one flight up, with Uncle Libish and my cousins. We walked through a small kitchen, past a tiny washroom, and into a dining room that faced a brick building. There was a small room with one bed off the kitchen where we would all sleep. By the time we got to the master bedroom, my cousins wanted our attention.

"Come upstairs and see where we live," Cousin Sally urged. My sister and I followed our cousins. Their apartment had more bedrooms and furniture. I wondered why we were not staying up there.

"Look at my bedroom," Cousin Lola said. We followed her into the small room with a linoleum floor that she shared with Miriam. It was nice.

"Do you want to dance?" Sally asked. She was already in high school.

"Okay," my sister said.

We went into their living room, where they had a portable Victrola turntable and a stack of record albums.

"Do you want to hear Perry Como or Frank Sinatra?" Miriam asked.

We had never heard these names. It seemed odd. After so many years apart, we were almost strangers. When we were younger, it seemed we had all spoken at the same time, the words almost on top of each other. Now one of them spoke at a time, more politely.

"You'll like school," Lola said. I listened carefully, since we were the same age. But then she went on to talk about things I did not understand. "Some kids were making out last week in the middle of the school. One boy even said something sexy to me."

"Really?" I said, trying to keep up. But I didn't know anything about boys.

I was encouraged by how quickly my cousins had adapted, and at the same time, I was in awe of them. They viewed themselves as already being Americanized. We were the "greenhorns."

Over dinner, I heard how difficult it was to make ends meet in America. In Europe after the war, food and lodging, however modest, had been provided by relief organizations. In America, it had come as a shock to my relatives once again to rely entirely upon themselves. Uncle Max, who had always been social, had found work in a retail clothing store for Yiddish-speaking customers. Aunt Sonia continued to sew. Feisty Aunt Tsivia also found work sewing. Uncle Libish worked in a factory that made fur trim for accessories like hats and shoes. Uncle Norman and Uncle Henry lived nearby and came to dinner that evening, too. Henry was working in a factory, as a presser. He was a hard worker and talented with his hands, but still not too talkative, so the job was a good fit.

Uncle Norman, the youngest, seemed to have adapted the best. He worked near the pier in a general store that catered to immigrants when they first arrived. His ability to speak Italian served him well, as there were also a lot of non-Jews coming over from Italy. My father's other brother, Benny, had moved with his wife, Dora, to Chicago. Everyone missed Uncle Benny, but they understood why he had not wanted to pass up the opportunity to work in the grocery store of Aunt Dora's uncle.

"Every morning we get up early and go to work," Uncle Libish said. "Don't let anyone tell you that it's easy to become a success here. I promise you it's not."

"I won't," my father said. He used to always have a comeback to his brother-in-law's comments. Now he seemed at a loss, while Uncle Libish looked so confident.

All my aunts and uncles appeared to have adapted. There was a pal-
pable distance between our family and the others that had not existed in
Europe.

I kept hearing my uncles say, "It's very hard here" and "You have to
work very hard." I didn't hear any hope extended, which made my blood
boil.

"How do you get started?" my father asked as he cut his chicken into
pieces.

"You have to start at the beginning," one of my uncles said.

"It's not like you just arrive and own Macy's department store, you
know what I mean?" Aunt Sonia told Clara.

"Of course," Clara said, but she didn't look happy.

For dessert, Aunt Sonia served a delicious gooey white cake with choc-
olate frosting and sprinkles. It was the first store-bought cake I had ever
eaten. I talked mostly to my cousins, but I still overheard snippets of the
adult conversation. Passing references were made to the old way of life and
to my grandfather Aharon, who was sorely missed. I hoped that the con-
versation would lead somebody to mention my mother. I still was repress-
ing terrible feelings that drained much of my energy, and I fantasized that
my mother was my guardian angel, keeping me alive. But nobody said
anything about her.

The following morning, my aunts and uncles went to work, and my
father and Clara left for a while, too. My cousins were excited to have the
house to ourselves. They took out bread and butter, which we ate as we
talked.

"Are you excited about Thanksgiving?" my cousin Lola asked.

"What's Thanksgiving?"

"You don't know about Thanksgiving? It's a holiday on a Thursday,
and we eat turkey," Miriam said.

"Do you like turkey and pumpkin pie?" Lola asked.

My sister and I stared blankly. We had never had either one.

"Help me clean up the kitchen and I'll tell you everything you will
want to know about the holiday," Sally said.

That week, we celebrated our first Thanksgiving in Brooklyn. I wasn't hungry, but I watched everyone else enjoying the festive meal. My father seemed happy to be reunited with his sister and brothers. Later that evening, however, Clara expressed doubts.

"They treat us like we're second- or third-class citizens," she whispered to my father, back in our tiny room, after the others had gone to sleep.

This was a shock to me, because it seemed that so recently we were a highly respected, special family.

"Maybe they're afraid we will ask favors of them," my father said.

Up until then I had been certain that people who survived together would remain close. Now I wasn't so sure. In Europe my uncles had been dependent on my father, and now, it seemed, when we were desperate, no one was offering us assistance.

After a week or so in Brooklyn, we went to stay in the Bronx with Clara's kind, plump old aunt Yetta and her thin husband, whose name I no longer remember. They had come to America as teenagers, and while their apartment was small and simple, to me it was a palace.

"Look, Sara. We're so high up!" I told my sister, as we stared out the window, watching rain fall onto the pavement.

"We've never been in a building this tall!" she said.

Aunt Yetta prepared huge breakfasts with bagels, smoked fish, cheeses, and many desserts. I still wasn't hungry, but after I heard Clara gossip to her about how unruly and sickly I was, I felt I had to be on my best behavior.

When Aunt Yetta's two sisters came by to visit, dressed stylishly in fur coats and jewelry, the elderly women sipped tea and complained about their grown children.

"They're too Americanized," one of them said.

"Who can get along with them when they think they know everything?"

"It's another world here," the eldest of the three sisters lamented. She wore a black shearling coat and old-lady lace-up boots. We called her

Tante Sura. "You'll see," she said to Clara. "American children are different."

Tante Sura took Sara and me shopping one day. "To prepare for school, you should speak English as much as possible," she advised us on the subway ride.

"Okay." I was shy, and mostly responded "Yes" or "No." I also assumed that since she was Clara's relative, she was negatively predisposed to me. From the subway station, we had to cross the street to get to the store. The stoplights changed so quickly it was frightening, and the store itself was overwhelming.

"I can't believe there are so many clothes in one place," I said. This may have been my first time in a retail clothing establishment.

"I hope we don't get lost," my sister said.

"Just stay close to me, girls," Tante Sura said, guiding us over to the escalator. I held on tightly as we stepped onto the moving stairs.

We walked by the racks of clothes, making our way to the preteen department in the basement. Everything seemed so big, and I felt so minuscule.

Tante Sura bought us underwear, blouses, and shoes. "Now, let's find each of you a pretty dress," she said, making a beeline for the dresses. "How about this one, Ruchel?" She held up a blue taffeta dress with a Peter Pan collar and a red ribbon with clip-on cherries in front. "Do you like this?"

"It's gorgeous," I exclaimed.

"Try it on," Tante Sura said, pointing to a fitting room. I loved dressing up. When I came out, my aunt smiled. "That looks so cute. Should we get it?"

I was excited to be buying American clothes of my very own.

One afternoon, my sister and I were sitting in Aunt Yetta's den, talking to some visiting relatives, when a man and woman I didn't know walked in. The woman looked like a princess, with sparkly brown eyes, long lashes, dark, curly hair, and fuchsia lipstick. She was dressed in an elegant outfit, beautiful shoes, and a fur coat. She walked right over, smiled a big, toothy grin, and spoke to us in Yiddish.

"Hi. I'm your cousin Margaret. Welcome to America," she said.

"Thank you," I said. Despite her Hungarian accent, I loved her throaty voice. And her interest in us made me feel important. We explained that we had not yet been to school because we had to find an apartment first. She assured us that we would love school once we got settled.

There was a vague sadness about Margaret. Later, I heard that she had been in the concentration camps but managed to come directly to America afterward. I'm not sure whether her husband had rescued her or they met after the war, but he was reputed to be wonderful to her. Apparently Margaret suffered from depression and was going for psychiatric help. Maybe that was why I identified with her so immediately.

"You'll come to love your new homeland," Margaret said, before she left.

"Thank you," I replied, dutifully. But loving America seemed doubtful. I had no friends and no home. At twelve, I was not only an immigrant but a girl without a mother. I felt like a third wheel everywhere I went. Under these circumstances, I was not sure I could find happiness in any homeland on earth.

10

But We Just Got Used to It Here

We found a tiny apartment on University Avenue, in the Bronx. The building was old, but it had lovely architectural touches such as elegant crown moldings.

"We have to walk up five flights?" I asked, panting, as we ascended the spiral staircase.

Sara got to the top first. "Wow! You can see all the way down. Ruchel, look."

"No. We're too high. I'm scared to look." I moved away from the stairway.

Inside our new apartment, I rubbed my hands on the beautiful glass doorknobs in the living room. "Where are we going to sleep?" I asked my father. He pulled a bed down from out of the living room wall and said that my sister and I would sleep there.

Young Sam got to sleep with his parents in the master bedroom. Even if I had a terrible nightmare, I never went in there during the night. I knew that I would not get any sympathy from Clara, and God forbid my father tried to comfort me—Clara would get mad at him.

The apartment had a tiny kitchen, with a colorful linoleum floor. Off to one side was a white rectangular table with chrome legs. Every Friday,

Clara scrubbed and waxed the linoleum floor in anticipation of Shabbos, and over dinner, she told us how exhausted she was as a result.

"Thank you, Clara," my sister dutifully said one Shabbos.

"I noticed you girls didn't put away your bed this morning," Clara added.

We stared down at our soup bowls.

"Sara and Ruchaleh, try to be more helpful," my father said. He himself took care of many of the family chores, but it sounded like that might change. "I won't have as much time to help out here, since I got a job today," he added, with less enthusiasm than I would have expected. Clara did not seem terribly excited either.

"Congratulations, Tatu!" I stood up to give him a hug.

"Are you working with our uncles again?" my sister asked.

"No. Not yet. It's a job in a factory downtown. They make clothes." My father had always been independent, his own boss. Now he would go to work in a sweatshop.

On a beautiful, sunny day in December 1949, an aunt of ours named Ida took Sara and me to register for school. Aunt Ida's husband had sponsored our family to come to America. As I walked into the huge old junior high school, P.S. 82, my heart pounded against the wall of my chest. I felt little and afraid. My legs shook so badly that I thought I would sink to the ground. I had no inkling of what to expect from school, and I didn't see how I would be able to concentrate with the cloud I constantly felt over my head. I still spoke only a few words of English that I had picked up from my Brooklyn cousins and a teenage neighbor in our apartment building, who had showed me how to wear my hair in "American" styles.

We walked down endless corridors to get to the principal's office. Inside, a tall, stout woman with salt-and-pepper hair, dressed entirely in black, introduced herself. In a stern manner, she proceeded to discuss our class placement. When she looked at me, she said, "After examining your test results, I have decided to place you in the seventh grade, with the children your age. But you will have to work very hard. If you do not keep up, we will be forced to move you back to the first grade."

Aunt Ida translated as the principal moved her lips. "She is saying that you may not wear dungarees, and you must do your homework."

"Okay," I said. All this was Greek to me.

After registration, Aunt Ida brought us back to her apartment, where her husband, our great-uncle, joined us. He asked what names we had used to register.

"Ruchel and Sara," Sara said, unsure if this was a trick question.

"You will need American names now," he said firmly.

My parents had not chosen my name arbitrarily. It was in memory of my father's maternal grandmother, Ruchel. Still, it did not occur to me to disagree.

"What about Rachel?" Aunt Ida proposed, sensing we were uncomfortable.

"It's still too Jewish," her husband said.

"How about Sarah for me?" my sister suggested, pronouncing it Sair-a rather than Saara, her existing name.

"No. Too old," the old man said. "I know. Sandra and Rita."

"Okay," my sister said. I nodded in agreement, too.

"Good. Those will be your names," he declared, looking pleased. The magnitude of this proclamation was lost on me at the time. Rita and Sandra would not only be our names at school, but before I knew it, this is what we would be called by everyone aside from our father, for the rest of our lives. Only years later would I regret the choice. There would be times later in life when I would try to revert to calling myself Ruchel or Rachel, but neither seemed to stick.

We walked to school by ourselves from the first day. It turned out to be a harrowing experience. We froze at the four-way intersection where multiple traffic lights seemed to point in all directions. We tentatively stepped off the curb, but then jumped back as vehicles sped toward us. A kind middle-aged man came along and walked us across the street; then we continued on our way.

In my first class, English, I felt so lost and frightened that I could hardly feel my legs. I tried not to make a sound when I sat down, to avoid calling attention to myself. Then to my embarrassment, my nose began to run because I had a cold. The teacher, Mr. Donkelman, came over and spoke to me quietly, in Yiddish.

"I fought the war in Europe," he revealed.

I appreciated his kindness, but I didn't want anyone to overhear that I was from Europe.

"You're a very pretty girl. You should sit up straight like you're proud," Mr. Donkelman said. Then he handed me a Kleenex.

My homeroom teacher, Mrs. Bell, smiled a lot. She was a big, chubby woman, with a pure white face, blue eyes, and blue-white hair. She wore purple lipstick and round patches of hot pink blush on her cheeks. Because of how ridiculous she looked, I promised myself that I would never wear rouge.

I soon caught on to every subject, except for math. My math teacher was a hateful person, and I heard that she particularly disliked Jews. She was skinny, with gray hair and faded blue eyes. She never explained anything to me and rarely called on me when I raised my hand to ask a question. My father was good at math, but I usually didn't dare ask for help. Besides being impatient, he worked long hours during the week, and after washing clothes on Sunday he seemed to have no leisure time. On the rare occasion that he tried to help me, Clara had a fit. And God forbid he felt ill or had some pain after I asked for help, Clara would say to me, "You see? You see what you did? You're going to give him a heart attack yet."

I was always afraid that my father would have a heart attack. In fact I was preoccupied with death, and all the talk at the time about polio exacerbated my fears. One evening, the family was in the living room when my father came home, upset.

"Mr. Rich still won't give me overtime," he said to none of us in particular.

"Tell him he promised you," Clara said, already sounding annoyed.

"I did. I told him I counted on extra pressing time."

"Well, tell him that you are capable of running his operation," she instructed her husband, *as if* talking to a disobedient adolescent. She was growing increasingly frustrated with his inability to gain any traction in this country. The adjustment seemed to demand too much from him. Each day, he was a bit more diminished. I felt hurt that my uncles were not helping him more, and guilty that I couldn't make things better.

My father's sad countenance brought to mind the beggars I had pitied as a child back in Poland. As he tried to reason with his wife, I obsessed about the burns on his arms from the hot irons at the factory and the exhausted look in his eyes. "Clara, I'm working hard. It's not so easy in this country to start over," he said.

"I'm going to finish my homework in the kitchen," Sara said, extricating herself.

"Then try something else. Stick up for yourself at work and stop being such a shmatte [rag]." By now Clara was screaming, trying to pick a fight. "You're not the only one who had a miserable day. The brats wouldn't help me at all." My brother Sam, pushing a toy truck around the floor, looked over at me.

My father's face by that point was almost white. Certain he would have a heart attack, I ran from the room, covering my ears. I felt like I was dreaming. This was not my life.

At first I was as lonely at school as I was at home. But after a few weeks, kids began to talk to me and offer help. I met Marsha while walking home from school one day. As it turned out, she lived in my building. Soon this smart, athletic, tall girl with curly, reddish blond hair and pale skin became my best friend. Marsha was fun to be around, and I always felt welcome in her home. Many nights after dinner, I would go over to play games or watch television.

"Don't be afraid, I'm right here watching," Marsha would call upstairs to me, in her Canadian accent. "But hurry! The show is about to start."

"Okay. I'm coming," I would yell loudly, mostly for my own benefit. I always ran down the stairs as fast as my legs would go because I had heard stories of how little girls got raped in apartment stairwells and lobbies. Inside, we would often plop down in front of the television set and watch shows like Man Against Crime, with Ralph Bellamy. When the show was over, Marsha's brothers would compete for my attention.

"Rita, come see my stamp collection," her older brother said one evening.

"No. She wants to see my comic books," the younger one insisted.

"Just ignore them," Marsha advised.

But I was fascinated by their collections because I had never seen such things. In my home, no one would have had the time or energy for these enterprises. I began to learn about healthy families by spending time with Marsha. "I'll be there in a minute. I'll just take a quick look," I called to her.

"Okay, but hurry. Then we'll play dominoes," Marsha said. She and her family were always playing games. I was drawn to them as a flower turns toward sunlight.

Marsha introduced me to her friend Arlene, who lived in the apartment building adjoining ours. I would count the minutes until the end of school on Fridays, when the three of us would get together. Sometimes we went back to one of their homes and danced. They taught me to jitterbug as we listened to singers like Bobby Darin and Tony Bennett. I was afraid to bring friends to my home because of the constant tension. Clara wouldn't even say hello if she was not in a good mood.

One Friday in the spring, Marsha, Arlene, and I decided to see a movie at the Park Plaza Theater, which was close to our school.

"My Foolish Heart is playing," Marsha said.

"Is that okay with you?" Arlene asked.

"That sounds good," I said, not revealing that I had never been to a movie before.

Normally, Arlene and Marsha would have ridden their bikes, but since I didn't know how, we all walked. "Do you like any boy yet?" Arlene asked along the way.

"No," I said, embarrassed by the topic.

"Boys are silly," Marsha said, good-naturedly.

At the cinema, we settled into our seats just as the movie was beginning. I relaxed, soaking in the entire experience. I found myself studying Susan Hayward for tips on how to look and dress more glamorously. My spirits lifted as I was transported to this other world. Afterward, I couldn't wait to go back again. Movies gave me a means of escape and made me hopeful about life.

Another bunch of kids asked me to join their club, the Furies. I felt that I must have been doing something right to get their attention. These kids were Jewish and very popular. Our club colors were royal blue and yellow, and we each had a nickname.

"We'll call you Ricky," one of the Furies, Pearl, announced. She was like an earth mother and took control of decisions like these.

"Okay," I said. Gradually, by emulating my friends, I learned to have fun. This was no easy feat, since my father still held the view that frivolity was a waste of time. One Saturday afternoon, for example, my family was relaxing in the living room. I started humming and doing a waltz by myself, hoping to cheer up my father and infect him with my spirit. Clara looked up and smiled. But my father just shook his head, annoyed.

"Okay, that's enough," he said. The gentle tone in his voice indicated some pride he must have felt in me. But he couldn't smile, as if he thought it was a sin to be lighthearted.

"I'm just having fun," I said.

"Oh, don't be silly," he said. I walked out of the room, dejected.

When I was sick with strep throat, as I often was, it was not uncommon for me to go all day without food. I prayed for my father to return home to give me water or make me more comfortable. At thirteen, when I had my tonsils removed, my father arranged for me to recuperate at Aunt Ida's.

"I want to stay at home with you," I told him. I had come out of surgery, and he and Clara were visiting me.

"Clara can't take care of you," my father said sadly.

"Can't you take care of me?" I asked my father, even though I knew the answer.

"*You know I have to work, Ruchaleh,*" he said softly.

"*And be nice to your uncle while you're there,*" Clara added. "*He can do good things for us.*"

"*I am nice.*"

My father brought me to my great-aunt and great-uncle's apartment directly from the hospital. I had been recuperating there for a few days when Aunt Ida went out to run some errands.

"*I'm leaving cold juice on the nightstand, and I'll be back soon. Just let your uncle know if you need anything,*" she said, standing beside my bed.

"*Okay.*"

After Aunt Ida left, my uncle appeared in the room. "*How's my beautiful niece?*" he asked, coming over to the bed.

"*I'm getting better.*"

"*Let me feel your head,*" he said, sitting down at the side of the bed and reaching over to stroke my hair.

My heart began to beat quickly, in panic mode, as my uncle slowly slid his hand down from my face to rest on my lower belly.

"*What a nice girl,*" he whispered.

I tried to smile, remembering Clara's edict to be nice to the man who had sponsored us to come to America (not to mention selected my American name). Again, I felt totally paralyzed; I was unable to escape, with no one to turn to. When my great-uncle's fingers brushed against my private parts, I forced myself to make noises. I think that scared him.

"*I better let you rest now,*" he said, getting up to leave the room.

Years later, I learned that other cousins of mine had also thought of my great-uncle as "a dirty old man." I hated him after this. I was also furious with Clara for sending me there when I suspected that she knew of his unsavory character. Maybe my father was complicit as well, although I couldn't be angry at him.

There was, however, a schism developing in me with respect to my father, a break in my heart. My deep feelings of love were increasingly coming in conflict with my unmet expectations. I began to lose respect for him, and trust. I became aware of the way he would almost sneak into my bedroom at night to tuck me in, like a married man stealing away to be with his mistress. Even if I were bursting with unhappiness about some school matter, my father would look at me with concern but then just say, "Shhh." He would not take the time to ask about my day or sit on my bed and talk. He was always listening for Clara's call to him as he hurriedly kissed me on the forehead and rushed out of my room.

Since nothing was really discussed openly in our home, it was not surprising that my father and Clara never talked to us about sex or dating. One evening, just before I turned fifteen, my sister and I took the subway into Manhattan on a double date with two boys who were a couple of years older. I no longer recall how we had met them, but we saw a Broadway show together, and then they escorted us on the subway back to the Bronx. They were very nice and perfect gentlemen. When we got home, at midnight, my father was pacing.

"Where were you?"

"We told you we were going on a date," Sandra said.

"It's midnight. Do you know how exhausted we are?" Clara asked.

"We're sorry," I said, feeling bad and hoping to end the conversation.

"What did you girls do? Why are you so late?" my father screamed.

"We came straight home after the show. I swear," I said.

"You girls ought to be ashamed coming home this late; girls your age doing I don't know what. I'm surprised you don't know better," Clara shouted.

How would we have known anything? I knew almost nothing about boys, and Clara's words made me afraid that something could have happened.

"We didn't think there was anything to worry about," I said loudly, trying to get them to listen.

"Shh, you'll wake Sammy, and then I'll be up all night, thanks to you," Clara said.

Rita Gamss (left), Norman Gamss,
and Sandra Gamss, circa 1951,
New York.

Sandra and I were both still sobbing as we ran out of the room. I didn't sleep all night.

Occasionally we would get together with our Brooklyn relatives. But it was always bittersweet. I longed for the close relationship we had had back in Europe, but instead there was distance. My uncles were moving on with their own lives in America. One afternoon, Uncle Henry and Uncle Norman came to visit. Uncle Henry brought a lady friend, with whom he seemed serious. She and Clara went off to talk, and Uncle Norman began dancing with Sandra and me. My spirits soared in the arms of my favorite uncle. There was something holy about him. But the reverie was interrupted when I noticed my father in a heated Yiddish conversation with Uncle Henry.

"But her nails are painted red," my father said.

"I don't see a problem with that," Uncle Henry said. He sounded annoyed. I had never seen him get angry at my father.

*Uncle Norman tried to distract me. "Let's keep practicing the waltz,"
he urged.*

*"There's nothing wrong with her!" Uncle Henry said. It had never
occurred to me that his quiet voice could get loud. I had simply assumed
that having grown up in a family of so many children, his voice had been
permanently lost.*

"Why are they arguing, Uncle Norman?" I asked.

*"Your father doesn't realize that Henry and I are grown up now," he
said.*

*"I'm telling you what I think is best," my father was saying to Uncle
Henry.*

"She's my choice, Iche," Uncle Henry said, ending the conversation.

*My father was no longer in control of his brothers. I was proud of my
uncle for speaking up. But I could tell it hurt my father's feelings. Things
had changed. And things continued to change. Just as I was beginning to
get the hang of being a teenager after two years in the Bronx, my father
came home and announced, "We're moving to Chicago. I have an opportunity to go into business there."*

"Chicago?" I said, in utter astonishment.

*"Your father is going into the grocery business with your uncle Benny,"
Clara said. She seemed happy about the decision.*

"But we just got used to it here," my sister said.

*"It's a chance to start a better life," my father said. He still believed
that with the right opportunity, he could turn things around.*

*I wished we were staying in New York and that my father would go
into business with Uncle Norman or Uncle Max instead. But I had no say
in the matter, and it didn't occur to me to get angry. Besides, I, too, still
believed that my father would again be a success.*

*A few days before we departed, I decided to tell my friend Pearl a
secret. After English class, I pulled her aside in the hallway.*

"I have a crush, Pearl."

"On who?"

I took a deep breath. "Herbie." Once I said it, it felt real.

"Herbie?" she said. Then she smiled, putting her hand over her mouth.

I nodded.

"He's so cute!" she said. He was handsome. He had bright blue eyes, a beautiful mouth, nice skin, and dark hair that he greased back.

To my shock, the next day, Herbie walked right up to me in the hallway. He was wearing Levi's and a black leather jacket.

"Hi," he said, smiling.

"Hi," I said shyly.

"You should have told me sooner. I like you, too."

I wasn't sure whether he really liked me or he was just saying that. But it didn't matter. "It's too bad this is my last day here. We're moving," I said regretfully.

"Why didn't we get to know each other sooner?" he asked, looking into my eyes.

"It's too bad," I said quietly. I expected him to walk away, but instead he asked, "Can I kiss you good-bye, even though I don't know you that well?"

"Okay."

He kissed me softly on the lips. My first kiss. I felt more alive than I had in years.

"I'll write to you," he vowed.

"I promise I'll write back."

Then we hugged and walked away in opposite directions. I felt weak-kneed as I brushed away the tears in my eyes.

I was cheered up later in the day when my friends from the Furies met me outside my last class and handed me a gift. "What's this for?" I asked, surprised.

"It's to say good-bye."

"Open it, Ricky," one of them urged. I pulled out a beautiful lavender-colored blouse with a velvet tie and short, poofy sleeves.

"I love it," I said. "I'll wear it all the time in Chicago."

"We're going to miss you," Pearl said, with the others chiming in.

"I'm going to miss you more," I admitted.

"We'll write all the time," another friend said.

I finally had real friends, whom I adored and trusted. And a popular, nice-looking boy who liked me. Things might have gone much more smoothly for me if we had stayed in New York.

For months afterward, I dreamed about Herbie. We wrote four or five letters back and forth. Then one of my friends wrote to tell me that Herbie had a girlfriend. I wrote to him to ask if this was true. "Let bygones be bygones," he wrote back, whatever that meant.

11

Utterly Demoralized

It was February, in the dead of the winter of 1952, when we arrived in Chicago. I was utterly demoralized. Uncle Benny greeted us at Union Station and brought us to his apartment.

"Sholem Aleichem," Aunt Dora exclaimed as she opened the door. She was a rotund, large-busted woman with pretty skin. When she swooped down to hug me, brushing her short red hair against my face, she felt soft and fleshy.

"Aleichem Sholem," we said, which meant "upon you be peace."

"Come on in! You must be starving."

I took off my herringbone wool coat, which I had immediately found to be insufficient defense against the Chicago winter, and was introduced to my younger cousins, Linda and Eddie. Then we moved right into the kitchen for dinner. At the extended table, anchored down with bottles of soda pop and containers of potato salad from my uncle's store, my sister and I were talking to our cousins when Aunt Dora asked whether we were excited to start our new school.

"No, not really," Sandra said.

"We liked our friends in New York," I explained.

"You'll have friends here, too. It will just take time," Aunt Dora said.

Rita Gamss with cousins Linda and Eddie Gamss, 1952,
Chicago.

Her Czechoslovakian accent was similar to Clara's, but she emanated more
warmth and understanding. Then she looked at my plate and said, "You
eat like a bird. Maybe you'd rather have ice cream." Without awaiting my
answer, she brought a quart of Neapolitan ice cream to the table and gave
me a scoop. I wasn't wild about the flavor, chocolate, strawberry, and va-
nilla side by side in the same container, but it beat the potato salad on my
plate. Suddenly I became aware of my father's voice from down the table.
He was in conversation with his brother, Uncle Benny.

"That's not what you said in your letters," my father said. He was smiling, but his worried countenance had returned like a homing pigeon.

"I'm telling you, that's how we operate. That's why we're successful,
Iche."

The room seemed to grow quieter. My uncle looked around and with what sounded like forced enthusiasm said, "You all must be exhausted. Dora, let's take them to see their apartment."

My aunt and uncle had found us a nicely furnished apartment nearby, in the northwest part of Chicago. The red brick building was across the street from a park.

"Come see your bedroom, Ruchaleh," Aunt Dora called. I walked into a cold, teeny, porchlike room, with several windows and a small bed. One window faced my parents' bedroom.

"Oh," I said, disappointed.

"It's charming. You'll love it once you put your own things in there," Aunt Dora said.

As soon as my aunt and uncle left, my father and Clara launched into an analysis of the dinner conversation.

"Do you think they changed their minds?" Clara asked.

"No," my father said.

"He couldn't be serious that you would have to work on Shabbos."

"I'll never do that," my father said.

"But we've moved here already. Tell him he made a promise," she insisted.

"Clara, he knows that," my father said in a clipped tone.

I cried most of the night, too worried about my father to fall asleep. In the morning, we enrolled at Roosevelt High School. Just to get there, I would first have to walk ten blocks to the bus stop in the bitter cold, without adequate clothes or boots. Then the bus ride made me feel sick. When I finally got to school, freezing and dizzy, I felt ill prepared. Even though I was smart, I was embarrassed by my deficiencies.

I spoke English well by then, but math, in particular, remained a horror. I had missed too much school, and I could not concentrate on my homework because there was always an argument taking place at home. Moreover, I was not emotionally equipped to overcome learning challenges. I had not yet put the past behind me. I was carrying around dead people, still feeling responsible for what had happened to my mother and brother.

At first, I felt terribly alone. I remained distant from the other students. After being wrenched away from my great friends in New York, I was convinced that friendships were transient. I was also conscious of being different from the popular kids, who sported the latest fashions and bleached hair. I envied the girls I saw coming to school with their friends.

Even my own sister seemed to shun me. When I looked for her after school, often she had left for the bus without me. I would then walk the five or six blocks alone, feeling rejected. I found it hard to understand why she didn't need me as much as I needed her, why she did not even want to share her clothes with me. I sensed that Clara was trying to turn Sandra against me. She compounded any natural sibling rivalry that we might have felt. If Sandra punched me or fought with me, Clara encouraged it. Not that she was wonderful to Sandra, but I was her favorite scapegoat.

After a few weeks I met Susie, my first Chicago friend. She was from Hungary, and in class we noticed each other's accents. Both of her parents had survived the war in concentration camps. Susie was smart and wholesome, with blue eyes and sandy brown hair.

"Are you going out with anybody?" Susie asked me after class one day.

"No," I said.

"Me neither. Do you want to sleep at my house on Saturday?"

"That would be nice," I said.

Before I left home to sleep at Susie's, I wanted to make sure that my brother Sam was okay. I worried about him, still overlapping him in my mind with my brother Nachum. I found Sam in the living room, watching television.

"Sammy, before I leave, I want to take your temperature."

"But I'm not sick. Mama says you get sick more because you're so skinny."

"You were sniffling, and I want to be sure you're healthy," I persisted.

"Okay, but you're wasting your time," Sam said, sticking out his tongue.

I examined his throat and then gave a cautious prognosis. "It doesn't look red, but you should take a nap today. Colds can lead to pneumonia if you're not careful."

"Okay," he said, knowing better than to argue. "What's namoanya anyway?"

When I got to Susie's home, her parents were cuddled up together on the couch. "Are your parents always like that?" I asked. It was strange for me to see somebody's parents being so loving to each other.

"Like what?" she asked.

"I don't know. So happy together."

Susie laughed, probably not understanding what I meant. I laughed, too.

When summer vacation came, I spent more time with my new friends. One day, Susie and I were at the park with another friend, Louise, when the subject of birthdays came up.

"How are you celebrating your sixteenth?" Susie asked me.

"I don't know." I hoped she would change the subject.

Louise gasped. "You don't know?"

"We don't really celebrate birthdays in my family." The truth was, I was not even sure when my actual birthday was. I knew that I was born in the spring of 1937, on the Jewish holiday of Shavuot, which commemorates Moses receiving the Ten Commandments at Mount Sinai. Although this would have been on June 9 or 10 back in 1937, someone put July 6 on my visa when we came to America, and that became my birthday.

"That's weird," she said.

"Louise, that's not very tactful," Susie said.

"Religious Jews think birthday celebrations might tempt the evil eye," I explained.

"Well, you have to do something," Louise said, unable to imagine otherwise.

"It's not just any birthday. You're turning sixteen," Susie said, squeezing my hands in hers for emphasis. Then she had an idea. "I know, we'll have a party for you."

"That's a great idea," Louise said right away.

I could only imagine what my father would say. "I'm not sure," I told them.

"You have to say yes," they said, in unison.

It didn't take too much persuasion. I nodded.

"She said okay!" Susie said gleefully. Immediately, she began to plan. "First, let's go find you a great dress. I know the perfect store." As we walked across the park and past a series of small shops, the plans unfolded.

"Let's have ice cream at the party," Louise said. "I despise cake without ice cream."

"As long as it's not Neapolitan," I said. I had grown weary of the one flavor Aunt Dora kept in her home.

Suddenly, Susie stopped directly in front of a dress shop. "This is the store," she said. I looked in the window, and spied a yellow dress on a mannequin. It was sleeveless and cinched at the waist, with off-white and black bees embroidered all over.

"Look at that dress! Isn't it beautiful?" I said, turning to my friends.

"Let's go inside and look," Susie said, pulling me by the hand.

The dress looked small enough to fit me. Then I turned over the price tag and saw that it cost eighteen dollars.

"Is there any way you can pay for it?" Susie asked me.

I shrugged. "I can save up some of my babysitting money."

She and Louise whispered to one another. "We'll pay for some of it for your present," Susie said.

I was awed by their kindness. A week later, four or five of my friends came to our apartment for the birthday celebration. I wore my new dress, and we danced and talked.

"Now aren't you glad we had a party?" Susie asked.

"Yes, definitely."

"Is this really your first birthday party?" another girl asked me.

"I think so. At least the first I remember."

"Well, you'll always remember this one," Louise said.

For one afternoon, my life felt normal, happy, and calm.

Otherwise, at home, my world was in chaos. In truth, I was barely surviving. The pain and guilt I carried around felt heavier each day. If Clara had a moment when her mood was lighter, or even if she put a plate of food in front of me, I felt a surge of hope that maybe she liked me. "We're lucky to have her," my father kept saying. "Just do as she tells you."

Our apartment came stocked with a cabinet filled with novels. Before I made friends, I spent my rare quiet moments devouring classics like The Good Earth and Pavilion of Women. They became my reality. Clara ridiculed me for reading, because it meant that I was not helping her. One afternoon, I was sitting curled up in our living room chair, which was covered with protective plastic, reading Orwell's 1984, when she walked in the room.

"What? Are you going to sit all day? Get up and dust the furniture."

I ignored her and continued reading, afraid of an onslaught of criticism.

"What am I, your slave? You spoiled little brat," she shrieked.

Hurt, I started to cry. "I just want to finish this book."

"Do you see me sitting and reading? Of course not. Oy vey iz mir. Tell me why I have to do all the work?" She stood close to me, as if waiting for an answer.

I kept reading as I stood up and carried my book into the bathroom.

"You'll be the death of me yet," Clara shouted. For good measure, she added, "And your father's going to have a heart attack when he hears about this."

My anger gave way to guilt once again. I began imagining the fight she and my father would have that evening over me, and he was unhappy enough already. When my father refused to work on Shabbos, Uncle Benny had reneged on his promise to bring him into the grocery business. Once again, my father had found work in a sweatshop, this time ironing dresses with steam machines all day. Not wanting to add to his stress, I opened the bathroom door and asked Clara how I could help.

My feelings of loyalty, that a family bond is sacred, didn't mesh with the reality that many of my needs were being ignored. My father no longer bore any resemblance to the confident man he had been before the war. He was increasingly depressed and remote. Although he corresponded with his siblings in New York, he seemed more distanced from them as well. The only thing that remained the same was his commitment to religion, which often sparked its own tensions.

"Ruchaleh, Sammeleh, I'm thirsty. Can one of you open the refrigerator?" my father asked one Saturday afternoon.

"Papa, why can we open the refrigerator but not you?" five-year-old Sam asked.

"I can't turn on lights today," my father said.

"Won't the light go on if I open the door?"

"Sam, you know it will. But Papa thinks bad things will happen to him if he violates the Shabbos law. He knows that we will be okay," I told my brother.

It was into this environment that my younger brother Brad was born, in 1954. Although I quickly fell in love with him, his arrival was more troubling for me than Sam's had been. My father was hardly functioning. I didn't understand how he could have another child when he barely focused on those already there. He was fifty-two, and Clara was forty. They argued often and seemed so unhappy. Clara would tell us how she had been cheated out of life by marrying our father. Increasingly, I wished that I could be adopted by someone who would give me attention.

Aunt Dora and Uncle Benny had become enemies with my family after the grocery business fiasco, and I felt I should hate them as well. But their home was my oasis of sanity, one of the few places I could get some rest. Sometimes I stopped by there after school to take a nap. Depression and illness undoubtedly contributed to my constant exhaustion. I seemed to contract just about every cold, flu, or virus that went around. Also, I did not get enough sleep at home because of the constant arguing there.

"You let Ruchel walk all over you," I heard Clara say as I lay in bed one night, early in my junior year. She and my father must have been in their bedroom, which was adjacent to mine, and the walls were paper-thin.

"I was just helping her with a math problem," my father said wearily.

"A math problem? While I'm tucking two babies in by myself?" She sounded infuriated. Then I heard her footsteps stomping into the bathroom. "I'm going to faint. Help me!!!" she screamed, before slamming the bathroom door. The whole family raced in and found her on the floor with her head between her knees.

"What's wrong?" Sandra asked.

"Are you okay?" I forced myself to inquire.

The Gamss family in 1953. From left: Rita, Isaac, Sam, Clara, Sandra.

"Oh, my God. This could be the end," she said, her voice barely above a whisper.

"Clara? Clara, please calm down," my father said with a panicky voice.

Although we had been through this before, Clara was still convincing. She continued to gasp for air until she had everyone's sympathy and apologies for having upset her. Then she went off to bed without saying another word. My father was left pacing in circles. My sister and I were bewildered. Once again, I was too upset to fall asleep.

Returning to school the next day was a relief. I had recently met a girl named Marilyn, who would become my best friend. I liked her right away. She sang beautifully, played the piano, and was popular. I felt flattered when she asked me to join her club—the IDL's, which stood for the Ideals.

I also began to meet some boys. Apparently my figure, particularly my increasingly well-endowed chest, was attractive, because men would whistle when I walked by. One boy who took interest in me was Italian American and worked in the grocery store with Uncle Benny. I first spoke with him at Aunt Dora's and Uncle Benny's home after undergoing emergency surgery. I had been having some stomach pains and asked Aunt Dora to take me to a doctor after hearing stories about people having their appendix burst. Sure enough, the doctor sent me to the hospital for an emergency appendectomy. Afterward, while I was recuperating at Aunt Dora's and Uncle Benny's, beautiful roses arrived with a note to me from the Italian American boy.

"He wants to come visit you," Uncle Benny told me when he got home from work and saw the flowers in a vase near my bed.

"I don't think so," I told my uncle.

But the following day, as I was reading in their living room, there was a knock on the door. When Aunt Dora opened it, a cute boy with dark curly hair asked if he could see me. My heart started pounding.

"Ruchel, do you feel up to company?" Aunt Dora asked.

"Maybe for a couple of minutes," I said, nervously setting down my book.

"So are you feeling better?" he said, sitting across from me. "You look good."

"I'm better. Thanks," I said. I didn't want to say anything that would prolong the conversation, since I was hoping he would leave quickly.

The boy stared at me. "You're very cute," he pronounced, smiling flirtatiously.

I smiled shyly, thinking of what to say. "Your flowers were really thoughtful," I said.

"Oh, thanks. I didn't know what kind you liked, but I know every girl likes roses, right?"

"I think so." Then I yawned, trying to emphasize how tired I was.

"Can I see you again?" he asked.

"We'll see," I said, meaning no.

It never crossed my mind that I could hurt his feelings, because I didn't think I was important. Besides, he was not Jewish, and I was not up to the struggle with my father that I assumed this would have led to.

A friend from school introduced me to a boy who was about three years older. I was attracted to him, probably because other girls liked him, and went with him for a walk in the park one afternoon. When it started to get dark, he hugged and kissed me. I struggled to free myself from his embrace. "Take me home," I said. To me, casually making out was scary and forbidden. Before we reached home, the boy asked me, "Can't you just let yourself relax?"

Most boys I spent time with asked me that in one way or another. I couldn't relax. Who could have, weighed down by my concerns? It wouldn't have mattered how I felt about him or any boy, because I had no idea how to have a relationship. Also, I was convinced that there was something objectionable about me, so even when I liked a boy, I wanted to get rid of him before he rejected me first. In my experience, nothing good lasted.

My senior year raced by. Two weeks before the prom, I still didn't have a date. I really wanted to go with this one boy, but I didn't dare let him know that I was interested.

"It's not a big deal. I just won't go," I told my close friend Marilyn, as we sat on her bed one evening.

"You can't skip the prom. We're all going out to dinner, to the dance, and then to breakfast at the marina."

"Well, I'm not going without a date."

"I still can't believe that you don't have a date. There are so many boys who would have died to take you, but you give off a vibe like you're not interested in them."

"I can't help it." I sighed, lying back on her bed. I closed my eyes and prayed that somehow someone would still invite me to go. I don't remember exactly how, but my prayers were answered.

I wound up going to the prom with a twenty-year-old boy from England who was visiting one of my friends, but we'd never even met. I wore a pink chiffon dress, which a neighbor loaned me, and was relieved to find a tall, nice-looking, and very polite boy come to pick me up.

"I like you very much," he said, in his British accent, as soon as we got in his car. His immediate interest in me was unnerving. Later, at the dance, when he tried to put his arm around me, I went numb.

"Did I do something wrong?" he asked.

"No. It's just that I barely know you," I said.

"Well, we can change that. Would you ever want to live in London?"

This question scared me half to death. I couldn't even think about leaving my father and family, even as my relationship with them continued to deteriorate.

In fact, I had little hope that Clara would accompany me to the upcoming mother-daughter tea.

"Is your mother going to the tea with you?" Marilyn asked one day at school.

"I don't know." I never corrected friends when they referred to Clara as my mom.

"*You better tell her about it soon. You still have to get a dress to wear!*"

That evening after dinner, I summoned up the courage to ask her. "*There's this special event for seniors at school, and all the mothers are coming, Clara. Do you want to go?*" I asked. My chest tightened as I braced myself for disappointment.

"*How can I get away for a tea?*" Clara asked, annoyed. "*I have a baby.*"

Tears poured from my eyes. I realized then how important this was to me. "*How can you not come? This is so special to me. I even bought us tickets with my babysitting money,*" I admitted.

"*I don't have the luxury you have to go to something trivial,*" Clara said.

The next day at school I told Marilyn that I was going to skip the tea.

She put her arm around me and said, "*You'll come with us.*"

I hugged her right back. Although her offer did not eliminate the devastation I felt at Clara's rejection, it still came as a great relief to me to be included.

At the tea, I sat with Marilyn and her family. I felt pretty, with my Italian-boy haircut and ice blue dress, but very sad. No one mentioned my mother or stepmother. People didn't want to embarrass me, so they didn't ask me about my family life. I never talked about it, even to Marilyn. She knew that I didn't like spending time at home, but she knew very little about my past.

As senior year drew to a close, I struggled to stay cheerful, but the world was closing in on me. I wondered whether I should be hospitalized. I had difficulty getting out of bed in the morning. I would suddenly tear up in the middle of a conversation. While most of my friends were choosing which colleges to attend, I was worrying that I would fail my math class and not graduate from high school. Everyone seemed to be moving on, but I had no idea what I would move on to.

I felt dead inside. There was only a hint of light that reminded me how much I wanted to live a "normal" life. That hint had to have been the power within myself—possibly little whispers in my ear uttered by my mother before she died, telling me, "You have to live, Ruchaleh, you have a lot to contribute. You have to survive."

Rita (center row, second from the left) with her club, the IDL's. To her left is her close friend Marilyn. Chicago, 1955.

12

I Might Even Marry Him

By the time of graduation, in June 1955, I had pulled away from my family and friends. One day I raised my head out of the sink after washing my hair. I looked at my face, close up in the mirror, and I hardly recognized myself. The eyes and mouth of the stranger in the reflection were angry. I was sure that I was losing my mind.

The unfairness of it all felt like a death sentence. Surely this wasn't the life I was meant to live. God had made a dreadful mistake. I was supposed to be loved, protected, and cared for, just like any other child. My classmates were going off to college, while I had no idea where I was headed. I wondered how I would ever gain the strength and wisdom to become a person in my own right. But even then, with my last ounce of energy, I visualized myself surviving. My instincts told me, "You can find your way out of this nightmare and build a future."

I went to see a young psychiatrist named Dr. Kitt.

"I just don't know where to begin." I had schlepped myself across town on three trains and was now sitting on a chair across from the slim doctor, neatly dressed in black pants and a button-down shirt.

"Just talk," he said.

He immediately made me feel comfortable, but before I could say a word, tears began to flow.

"I don't know what's wrong with me. I was shampooing my hair one day, and the water was too hot. When I stood up, I felt disoriented—disconnected from the world."

Dr. Kitt was calm and reassuring. "What's going on in your life?" he asked.

I described my family and our apartment.

"Tell me how it feels to live at home," Dr. Kitt said. I sensed his compassion. Yet I had been brought up to believe that talking about my family was disloyal. I also feared that admitting anger with my father could kill him.

I gave some very vague answer, to which he responded, "Do you realize that you have a lot of stored-up anger?"

I wondered whether he could read my mind. "I don't know why, but I'm sad and I cry all the time," was all I could confess.

Dr. Kitt then asked where I had been during the war. Again, I cried as soon as I spoke. I wasn't just telling him, I was telling myself. Until then, I had locked my past away. Particularly my brother's death. I don't think I had talked about him to anyone.

"And where is your sister?" He seemed very interested in everything I had to say. This encouraged me to keep talking.

"My sister just got married," I said. Then the tears came. "I feel so abandoned. The only thing we had was each other."

"So your sister's marriage has triggered this. It makes sense, because it sounds like she's the only person in your family you can communicate with."

I became hysterical. I wanted to talk to him forever, but the session was already over.

"I'm going to need to see you again," he told me. When I hesitated, he explained, "It's quite incredible that you can be so in tune with yourself and the world. But you've had a hard life, and you have a long way to go."

I wanted to see him again, but I didn't know how I would pay for therapy.

Again, he seemed to read my mind. "Since you just graduated, I'll work out something you can afford."

But money was not the only obstacle. I was not quite eighteen, so I had to get my father's permission to see Dr. Kitt. Back home, I pleaded with him.

"Please, Dad. I really need you to sign this form."

"No, Ruchel. You're not crazy. You don't need a psychiatrist."

"But he can help me. I do need him."

"I know you can pull yourself together. No."

My father could not understand. But Dr. Kitt did. He relaxed the rules, since my eighteenth birthday was just weeks away. To pay for the sessions, I got a job. Because I could barely function, I chose the least challenging secretarial position I could find. I don't know how I got to work or how I accomplished anything once I did. Every task was like hard labor. I remember one morning in particular, I was waiting at the train station, and I felt so despondent that I just stared over the ledge of the tracks, wondering if I was going to fall in. Desperate, I asked God to take over for me.

During this siege of depression, I felt as if an arrow had pierced my heart, and my life's struggle would be to extract it. I realized how much I missed the close family from my early childhood. I continued to pray for inner strength to guide me to be who I was meant to be. And I kept going, one day after the next, because somehow I knew there was a life that lay waiting ahead of me.

Meanwhile, Clara continued to drive me crazy, and I knew that I had to move out. One day, my sister, Sandra, came with me to see Dr. Kitt. I was so depressed that I just laid my head on her shoulder in the waiting room. In desperation, I said, "I don't know where to go, but I can't live at home any longer. Is there any possibility I can stay with you and Milt?"

"Okay," she said, after a pause.

"Are you sure?"

"It doesn't seem like you have a choice."

I didn't need to be a Philadelphia lawyer to see that my sister didn't really want me moving in with her and her new husband. But I felt much safer with her, and my father had drummed into my head that family helps family. So despite her reluctance and my guilt about leaving my parents and younger brothers, I moved into my sister's apartment and shared the rent.

Probably the person saddest to see me leave home was my brother Sam. I was a source of comfort and friendship to him. Clara had a temper and often was preoccupied with her own problems. Our father brought home candy and tucked his sons in at night, but he was usually working, in synagogue, or asleep. My brother Brad was still only a toddler. Sam and Brad would never know the strong, confident, and involved father I had witnessed as a young child. I felt bad leaving my brothers behind.

It took me a year of therapy to admit I had anger toward my father, and a lot longer to discover who I was. But in the meantime, Dr. Kitt helped to poke a hole in my depression. Rather than sinking further down, I began to heal. I was able to feel some warm rays of light peeking through the darkness. I felt myself bending toward the sun. I wanted to live again, not merely to exist.

As a start, I took a permanent job as a receptionist at a company called Allied Purchasing, in the merchandise mart where Sandra worked. The employees were lovely, and the office felt homey. But a situation that was comfortable compounded my guilt. My scars ran deep.

Alta, one of my new bosses, took me under her wing. She was an attractive Texan, in her sixties, with bright red hair and blue eyes. One day she called me into her office and closed the door.

"My husband Jimmy knows a kind man we want to introduce you to," she said.

"Really?" I tried to sound enthusiastic.

"Yes. He has gorgeous eyes and a smile to die for, and you can get him on the rebound because he just broke up with his fiancée."

"I'm just not ready for a serious relationship," I said, despite the fact that I had been having nightmares in which all of my friends were getting married while I, at the age of nineteen, was destined to become an "old maid."

At lunch that day, my sister encouraged me to reconsider.

"What have you got to lose?" Sandra said.

"I'm just not ready."

"He could be the love of your life," she said. "What are you waiting for?"

Over the next couple of weeks, Alta persisted as well. Finally I relented, and she set up a lunch date for the four of us. It was just before Labor Day of 1956 when Alta and I walked the ten blocks from work to meet her husband and their friend at Fritzel's, a well-known Chicago restaurant. I wore high heels with my new dress, so my ankles were killing me on the way. I also had butterflies in my stomach. But I did not let on that going to a fancy lunch on a blind date was anything unusual. Before we walked into the restaurant, we peeked in through the window.

"See that dark-haired fellow near the bar?" Alta asked, pointing.

I saw a tan, well-dressed man. He was shorter than I had pictured him, but very handsome. "The one in the herringbone suit?"

"Yes. That's him!" she said, proudly.

By the time we got inside, my date and Alta's husband were seated at a table. They stood up to greet us, and Alta jumped in to introduce everyone.

"Frank, Jimmy, I'd like you to meet Rita."

"Hello," I said, to neither in particular.

"Hi," Frank said. He seemed a touch nervous.

"Ooh, it's nice to meet you," Alta's husband, Jimmy, said good-naturedly. He was tall and striking, with salt-and-pepper hair. I could tell he was a flirt. "So you two work together?" he asked as we got settled.

"Alta is my boss," I clarified.

"Honey, you sure pick good-looking employees," he told Alta before winking at me.

Over sweet-and-sour meatballs and salad with the first heart of palm and avocado I ever tasted, the conversation was casual. "My family owns a department store," Frank said, after Alta prompted him.

"Wow."

He smiled. "It's not Marshall Field's. Just a small one. So tell me about yourself. Where did you go to high school?" he asked me.

"Roosevelt," I said. I wanted to deflect the subject before anyone asked about my history. "What do you sell in your store?"

After more casual conversation and dessert, Alta gave Jimmy a meaningful look.

"We'll just leave you two alone to get to know each other better," she said. "Take your time."

"So if you'll excuse us . . . ," Jimmy added, giving me another wink.

When they left, I was surprised by how comfortable I felt with this man. We talked for a few more minutes, and then he drove me back to work in his turquoise-and-white Oldsmobile convertible.

"It was super meeting you. I'd like to see you again," he said when he pulled up in front of the merchandise mart.

"That would be nice."

"How about Saturday?" he said, touching my hand.

"Fine. That should be fine."

Back at work, I went straight to Sandra's office.

"How did it go?" she asked.

"He was so sweet. I might even marry him," I said, not realizing what had come out of my mouth.

"Really? Are you kidding?" I could tell she was surprised.

"I'm not saying that I will marry him. But he's adorable, and he made a very good impression." I still thought I should work through my distraught feelings first, as if I could do that in a week or so.

I next saw Frank on Labor Day. When he arrived to take me to dinner wearing a felt fedora, I was taken aback because he looked older than his twenty-four years. But at the steakhouse, his warmth and attraction to me kindled my affection. Over liver with grilled onions and mushrooms that was out of this world, we sat together, feeling very close. He reached over and tenderly held my hand.

"Now where exactly were you born?" Frank asked.

"Poland. Have you ever met anyone from Poland?"

"Not that I know of," he laughed. "But I've been to Korea."

"Really?"

"Well, I've flown over it. When I was in the navy." He went on to talk about his friends and close family. The mention of his parents reminded me of my problems.

"There's something I really should tell you," I said.

"You can tell me anything."

"I'm seeing a psychiatrist."

"That's fine with me," he said right away.

Frank was so smitten that everything I said was okay, rather than an impetus for further conversation. In actuality, I don't think he even knew what a psychiatrist was, not to mention understanding how difficult the road in front of me was going to be.

"Sometimes I experience moods of depression. And I understand if you don't feel comfortable with that," I tried to explain. I didn't want to pull the wool over his eyes.

"That's okay. Assuming we continue to see each other, I would be there to support you," he told me, without any judgment in his voice.

"Are you sure?"

"Yes. Anyway, I love your accent," he said. "It's so, ah, mysterious."

Frank was soon calling me every day, and we saw each other as often as possible. In late October, we walked out of a restaurant after dinner and it began to snow. Frank put the collar of my black coat up around my neck and kissed me.

"I love you," he said, for the first time.

He was so wonderful. He made me feel like a person with possibilities.

Still, I was not yet ready to use the word love. "I really enjoy your company," I said instead.

Frankie, as I began calling him, became my life. I couldn't wait to see him. He was not the type to pry or ask a lot of questions about my past, so I kept things light, revealing only bits and pieces.

I brought Frankie to Shabbos dinner to meet my family a few weeks into our relationship. He sat beside me and looked very handsome in a dark gray striped cashmere suit. I was tense and had to keep reminding myself to breathe.

Before the prayers, my father smiled at Frankie and handed him a yarmulke. He smiled sweetly back, placing the round skullcap awkwardly atop his head. My father and Clara liked him right away.

"What do you do?" my father asked, as we got started on the chicken soup.

"Pardon me?" Frankie asked.

"What do you do, for your work," he repeated, more slowly. He spoke very little English, but was trying hard to make himself understood.

"Oh. I work in my family business," Frank answered.

"Very nice," my father said. He sounded impressed.

"He works very hard," I interjected, wanting to enhance their impression of him.

"I'm sure he does," Clara said, as if Frank were a knight in shining armor.

"Were your parents born in this country?" my father wanted to know.

"Yes but my grandparents were from Russia and Hungary," Frank replied. To my surprise, Clara was smiling warmly at me. I felt myself becoming more important in her eyes by having attracted such a handsome, charismatic man, who also seemed to have money. Presumably he could take care of me, and perhaps my father and her as well.

"Isn't Rita pretty?" Clara said. I thought I might be hallucinating. She had never complimented me like that before.

The evening went better than I could have imagined. My father and Clara probably would have preferred that I fall in love with someone more religious, but they didn't dwell on it. Little did they know that the first and probably the last time Frankie had been in a synagogue was on his bar mitzvah day. Nor did they know that by that point I, myself, had built up a great deal of ambivalence about the role that religion would play in my own life. I still believed in God and appreciated Judaism within a happy family, but I had lost my mother and brother because we were Jewish. Moreover, in America, my father's strict adherence to religious law had further distanced him from our family and made it harder for him to assimilate.

Not long thereafter, Frankie's parents hosted a gathering in their basement recreation room for the extended family to meet me. When we arrived, we were greeted by a stocky, stylish-looking woman with black hair but for a gray streak in front.

"Frankie, you're here!" the woman said, greeting her son with a hug.

"Mom, I'd like you to meet Rita," he said casually, with a big grin.

"How do you do, Mrs. Lurie?" I said, trying to sound confident.

"It's very nice to meet you," she said. Her name was Gertrude. She was wearing a lot of makeup and the dark lipstick that was fashionable at the time.

Frank's father, Leo, soon appeared beside his wife. "You're very pretty," he observed. I was wearing a blue jersey sheath dress that I had bought for the party. "And what an interesting accent. Where did Frankie say you were from?"

"From Europe. Poland originally."

"Oh, Poland."

This was a new experience for me, being at a party as someone's girl-friend. But I felt surprisingly calm and collected. As we sat holding hands in one of the upholstered armchairs, I looked around and observed his relatives, drinking and eating from the buffet. Frank's brother, Buddy, was there, with his wife, Renee. So were Aunt Rose and Uncle Rudy, who lived in the upstairs duplex, and their four grown children. I felt so guilty. Here I was enjoying being with a family, while I felt so despondent about my own.

These same pangs of guilt returned in December, at Frank's family's Christmas party. Celebrating Christmas was foreign to me. Exchanging gifts was still new to me, too, but easier to adapt to. I gave Frankie a lightweight black leather jacket that his brother's wife, Renee, had helped me select.

Then he reached into his jacket pocket and pulled out a small box. "And I have something for you."

I unwrapped the gift, opened a box, and discovered a gold Lucien Picard watch inside. "It's gorgeous," I said, draping the band around my wrist to admire it. Then a cloud drifted in. I wondered what I was committing to. "But I am a little confused," I said.

"Confused about what?"

"Well, what exactly does this signify?"

"It's just a present that I wanted you to have," he said.

I relaxed immediately. "That's what I thought. I just wanted to be sure."

Two weeks later, in early January of 1957, I was alone at Sandra and Milt's apartment when Frankie came to pick me up for a date. I answered the door, and he led me into the living room. Then he turned to me and said in a serious tone, "There is something I want to talk to you about. Do you mind sitting down?"

"No. Sure." I didn't even have time to think about what Frankie was going to ask me before he knelt down on one knee and slipped an engagement ring on my finger.

"Will you marry me?" he said.

I was excited and shocked. Even though he had dropped hints about marriage, the proposal came sooner than I had expected. I briefly panicked that he knew too little about me and considered saying that I wanted to think about it. But I looked into his hopeful eyes, and I knew that I loved him. I knew that he loved me and that in his eyes, I couldn't do anything wrong.

"Yes, of course," I said, elated. Then out of my peripheral vision, I noticed the shadow creeping in. "Frankie? Are you sure?"

"Of course I'm sure."

"Because if you think you're ever going to leave me, do it now. I couldn't deal with being rejected."

"I could never leave you. I love you." He wrapped his arms around me and held me gently against him. "I hope you don't leave me," he added.

After our engagement, I began spending time with my future sister-in-law, Renee. We were very different. She had grown up as an only child with doting parents. She was also very glamorous, with platinum blond hair and a fancy wardrobe. Still, we became friends. As we shopped for a wedding gown and clothes for my honeymoon, Renee tried to tutor me about Frankie's family. "Gert will expect you to call every day and have dinner with her on Monday and Thursday nights, when the boys are working," she said.

"Really? You call your mother-in-law every single day?"

"Honestly."

"Okay . . ." I worried about all of these expectations from a group of strangers. I didn't want to be controlled by them.

"Oh, I almost forgot the most important thing. Aunt Rose will expect you to run upstairs and say hello to her, too, every time you visit Gert," Renee continued. "I suppose because they're sisters."

The night before our wedding, Renee stayed with me at the hotel, and in the morning we got ready together. Frankie and I chose that particular hotel because it was the only kosher one we knew of in Chicago, and that was very important to my father.

I walked down the aisle in between my father and Clara. I'm sure they were happy for me, but all I felt was their pain. I kept thinking, "Is my father happy?" I wondered whether he felt bad that his new son-in-law had paid for the wedding. I took in the guests as I walked past them toward my soon-to-be husband. They all were friends or relatives of Frank's family. I had not even invited my best friends from high school. I had not felt that I had a right to, since my father did not pay for the wedding. Also, since the onset of my depression, I had lost touch with them; I had focused my scarce energy on planning my new life. As we neared the chuppah, the wedding canopy, I saw Frankie, smiling at me. I knew I was making the right decision. The elderly rabbi began speaking.

"Thirteen years ago, I performed the bar mitzvah of the groom. And as a young rabbi I had the privilege of officiating at his parents' wedding . . ." The rest of what he said was a blur.

"I do," I heard myself say. Then Frankie stomped on the wineglass, and the guests cried, "Mazel tov!"

A champagne brunch reception followed. There was a sense of excitement somewhere in my mind, but most of what I could feel was tension. After we cut the scrumptious black-and-white wedding cake, I walked over and took my father's arm.

"We're supposed to dance now, Dad."

"Good," my father said. As we waltzed, I noticed how handsome he still was. We both knew that someone was missing, but neither of us mentioned my mother.

"Mazel tov," Clara said, appearing beside us when the dance ended.

Rita and Frank Lurie. Chicago, 1957.

As we all three hugged awkwardly, Uncle Norman came to my rescue. "May I have a dance?" he asked. He was my only uncle from New York at the wedding, and I couldn't wait to dance with him.

"I'm so glad you're here," I said, as we fox-trotted to the music.

"What? Miss your wedding? Are you kidding?"

"I wish I could see you more often. I really miss you." Uncle Norman was now married and had recently become a father. He still worked hard in his store at the pier, but he had returned to his religious roots, and he no longer worked on Shabbos.

"I know. It isn't easy," he said, squeezing my hands as we danced.

*Rita Lurie and Isaac Gamss,
in a father-daughter dance at
Rita's wedding, Chicago, 1957.*

*Frankie and I flew to Florida for our honeymoon. On the plane, I wore
a navy blue Valentino skirt that attached to a white and navy polka
dot blouse with a blue bolero jacket. Long white leather gloves and navy
leather shoes completed the outfit. When we walked into our suite, it
was covered with orchids. I could not believe that this was going to be
my new life. I felt like I was a princess, living in a fantasy.*

*"All I want is for you to be happy," Frankie said, kissing me. "And
while we're here, you should buy whatever you want. We're only on our
honeymoon once."*

*We sat at the hotel pool, getting to know other honeymooners. We
liked them so much that we rarely went to dinner alone. It was when we
were alone, however, that I became more aware of the gap between us. We*

came from very different worlds. Absent were the meaningful conversations between us to which I had looked forward, where we poured out our hearts to each other and felt utterly understood. We had spoken nearly every day over the previous nine months and learned many things about each other, but we had not yet connected on that deeply intimate level that I longed to be known. I only hoped everything would be all right when my husband finally saw the war that was raging inside me.

13

A Wonderful Mother

Back in Chicago, life was exciting. We went to fancy restaurants and rented a luxury apartment where we entertained our interesting new couple friends. I felt proud that I could hold my own with them. I wanted to share my new comforts with my family, and fantasized that Frank would say, "Let's give them our money." Yet I knew we were living a nice life because Frank had saved money since he was ten years old; we didn't have huge savings.

Frank and I spent a lot of time around my in-laws, which intensified my own issues of loss and deprivation. I could not see how my father and Clara would ever mix with Frank's parents. Even I felt like an outcast around them. I sensed that they expected me to just waltz in and adore them, to be the perfect daughter-in-law, but my life hadn't prepared me for this. And they didn't make an effort to get to know me. Maybe this was impossible—the truth was, I was still in hiding. I continued to feel possessed by dybbuks, the demons that my parents had told me stories about as a young child.

A few months after our wedding, Frankie and I were sitting on the sofa in our apartment when I experienced a strange pain in my lower abdomen.

"Do you think I could be pregnant?" I asked.

"I don't know, Ree. Maybe you should make a doctor's appointment."

"With who?"

"Your gynecologist, I guess."

"I've actually never been to one," I said.

That week Frank went with me to my first gynecologist appointment. After an examination, the doctor told us that I had a cyst on my ovary the size of a grapefruit that needed to be removed right away. The procedure apparently went well, but the day after, I began hemorrhaging and was rushed back into surgery. I awoke afterward to a hushed conversation between my mother-in-law, Gertrude, and her sister, Rose.

"It's terrible that her father isn't here."

"Can you imagine? Poor girl," Aunt Rose whispered back.

I wanted to yell at them, "If he could be here, he would!" I knew how hard my father worked. Who were they to judge him? Besides, I probably never had revealed to him the seriousness of my surgery, not wanting to put more stress on him. But instead of defending him, I pretended to be asleep, and worried that I was letting him down.

Only in retrospect did I realize that in the weeks that followed, Frank had seemed preoccupied. Then one day, he walked into our apartment looking pale and worried.

"Frankie? What's wrong?" I asked.

"It looks like we're going to lose the store." He sounded like he was in shock.

"I don't understand. I thought it was doing well."

"It was. But we just can't compete with the new discount appliance stores. They keep growing, and they're giving their merchandise away for no profit. We're filing for bankruptcy."

"I can't believe it," I said, trying to sound calm.

"You don't have to worry, honey. Buddy and I already have an interview set up to start something new."

For some reason, I wasn't too upset. Frank had said that he was a good salesman, and I trusted that he would find another job. Just days later, I was cooking dinner when Frank came home and asked, "Ree, how would you feel about moving to California?"

"California?" I had to sit down to absorb this.

"Buddy and I have an opportunity to go into the maintenance business there, cleaning department stores," Frank said.

"Does that interest you?" I asked, surprised.

"Well, it sounds like the business has a lot of potential. And Los Angeles is supposed to be super," Frank said. "The weather is perfect all year long, and we'll make enough money so that you'll be able to come back to Chicago to visit whenever you want."

"I guess it could be exciting," I said, trying to convince myself. After all, I had never wanted to move to Chicago in the first place.

Had things been better with my father and Clara, I'm sure I would have been more hesitant. But they were still intolerable. All of my instincts told me to pull further away in order to preserve my sanity. Just to be sure, I went to see my psychiatrist, Dr. Kitt.

"Would it be very harmful for me to move away?" I asked.

He considered my question before offering an opinion. "In the best of all worlds, it would be great if you stayed here and worked things out with your family. But the likelihood of that happening is extremely remote. You have to balance the guilt you'll feel now if you leave with your long-term well-being."

Was he saying I should go? "Will I be doing something wrong?" I asked.

"No, Rita. You and your father don't have that type of relationship. He barely knows you. I am sure you'll feel relieved being farther away. You'll discover answers within yourself."

Buoyed by Dr. Kitt's encouragement, I brought Frank with me to break the news to my father and Clara. It was a warm summer Shabbos evening. As we sat at the dinner table, watching Clara light the candles, I was acutely aware of the butterflies in my stomach.

"Frankie, come hear my new record album," Sam said. It was amazing to think that he was already nine years old.

"Sammeleh, let him take a few bites of food in peace first," Clara told her son.

"Rita, can you throw the ball with me if Frankie plays with Sammy?" four-year-old Brad asked, holding up a large plastic ball.

"Sure," I said. I would miss my young brothers.

"First, we have an announcement," Frank said. I took a deep breath.

"What kind of announcement?" my father asked, smiling at Clara.

Oh, no. They think I'm pregnant! "Frankie has a terrific business opportunity in California," I blurted out.

My father's face grew gray and taut. It seemed as if I were viewing him through a time-lapse film process. "What does that mean? You're traveling to California?"

"Actually, Dad, we're moving there."

"But Rita can come back and visit as often as she wants," Frank said.

My father smiled stoically. Even Clara seemed confused. I wanted to tell them that they could come with us. That we would send money. That I was sorry for leaving. Tears rolled down Sam's cheeks as he concentrated intently on cutting up the matzo ball in his chicken soup.

"Honey, maybe you and Sam can go listen to music now," I suggested. Sam didn't even look up.

The good-byes were difficult. At the end of my last session with Dr. Kitt, I shook his hand and thanked him for all he had done for me.

He smiled. "Keep in touch. I want to know how you're doing," he said.

"I will." But even as I said it, I doubted that we would ever speak again. Becoming estranged felt completely normal to me.

Just before Labor Day, in the sweltering heat, Frank and I left Chicago for Los Angeles. Hour after hour, tears pooled in my eyes as we drove westward. The temperature continued to climb. Frankie and I thought *we would die of thirst. By midafternoon, my tears had evaporated in the scorching heat.*

We settled in Hollywood, in the same brand-new apartment building as Buddy and Renee, my brother- and sister-in-law. A couple of months later my in-laws moved out west as well, reawakening me to the void in my relationship with my own family. By late December 1958, just before New Year's Day, I left ninety-degree Los Angeles and went back to Chicago to see them.

The plan was that I would spend a week there. I visited friends and my siblings, and I met my baby niece, Sandra's daughter Lauren. But with my father and Clara, it became an endurance contest. The conversations were superficial. Although they probably wanted a loving relationship just as I did, the impression they conveyed was that I had shortchanged them by moving away. All of the pain and feelings of deprivation I had experienced in that household returned full force. I called Frank at the end of my third day there.

"I think I'm ready to come home."

"That's wonderful. But why?"

"It is fourteen degrees, and I didn't pack warm enough clothes."

"Why don't you buy a warmer coat?"

I was silent for a moment or two. "It's not just that. Nothing is ever going to change here."

Back in Los Angeles, Frank and I were eager to begin a family. Right around the time of our second anniversary, we were walking in the farmer's market one Saturday, past the rows of fruits and vegetables, when I had to sit down.

"Rita?" Frank said. "Are you okay?" He followed me to one of the benches.

"I don't know. Just looking at the roast beef sandwiches made me nauseous."

"Maybe you're pregnant."

The following Monday, we were waiting anxiously in the obstetrician's office. When the gentle, soft-spoken doctor walked in, he was smiling.

"You're not sick," he said.

"I'm not?"

"No. You're pregnant."

"Really?"

"She's pregnant?" Frank asked, his voice sounding so excited.

"Yes. You're pregnant. Go home and enjoy it."

We sprang up and hugged each other. As we left, we also hugged the doctor.

"We're going to have a baby!" I kept saying. We were smiling and holding hands on the way to the car.

"It's just fantastic!" Frankie was so thrilled.

I could not believe that my body was capable of making a baby. "It's a miracle! A new beginning."

Predictably, however, my excitement soon gave way to inner turmoil. I began to question whether I deserved the joy that a family would bring. I worried that I could not set aside my unresolved anger. At twenty-two years old I still felt unprepared to nurture a child. Everything inside of me was screaming, What about me? When do I get to be treated like a child? I wondered how I would have the energy to nurture a baby who would be entirely dependent on me, when just facing my own anxieties was so exhausting. I lay awake at night and prayed aloud that I would overcome my fears and be a good mother.

Frank overheard me one evening. "You will be a wonderful mother," he said.

"How do you know?"

"I see the way you talk to the baby now." He put his arms around me. "Just today, in the car, when the baby kicked, you rubbed your belly and said, 'It's okay, we're almost there.' "

"I guess I did," I said. Whenever something upsetting occurred, I reasured the baby as well.

"And you already tuck the baby in each night so sweetly," Frank added.

"I do?" I didn't think he had noticed.

" 'Good night, my sweet baby,' " Frankie said with a cute smile, imitating my voice. "Then you kiss your hand and place it on your belly. Right?"

After the first trimester, these fears subsided. I decided that I would not waste my opportunity to create a family the way I pictured one should be—loving, healthy, and always there for one another. Inside of me, a candle was burning bright, and I needed to fully absorb its warmth. I looked forward to having someone of my very own to provide all the comforts of which I had felt so deprived; someone else to love, hopefully share my feelings with. Even with Frank, I still had not revealed many painful things. I began to focus on these thoughts rather than on the negative ones. While I still was anxious, I had never been so excited in my whole life.

Shortly before the baby was born, Frankie and I realized that children were not permitted in our apartment building. We had heard about new homes being built in a nearby suburb, the San Fernando Valley, and one evening we used flashlights to look through the windows of one of them. It was a three-bedroom, two-bath tract model set atop a modest hill at the end of a tree-lined cul-de-sac. With no time to spare, we bought it that night.

At 12:30, just after midnight, on February 13, 1960, our baby arrived. When the nurse brought her to me, I couldn't clear my mind from the anesthesia. As if in a dream, I heard her say, "You had a beautiful little girl," and I looked at her out of the corner of my eye. Then I fell back asleep. An hour or so later the nurse brought her back in, and I still couldn't focus. Maybe I was afraid to meet her. When I finally woke up, my roommate, a young Israeli woman, was propped up in her bed, staring at me. "What's wrong with your baby? Why aren't they bringing her in to you?" she asked.

I panicked. But within minutes, the nurse carried the baby back in and placed her in my arms. I held her, but it wasn't the way I had imagined. I had to convince myself that she was my child. I did not feel the love pouring out. Soon Frankie came in.

"Can you believe it?" he asked, beaming excitedly.

"No," I said groggily. "She is a miracle."

"Not just that, she looks just like me. Squashed down into a baby!"

I laughed and began to relax. A feeling of love took over. I suddenly realized that I had not yet called her by her name.

"So you still like the name Leslie, right, honey?"

"Yes, it's official. I already told everyone the news."

Then the sadness swept in again. I thought about how far away my family was. I especially missed my mother, and then I remembered that we had decided that the baby would be named for her. "Her Yiddish name is going to be Leah, after my mother, remember?" Frankie took my hand and told me that yes, of course he remembered.

We brought the baby home on a sunny day. The daffodils I had expected in April were already blooming. Immediately, I got this pang—what am I going to do now? How am I going to protect her? I still felt so uncertain of my own existence. Meanwhile, the baby communicated to me from the start that she had needs of her own. For three months, she cried nonstop. I carried her around day and night.

"She's so sad," I told Frankie each evening when he got home from work. His industrial housekeeping business had not panned out, and he was now a sales manager for a decorative pillow manufacturer. I handed the baby over to him like a hot potato as soon as he walked in the door.

"Honey, the doctor said it's just colic, and it's not unusual."

"I'm not so sure. Maybe she's angry with me. Maybe I make her uncomfortable. Maybe I don't have as strong an attachment to her as I should." I would sit in the rocking chair in the nursery and rock back and forth. All of the grief, anger, and disappointment that I had pushed away returned like lightning.

"How could you make her uncomfortable? You hold her day and night," Frankie said. He carried the baby around, bouncing her in his arms as he tried to reason with me.

"Maybe I'm transmitting my anxieties to her." I convinced myself that Leslie would not get the love that she needed until I exorcised the badness inside of me. I went so far as to think that maybe if I got a lobotomy, I wouldn't be so preoccupied with my wretched past. Frankie put his arms around me.

"That's ridiculous," he said wearily. Sometimes, in exhaustion, he would sit down with the baby on the floor.

"I'll take her," I would say, immediately swooping her out of his arms. I had to ensure that Frank's frustrations did not affect our child, even when I myself felt numb.

"Rita, you need a break. Let's get a babysitter and go out to dinner tonight," Frankie said one evening.

"Honey, we can't get a sitter. No one else knows how to comfort Leslie."

Frankie knew that it was hopeless to try to talk me into leaving my baby. Miraculously, after three months, her colic disappeared. By six months, I felt this great attachment to her. As I looked into her big, beautiful dark eyes and my feelings of love poured out, I could actually feel her love flowing back, directly into my heart. This made my spirit soar. I grew determined to be a wonderful mother. This way, my child wouldn't suffer for me having been a survivor, and no one could doubt that I was capable of living a good life. Well, almost no one.

My father and Clara came to visit not long after this. I had high hopes this time. I had lamented not having more family around to share in our joy, and my new therapist encouraged me to express my feelings to them. Still longing for their approval, I planned to cook food they loved and be a warm hostess. But from the minute Frankie brought them from the airport, there was tension.

"Wait until you taste Rita's chicken, it's out of this world," Frankie told them, inhaling the savory aroma as he carried their suitcases into the spare bedroom.

"Do you have cottage cheese in the house?" my father asked.

"Don't worry, the chicken is kosher, and I bought a pan to roast it in," Frank said.

"But your dishes aren't kosher. Your kitchen isn't kosher," Clara said.

"Cottage cheese will be fine, if you have some," my father said.

For five days, my father subsisted on fruit and cottage cheese. By the fourth day of their visit, as we sat in the backyard while the baby napped, I decided it was time to talk. I felt that if they could understand me, our relationship would move to a stronger footing.

"There are things that we should talk about," I said, trying to remain calm.

"What, we haven't been talking?" my father asked.

"No, Dad. Not about some matters that are important to me. I want to know whether you understand why I've been so hurt and angry over all these years."

"No, we don't know. I don't know," my father said.

"I can't even imagine," Clara added.

My therapist had urged me to be direct. "I wasn't treated right. I didn't feel taken care of. When I was sick, I had to go to someone else's house, and even before that . . ." My voice began to quiver.

"My life wasn't any better," my father said, interrupting me mid-thought.

"I know," I said.

"And you weren't an easy child," Clara added.

"I'm sure I wasn't, because I was sick and unhappy." By then I was crying.

My father and Clara were upset, too. They probably had their own dreams that with the birth of a new generation, we would become one big happy family. But that wasn't happening.

"We did the best we could," my father said.

"I never felt like I was even a part of your new family," I sobbed.

"You didn't appreciate what a good mother I was," Clara said. She was *practically screaming by this point.* "You have no idea how lucky you were to have me."

"We did the best we could," my father repeated, with tears in his eyes.

While it was liberating to discover that no one dropped dead on the spot because I expressed my feelings, it was clear that the conversation wasn't going anywhere. They would never understand what I had been feeling, so why prolong the agony? "I think I hear the baby crying," I said abruptly. I got up to see if she had awakened from her nap.

A day or two later, they were gone. I wouldn't see my father again for more than eight years.

PART II

My Own Voice

(1960–1997)

Rita and Frank Lurie, Miami Beach, Florida, 1959.

14

On My Watch

I WAS BORN in 1960, just sixteen years after my mom, Rita, left the attic. In a photograph of my parents taken in Miami Beach the year before, Mom looks like a movie star. Her one-piece swimsuit shows off her slender but voluptuous figure. Her pale skin and delicate features, framed by dark hair in a short pixie cut, are reminiscent of Audrey Hepburn's. She is posed on a diving board beside my suntanned father, his white teeth glowing as he grins from ear to ear. To the casual observer, there is no trace of Mom's inner turmoil. But staring at the photo, I see it in her tentative smile and the distant look in her eyes. I always knew it was there.

My memories from early childhood are more tenuous than Mom's, hovering in the foggy recesses of my consciousness like delicate soap bubbles, ready to pop if I pay them too much attention. Perhaps these recollections are so fragile because I have so many of them, crowding one another out. Unlike Mom's, my own childhood was not abruptly aborted. Many of the relatives I met as a young girl remained in my life. Their evolution over the years helped inform my first impressions, and rendered them less nostalgic than those enshrined in Mom's memories.

Despite having been saddled with a colicky baby, Mom was determined to be a model mother. She read every parenting book she could get her hands on, collecting them like trophies in the cedar bookcase that Dad built in our den. Before I could read Dr. Seuss I had heard of Dr. Spock, the acclaimed baby doctor, because most of the books on the shelf bore his name. Mom's research and keen intuition led her to create a routine for me from the very beginning. In the mornings we went to the grocery store and on an excursion like a walk to the park. We would return for lunch and my nap, during which time Mom did chores around the house. Never a day passed, Mom boasted, that she didn't give me a bath before dinner. Cleanliness was truly next to godliness for her. Then, after dinner, came Mom's favorite part. She loved snuggling with me and patting my back as she put me to sleep at night.

Leslie and Rita Lurie, Los Angeles, 1962.

During my first few months, all of our excursions were on foot. Well, on Mom's feet. I was in a stroller, being pushed through our neighborhood along the long concrete sidewalks, past the single-story ranch homes set behind small rectangles of grass. Mom had not yet learned to drive. From what I've been able to glean, Dad tried to teach her, but when she drove over a curb and onto a neighbor's lawn, he mumbled something about divorce. They ultimately hired a professional who taught her in short order.

It was a predictable suburban world that I was born into. My parents knew their butcher, pharmacist, and each gas station attendant by name. Although Mom resolved from the outset that I would never suffer because she had been a Holocaust survivor, I still never felt safe. Whether I inherited her posttraumatic chemistry or simply overheard pieces of her past that may have slipped out before she realized that I was always watching, I seem to have been born braced for that terrifying moment when the world I knew would come to an abrupt, untimely end. In self-defense, I clung to her.

I was two and a half years old, and I gripped her soft, smooth hand tightly. Mom was leading me down the dimly lit corridor of a local synagogue to my first day of preschool. I was "dead girl walking." When we arrived at the classroom, I saw other children hug their mommies good-bye and boldly go inside. Why were they approaching their executioner so calmly?

"Mommy, I want to go home."

"When school is over, we'll go home," Mom said.

"I'm not going in there." Tears streamed down my cheeks. A young teacher came out of the classroom and whispered something to my mother. Mom said something back, looking concerned. Then she turned to me.

"It's time to go into the classroom." Her voice was more serious than usual.

Again, the tears flowed. "Will you stay?"

Mom glanced over at the teacher but then seemed to think better of awaiting her response. "Okay, Leslie, I'll stay for today."

Inside, we sat down in tiny chairs with the other children. Mom, six months pregnant, looked as uncomfortable as a kid in a catcher's mask. The next day, back at school, I again refused to let go of her hand. This time, however, the teacher insisted that Mom wait outside the door.

I don't remember what we did in class that day, or on any of the subsequent days. I don't remember getting to know the other children. I never took my eyes off the tiny rectangular window set in the wooden classroom door, and the dark, liquid eyes peeking lovingly back at me from the other side—eyes that hovered permanently between joy and sorrow. Like missile-tracking radar, I was constantly locked on to her whereabouts. Not only did I need to ensure that she didn't leave the building, but I knew somehow I had to make certain that on my watch she didn't disappear entirely.

MY SISTER, GWYN, was born in 1963, and two years later, my brother, David. Mom's days were now devoted to the three of us. At our doctor's checkups, she viewed the pediatrician's proclamation that we were in "perfect health" as a validation of her devotion. While many young mothers of that era were espousing the importance of putting their own needs ahead of those of their family, Mom wasn't buying it; she knew how badly she had been hurt by not receiving enough love and attention.

One day after school, when I was six, I found her in the kitchen preparing dinner. Although she had spent the day doing chores and taking care of my siblings, she was stylishly dressed. Every hair in her bouffant do was in place. I never saw my mother sweaty or dirty. I sat down at the round white kitchen table and gazed at her as she poured enormous measures of innovation and love into one of her elaborate, delicious creations.

"What's for dinner?" I eagerly asked.

"You'll see."

"Tell me what it is."

"I'm preparing a special concoction."

"Special concoction" was Mom's code for a new dish that she was creating. "We're not having triangle tip roast?"

"I'm making something called beef stroganoff. You'll love it," she said.

"When will it be ready?" I asked.

"Pretty soon. When Daddy gets home."

There were many situations in which Mom felt tense or lacked confidence. She was not a member of the PTA or one of the Brownie leaders, whom she viewed as insiders. So when she was in the kitchen, where she seemed so accomplished, I often felt a sense of relief. I could go off duty. Except that on this day, Mom seemed preoccupied.

I had not yet been told about the Holocaust. But even at that age, a good deal had undoubtedly been communicated to me. I sensed Mom's fragile quality and profound sadness, and was mastering the skill of lifting her spirits. I knew that she would sacrifice anything to comfort me, and that I needed to do the same for her.

"It smells delicious. Whatever it's called," I said.

"It will melt in your mouth," Mom said, looking over at me with pride.

When I said the right thing, it made us both happier. If I could just figure out how to give her what she needed, maybe she could let go of the heavy burden she seemed to be lugging around all the time.

Taking a deep breath of the rich, complex aroma from Mom's stroganoff, now bubbling on the stove, I felt my mouth begin to water. Our family dinner would magically erase the worries of the day. That evening, as usual, we gathered together in our cozy kitchen, around the table brimming with sumptuous, delectable dishes, with Mom nurturing all of us in the way she felt most adept. I forgot that something had been troubling her.

After dinner, however, as I went into the adjoining den, leaving my parents alone in the kitchen to clean up, I overheard Dad asking Mom what was wrong. She said something about wanting to move. I couldn't believe it. Why would Mom want to leave our beloved home? To my relief, Dad had the same question.

"What's the problem with where we live? The schools are terrific, and where would we move to anyway?" he asked.

"It just doesn't feel like home to me. I don't know how to explain it."

"You're friends with so many of the neighbors. You gals go marketing together, and take the babies to the park—"

"And I love it here. This is our home!" I couldn't resist calling from the den.

"Leslie, Daddy and I are having a conversation. Have you been listening?"

"No." I smiled to myself.

"You have ears everywhere," Mom said. Then she went back to her conversation with Dad. "I don't expect you to understand. But I feel different from everyone here. I don't have friends who satisfy my heart and soul."

"Things will get better," Dad promised.

From the other room, I vowed to help make that happen for Mom.

15

Bread Crumbs

IN THE SUMMER of 1967 my family as I knew it expanded when Mom's first cousins, Lola, Miriam, and Sally, flew out from New York for a visit, with their husbands and children in tow. On a hot Sunday afternoon, the ten children played outside while the adults, including Mom's sister Sandra, chatted in our wood-paneled den. After a while, my nine-year-old cousin Lauren, Auntie Sandra's older daughter, and I came inside.

"I still can't believe we have so many cousins," I said.

"I'm not surprised. I've known about them," Lauren said.

We sat in the kitchen and drew pictures, but then we grew curious about what was going on in the next room.

"Why do you think they're so quiet in there?" I asked.

"They're probably talking about things they think we're too young to hear about."

"Let's go listen anyway. We can show them the drawing you made. It's amazing."

We looked for every opportunity to slip in and out of the den, where the adults were talking. Each time we made an appearance, the conversation seemed to have grown more serious. Eventually no one even noticed us.

Los Angeles, 1967. Family reunion, with the New York cousins. From left, Sally Frishberg, Rita Lurie, Lola Goodstein, Sandra Weiss, Miriam Silver.

"How is your mother doing?" I heard Mom ask her cousins. Her voice sounded strange. Years later, Mom would explain that the mention of Aunt Tsivia stirred painful feelings of her own losses.

"She's still working," Cousin Lola said. Lola was thirty at the time, like Mom, and petite. That day she had her hair pulled back in a ponytail and was wearing a hot pink short-sleeved blouse. She had married a successful businessman and was raising two young daughters. "Sandra, Rita, do you have any contact with Clara?" she then asked.

I realized then that Mom rarely mentioned Clara's name. I had never heard anyone ask Mom about her stepmother before.

"Once in a while," Auntie Sandra said, turning to Mom with a pensive smile. Like Mom, she had dark brown hair, below her shoulders and always styled. She was pretty and had the softest skin I had ever felt, but she did not put herself together as dramatically as Mom.

"It's all very surface," Mom clarified. As usual, she was dressed in the latest style with an animal-print-patterned jumpsuit, her hair coiled in a French twist. "To get to real feelings is too painful."

"I'm sorry to hear that," Sally said. She still seemed to be the leader of the cousins and spoke as directly as she put herself together. Her brown, curly hair was cut short and neat, in contrast to the elaborate hairdos of her California cousins.

"It's unfortunate," Mom continued, "but Clara's presence only accentuated the feelings of emptiness we carried around after losing our mother." They shook their heads. My cousin and I went back into the kitchen. Lauren was still toting her drawing, never having been given the opportunity to show it off.

A short while later, when we next dared to reenter, the tone in the den had grown more intense. Cousin Sally was recounting memories of feeling terrible fear and hunger during the war. I looked down to the other end of the couch. Dad and the four other husbands were listening intently. The den, never a bright room, felt even darker that afternoon, with only bits of light filtering in through the closed blinds.

"Frankie has never really heard me talk about this time in my life," Mom said.

"You're hearing it now," Auntie Sandra said to him. She smiled, but she dabbed tears away with a tissue.

Ultimately, Mom recounted her own mother's final moments—how Leah had lit candles on Shabbos, looked around the room, and then lain down one last time. No one could believe she remembered so much. Her recollections seemed to jog the memories of the others. They were all in tears, like the audience at the end of *Love Story*, but we didn't quite understand why. Then someone noticed that all of the children had made their way into the room. The eleven of us stood there, in silence.

"Should we go outside and take some photos?" Dad suggested. Everyone jumped up at once.

After that weekend, I had more questions. So did my cousins, Lauren and Karen. When I next went over to their house to play, they made references to "the Holocaust."

"What happened to your mother during the Holocaust?" I asked Mom that evening, back at home. Although she seemed surprised by the new word in my vocabulary, she tried to answer my question. Not only did she believe I was better off learning about her past directly from her, but she was concerned that if she avoided my questions, I would come to imagine that she held deep secrets relating to me! Still, as Mom provided answers, she paid close attention to my reactions, taking care not to tell me more than she thought I could process. The primary message that I took away was that I was safest with Mom. And like Hansel and Gretel in the forest, I needed to always be sure that I knew how to get back home.

One summer in the late sixties, we headed south for a family trip to a modest resort called Vacation Village in San Diego.

"Let's make this a safe, happy, healthy vacation," Mom said from the front passenger seat.

There was no response.

"Okay?"

"Okay," my brother, David, said. He was wearing green shorts and a cream-colored T-shirt, with tortoiseshell-framed glasses over his large dark brown eyes. Although he was five years younger than me, he was good at keeping the peace.

"How do we *make it* a healthy vacation?" Gwyn, whom we still were calling "Winnie," asked. She had shiny brown hair, beautiful dark eyes, and an impish smile that was already short two front teeth, one from a daring leap off of her bed at eighteen months, and the other the following year, from tripping onto a sprinkler head as she sprinted with wild abandon around the cul-de-sac.

Mom jumped on that question. "Well, we can wash our hands before we touch food, get plenty of sleep, and be aware of our surroundings in the ocean."

Lying down in the back of our station wagon, I briefly considered whether Mom's list of precautions could forestall the early demise I so dreaded. As we headed up the on-ramp to the Ventura freeway, out of the corner of my mind's eye I could see that old shadow appear. I was overcome by a lonely sensation, suddenly distanced from my fellow passengers, who were excited to be embarking on a vacation. Who were all these people in the car? I wondered. Though they looked familiar, they didn't feel like the kindred spirits I had been with minutes earlier. I longed to be home, inside my refuge.

"Whuuhh!" Mom suddenly gasped, thrusting her right arm against the glove compartment to brace herself. "Honey, slow down." Mom was always a nervous wreck in the passenger seat. She frequently stomped her right foot on a phantom brake pedal when Dad drove.

"I see the car, Rita! He's fifty feet ahead of me," my father snapped. Although he rarely lost his temper, particularly at Mom, her passenger-seat driving annoyed him. Normally, Dad was funny and friendly, warm as a kindling fire. If Mom was the exotic caviar in our family, Dad was the macaroni and cheese. The rest of our family felt secure in his presence, and he was utterly content in ours.

"No, he's closer than that. It didn't look like you saw him," Mom said.

"How far is this place?" I asked.

"About three hours," Dad answered.

A wave of anxiety undulated from my left arm across my chest. How would I find my way back if we got separated, or if my parents abandoned me along the way? Worse yet, what if those people in the front seat weren't my parents at all, but kidnappers in disguise? Determined to secure a path home at any cost, I sat up and stared out the windshield, trying to memorize each large green freeway exit sign on our journey. "Woodman Avenue, Van Nuys Boulevard, Sepulveda Boulevard," I said to myself.

"Dad, can you switch to a better station?" Gwyn asked, as classical pieces poured relentlessly from the speaker in the dashboard. "There's no way I can listen to this carsick music the whole way."

"Yeah, I can't concentrate," I said.

"Concentrate on what?" Gwyn asked.

Valley Vista Boulevard, Mulholland Drive, Sunset Boulevard. "I just want to concentrate on the drive," I said cryptically. By now we were heading south on the San Diego Freeway. Like Mom's cousin Sally, out in the fields, I needed to keep track of where home was. The freeway signs on our road trips became my bread crumbs.

Gwyn was staring at me. "Are you sad?" she asked.

"No. I just miss being home," I said.

Mom twisted her upper body around to face me in the way-back. She couldn't bear it when one of us was troubled. "We're all together. Have you ever heard the expression, Home is where the heart is?"

She asked me that every time. "I guess I left my heart at home."

"Dad, can you pull over?" my brother suddenly announced. "I'm carsick."

I looked over at my brother, whose face was nearly as green as the freeway signs. "You better pull over fast!" I said, my heart pounding as I jumped from the way-back into the middle seats just in case Dad didn't react quickly enough. There was only one thing I disliked more than leaving home or being apart from Mom, and that was being anywhere near vomit.

Eventually, we arrived at the resort and made our way to the beach. It was late in the afternoon, and Mom was unusually relaxed. She always wanted our family to have fun and live what she viewed as a normal American lifestyle. This included visits to the zoo, movies, and dinners out. Mom experienced a childhood of her own by exposing us to these things. Taking us on vacation, however, made Mom particularly happy. She felt like we all were growing together.

"I love the ocean air," she exclaimed that afternoon, trying to inhale every last molecule. She turned to Dad, who was putting film in the camera. "Honey, breathe deep. It's so good for you."

Dad took a quick breath to make Mom happy.

"Frankie. Deeply. Through your nose. Feel the air expanding your lungs."

"Rita, I do," he said, turning the camera lens on her. Photography was Dad's hobby, and we were his favorite models. He was always taking pictures of us.

We picnicked, collected shells, and built sand castles. While the rest of us frolicked in the ocean, Mom planted herself along the edge of the shore, like a lighthouse. As the waves washed around her knees, she never removed her huge white-rimmed sunglasses or wet her perfectly coiffed dark hair, styled high in loose curls. Mom had never learned to swim. In a body of water, her arms tensed, as if she were a child awaiting a vaccination, and her legs stubbornly refused to float.

"Ree, turn around and smile," Dad said. Then he focused on us. "Come on, guys, can you all get in a picture?" Reluctantly, we came to the edge of the shore and posed. "Say cheeeese." Everyone smiled— except for me.

16

Magical Distractions

BETWEEN THE AGES of seven and eleven, Mom wandered throughout Europe. As her traumatized, fractured family awaited an invitation from some country to come and live permanently, she felt alone in the world. One generation later, I, on the other hand, spent my seventh to eleventh years nestled in the cocoon of the only home in which I had ever lived, amid a loving family. An all-American girl in the most powerful country in the world, I was still watchful as a sentry, on guard against the demons of Mom's past.

Saturday nights were my parent's "date nights." Before they left the house, I would sprawl across their twin-beds-pushed-together-to-form-a-king-size-bed, gazing over at Mom as she got ready.

"Do you *have* to go out tonight?" I would ask, dreading the inevitable response.

"We're just going to dinner, and we won't be home late," she promised in a compassionate tone. Then, looking at my plaintive countenance, she would add, "When we get back, I'll come in your bedroom and kiss you good night."

"*Please* can I come with you?"

Seated at her vanity, shapely bare legs crossed, Mom methodically applied makeup with her elegant, pale, smooth fingers tipped with long, brightly polished fingernails. "Daddy and I need a little time alone with each other," she would explain. I couldn't understand how this "need" trumped my desperation to remain in their orbit.

Mom probably spent forty-five minutes, although it seemed longer, calmly applying foundation, the perfect blush, lipstick, and eye color to her lovely face. Each week I watched from my bedside seat, mesmerized, with butterflies in my stomach. And I hoped against all hope that she would abruptly abort her plans and stay home. Nothing else would dispel the impending sensation of falling off a cliff that was rising within me.

"Rita, hurry up, we're late," Dad inevitably called from some other room.

"Coming," she would shout back, continuing to adorn herself.

Dad was forever waiting for Mom, who hated to be rushed. She was finally free to move at her own pace, and she did. Sometimes she tried to push me, however, to move beyond my comfort level.

MOM DID NOT want me to be an outsider. When the other nine-year-olds were joining Girl Scouts, Mom thought I should, too. From day one, I had my doubts. Besides delaying that blessed moment when I got home, scouting stifled my individuality. That "one for all and all for one" spirit was a better fit for those lucky enough to have been born with more trust in rules and groups. I was warier. For three or four weeks I dejectedly sat at the meetings, biding my time. Then one afternoon, everything changed.

"Now that you are Junior Scouts," our troop leader said, "you'll have the opportunity to delve into a wide variety of girl-friendly hobbies. These activities teach leadership and responsibility." We were sitting in a small rec room at a local park. I was staring at the thumb on our leader's right hand, wondering what had caused it to permanently dangle like an overcooked noodle, when she said something that sparked my interest. "Along the way, you will be able to earn badges." As she mentioned a few of them, and what earning them entailed, I began listening closely. She finished with something like, "We certainly don't expect you to earn every one."

When I got home, I jumped onto my bed, flung open the Girl Scout handbook, and skimmed through the requirements for each badge. Over the following weeks, I checked off one task after the next. Even when a hobby particularly interested me, like photography, I never let the temptation to delve more deeply interfere with the overriding goal of earning a badge as expeditiously as possible. I found that my zeal to earn as many badges as I could distracted me from worrying about the upcoming Scout campout (which I had no intention of attending), as well as the time away from home that Scout meetings demanded. The world felt much safer when I was on a mission.

The first badge ceremony, a few months later, was exciting. In the park auditorium parents sat on risers behind their daughters. The leader began calling the Scouts up, one by one, to receive the badges they had earned. One girl received badges in cooking and science. The audience politely applauded as she went up to receive them. Another girl earned the first aid badge. One of my troopmates collected four badges, for which she received louder applause. Before the leader announced my name, she chuckled. "Our next Junior Scout has been very busy," she said. I had earned badges in art, first aid, careers, and something related to being a model citizen. I earned a badge in pet care without owning a pet, and a travel badge while disdaining being farther away from home than Disneyland. I had collected twelve badges in all. To my utter surprise, this was far more than any of the other girls had earned.

As I returned to my seat, my parents beamed. I particularly loved Dad's reaction, because I sensed that he better understood this type of all-American achievement. Mom always seemed proud of me, often unduly so. But Dad's enormous smile that evening, and the pleasure he took in my actual accomplishments, was probably my sweetest reward.

By the next meeting, I no longer wanted to be a Scout. The magical distraction of the challenge of earning badges, talismans against all disaster, had worn off. Mom tried to dissuade me from quitting. She refused to pick me up from the nurse's office the first couple of times I called to come home with the sorts of vague maladies she knew I never suffered. But by the third week, she relented. Mom had more immediate worries.

Dad had been standing on a ladder, painting the trim of our pale yellow house, when the paintbrush slipped from his hands. He climbed down, picked up the brush, and returned to the task. Then he dropped it again. He was very handy, always building and fixing things around the house, and his clumsiness was uncharacteristic. Dad's muscles continued to weaken over the next few months as doctors struggled to identify the ailment. One day, Dad came home from work limping.

"What happened?" Mom asked as soon as she saw him. She looked scared.

"Nothing. I fell." Dad never wanted to alarm Mom.

But her radar was highly tuned. "Fell where?"

"On an escalator. My legs just gave out."

"Frankie, we're calling the doctor. Now I'm really worried" Mom said.

The following week, Dad looked thin and frail, in a white turtleneck and loose slacks, as he and Mom left home to go to the hospital. By that point, an ophthalmologist had diagnosed the illness as myasthenia gravis, a potentially fatal neuromuscular disease. Dad was about to undergo surgery that would either save his life or end it. In her neverending effort to protect me, Mom neglected to mention the risk that Dad could die.

Still, I knew that Dad was very ill. I was worried, but not panicked. It was Mom whom I could not live without. Fathers, I was convinced, could not replicate the emotional security and nurturing that mothers provided. Unbeknownst to me, I had become the third generation to suffer from maternal separation anxiety. Not only had Mom never recovered from losing her mother, Leah, but Leah had never finished grieving the childhood loss of *her* own mother. In any event, the fathers in our family survived. I knew that Dad would recover. And if, God forbid, he didn't, I was braced. I had prepared for the loss of a parent my entire life.

Three weeks later, I was deeply relieved to come home from school and find Dad in the master bedroom, back from the hospital. I gently gave him a hug and lay beside him. Although it would take many more years for him to regain his full strength, I never heard him complain. And I never heard Mom do so, either. Here she was, thrown once again into extreme uncertainty, and yet I never heard her ask, "Why me?" or take any of her anger out on her children. In the long run, this event would prove to be one more enormous stress on Mom's already vulnerable system. But at the time, she rose to the occasion. I had the sense that more than ever, we were a family of survivors.

17

I Do Understand

IT WAS JULY of 1969, and I was nine years old, sitting in a small, dark, makeshift office. A man I had spoken to for the first time the previous evening was dialing the phone. When he handed me the receiver, I eagerly waited for someone I knew to answer.

He did. On the third ring. "Yell-ow?" It was my father. He pronounced "Hello" with a "Y" when he answered the phone.

"Hi, Daddy."

"Leslie?" He sounded surprised to hear my voice. "Is everything okay?"

"No." I looked over at the man, known as the camp director, and wondered how to communicate my message without offending him. "Can you come pick me up?"

"Tonight?" It was already nine o'clock.

"Yes," I said quietly.

"Hang on a minute." I knew what was coming next. "Reeee," Dad called to my mother, who presumably was in another room. "Pick up the phone. It's Leslie. It's Leslie! Pick up the phone!" he called again, louder.

The other line picked up. "Hi, Leslie," Mom said. In her simple greeting, I could tell she was happy to hear from me but worried about why I was calling.

"Mommy, please! I can't stay here another night."

Dad jumped in. "Leslie, camp is over tomorrow morning. I'm sure it's almost time for you to go to sleep, and in the morning, you'll get on the bus to come home. Besides, Winnie and David are already in bed, and we'd have to wake them up and—"

"Wait a minute, honey," Mom interrupted. "Leslie, what's the problem?"

I knew that Mom would give me an opening. And when she did, I pounced on it. "I haven't eaten all week. . . . I have no friends. . . . No one even talks to me." Like the Red Sea parting, tears miraculously began to flow as I spoke. The camp director looked at me skeptically. I turned my head away and said quietly into the phone, "Please come and pick me up. I can't wait until the morning."

"Leslie, hold on a minute," Mom said. After a few seconds, my father, still recuperating from his surgery, said, "Are you sure you can't wait until the morning?"

I thought hard. I felt guilty. But I forced myself to say the only word I could seem to articulate. "Yes."

"Okay," he said with a sigh of resignation. "We'll be there in a couple of hours."

For years I replayed in my mind that phone call and my escape from a five-day sleepaway camp just twelve hours before the scheduled time of departure. Yes, I had been homesick all week, and I had barely eaten. I had wondered why of all the students in my school, the principal had chosen me for this camp scholarship. Me, the child who probably least wanted to go. Nonetheless, it had not been an unmitigated disaster. I had gotten to experience my first night sleeping under the stars, in a sleeping bag on the beach, and I had learned to budget my tokens rather than spending them all at once, so I could buy candy each day at the cantina. I had even written an article in the camp newspaper testifying to the many friends I had made that week.

When the director found me at the camp carnival on the penulti-mate night, appearing to enjoy myself, however, and smugly asked if I still wanted to call home as he promised he would allow me to do, I felt com-pelled to call his bluff. I knew it would be my only opportunity. I always wondered what would have happened if I had stayed—if I had learned at the age of nine that I could survive for five days without my mother.

Although I would not learn this lesson that week, I didn't blame my parents for rescuing me. Once I got Mom on the line, I knew it was a done deal. She felt responsible for eliminating any suffering on the part of her children. In the course of researching this book I discovered that Holocaust survivors often mistrust outsiders and overprotect their own children, thereby interfering with the natural parent-child separation process.

Mom was certainly overprotective of all three of her children. When my brother, David, was in the fourth grade, for example, and felt that one of our neighbors in the carpool was a bully, Mom drove David to school separately and then came back to pick up the other kids. Mom's fears led Dad, also, to raise us in a gentle way that avoided provoking any unnecessary anxiety.

As a child, being well protected and overly adored were precisely what I wanted. But in later years it would extract a huge toll from me. I vowed that when I had children, if they called me from camp beg-ging to come home early, I would give them the gift of my confidence in their ability to survive. It never occurred to me that I would have a child who would insist that she could not—that I might have a daughter whose psychological or genetic makeup was so affected by my mother's Holocaust experience. I had no idea what a challenge it would be for me to fulfill this vow.

NOT LONG AFTER my return from camp, when I was ten, Grandpa Isaac arrived for a rare visit. This was his second trip to California, and the only one I would be old enough to remember. Mom spent the week tensely asking her father if he liked the food, if his room was comfortable, and if he noticed certain things about me, like how well I read. I could tell that she wanted him to compliment her more—and to compliment her children. It was hard for me to connect this small, serious man with a heavy accent to my warm, familiar mother.

Once when I walked by my bedroom, which my grandfather was temporarily inhabiting, I noticed him wrapping tefillin around his wrists. I found my mother in the kitchen and asked her what he was doing.

"He's praying in a traditional Jewish way. It's called davening."

"Oh. He's hard to understand. Do you think he understands me?"

"I'm sure that he loves you," Mom said.

That afternoon, she and Grandpa Isaac sat out on the patio talking while my siblings and I played cards.

Mom had seemed anxious since her father arrived. "Leslie is so smart. She's doing so well in school," I heard her say.

"Yah, yah," Grandpa Isaac responded brusquely.

I felt bad hearing this. Wasn't he proud of me? Mom later explained to me that some of her father's behavior was superstition. He was afraid to tempt the evil eye. The following day, I heard her pleading with him. "Do you understand what I'm saying? I want you to be happy for me."

He looked at her, sounding confused. "Happy. Happy. What's happy?"

"I don't know. But you do realize why I left home, right? That I missed my mother, and Clara didn't fill the void, and I needed help?" Mom looked at him, begging to be understood, released from her guilt prison. But it was not meant to be.

"You're okay now," he said softly.

At the end of the week, we all hugged good-bye at the airport.

"I love you, and I want you to take care of yourself. I'm sorry things weren't better for you," Mom told him, crying.

He also had tears in his eyes. "I love you, too," he said.

18

Sunday Inquisitions

GRANDPA ISAAC USED to spend Sundays writing letters to his siblings in New York and his daughters in California. Recently, I asked Mom what she did with those letters.

"I read them, Leslie, of course."

"I mean, did you save them?"

"No. I didn't," Mom said, shrugging her shoulders.

"That's too bad. I would love to read them."

"I'm sorry," Mom said, in the same I'm-not-at-all-sorry way I tell my kids that I'm sorry they have to go to bed on a school night. "But my father's short letters, primarily about the family in Chicago, pulled me back into his sadness." In contrast, I preserved every birthday card, report card, flattering photo, newspaper article in which my name was mentioned, and note passed surreptitiously in class, dutifully pasting them onto decorated scrapbook pages. Not only did I experience much that I wanted to remember, but I knew my life could end at any time. If I was not around, I hoped that my future children or grandchildren would have images and documentation of their roots.

No, Mom didn't make scrapbooks or collect souvenirs. She was more interested in looking forward, to capture the next moment and make up for lost time. I kept looking back for her. I carried a mental ledger of her life, always hunting for credits to balance her past.

It was on Sunday mornings that I learned bits and pieces about Mom's past. The years through which she suffered the most, the years she had no interest in documenting or reliving with her children, were the ones we relished hearing about. The snippets of information revealed on Sunday mornings turned our ordinary, loving Mom into some sort of superheroine, a person who had survived bullets and famine and, even more miraculously to me, the loss of her mother.

Sunday mornings at our home began with a trip to Weby's, the local bakery. Gwyn, David, and I piled into Dad's car to forage for tomatoes, onions, bagels, onion pockets, lox, cream cheese, and Mom's favorite, sturgeon. Then we hauled it all back home, set the round Formica table while bickering over who was doing more, and invaded the master bedroom, where Mom was still sleeping.

"It's time to wake up," I loved to announce as we entered the room.

"Breakfast!" David chimed in.

"It's the middle of the day," Gwyn would shout.

We made a good wake-up brigade and took pride in a job well done. Staring at Mom from the foot of her bed, we eagerly awaited the first signs of life. When they were slow in coming, we would lie down beside her. She felt warm and soft, and wore her distinctive morning aroma.

"What time is it?" she would murmur, rolling onto her back.

"It's after ten." And I couldn't resist adding, "It's late."

"It's not late. I was just in the best part of my sleep." We always seemed to interrupt Mom during "the best part" of her sleep. She was the last one in the family to fall asleep, perhaps dreading the nightmares that often intruded on her slumber, and the last to awaken. Once she reluctantly crawled out of bed, she made her way into the kitchen to scramble eggs. She would whisk them together with milk and salt, pour the mixture into a pan sizzling with margarine, which we all believed was healthier than butter, and patiently turn them over and over with a spoon until they were creamy. Finally, she proudly brought them to the table, evidence of her deep love for us.

"Did everyone wash their hands?" Mom asked without fail.

"Yes," we said.

"I'm serious. It's very important to wash your hands before you sit down to eat. You were at the bakery, touching God knows what, and that's how people get sick."

"We're not going to get sick," I would argue. But knowing that Mom would not be satisfied until we disinfected ourselves, we trudged over to the sink.

"Don't be so sure," Mom was still saying as she loaded her onion pocket with cream cheese, sturgeon, tomatoes, and onions. Whatever she ate always looked better than everyone else's. It sounded more delicious, too. She would savor each bite, chewing thoroughly, apparently never having forgotten those years of starvation.

At these Sunday brunches, with the sun streaming in through the opened shutters on the most relaxed day of the week, my thoughts often turned to Mom's past. I would wonder whether she, surrounded by all of us, was missing her own mother, Leah. I craved an intimacy with Mom that I sensed could not be achieved until I could picture how she had been with her mother. I longed for Mom to bring her memories of Leah to brunch, so we could get to know her.

Before I asked a question about Mom's childhood, an internal debate usually took place. *Is this a good time? There's never a good time. Why upset Mom now? Mom would want us to ask about her mother. Not now.* I remember one morning such a debate occurred when I was eleven. Trying to sound at ease, as if I were inquiring whether I could buy the brown suede saddle shoes I had been coveting, I asked, "Do you remember having breakfast with *your* mother?"

"Sure. Before the war," Mom said. She sounded neither upset by the question nor eager to prolong the conversation.

"The war when you were in Poland?" my sister asked.

Mom took a deep breath.

"Yes."

"What about in the attic? Did you eat with her there?" When Mom answered yes to a question like this, it reassured me and alleviated, to some small extent, the burden I felt to compensate for her mother's absence.

"We didn't exactly eat meals," Mom said.

Keeping my voice very even, I asked, "What did you eat?"

"Raw potatoes or onions. Nothing really."

"How could you eat raw potatoes?" my father asked.

"We were starving. We didn't have a choice, honey."

"I hadn't realized that they were *raw*," he said.

It always seemed odd to me that Dad knew so little about Mom's past. He was more concerned about her happiness than her history. Whether through a lack of fascination with people's inner thoughts or a respect for their privacy, Dad was rarely one to probe beneath the surface. Even when I was a teenager, he never seemed eager to discover what boy I liked or what I did when I was out with friends. As far as asking Mom questions about the Holocaust, Dad told me later that he had not been knowledgeable enough back then to know what to ask. But I continued to believe that he never wanted to upset her. Dad was a constant source of warmth, friendship, comfort, and support to Mom. He was the reliability that her life had lacked. I was not a chip off of his block. I needed answers.

"Did your mother die because she didn't have enough food?" I asked softly. I tried to stress that the sadness I felt was for Grandma Leah, not for Mom. If Mom thought I felt sorry for her, it might make her feel worse. I remained more keenly focused on her emotions than on my own.

"I'm sure she died of malnutrition," Mom answered.

"I thought your mother died in the war," inserted David.

"She did. There was a war in Poland, and we had to hide," Mom said patiently.

These conversations felt like rides down gentle rapids. They went quickly, the surroundings were serene, yet just around the bend there was always a possibility of capsizing. I felt particularly close to Mom during these times. The other mothers and daughters I knew bonded over shopping or favorite television shows. My mother and I bonded over our love for our mothers and a distant past we couldn't entirely comprehend.

During these Sunday inquisitions, Mom might have preferred to tell us more about her earlier childhood, when she milked cows or watched Grandma Leah bake challah. But I did not know there were such things to ask about, nor did she volunteer them. Until a quarter of a century passed and I interviewed Mom for this book, her childhood, in my mind, consisted of a Nazi invasion, an attic, a few raw potatoes, and her mother's devastating death.

"When you were hungry, did your mom give you her food?" Gwyn asked that morning.

Mom took on a sad countenance. She turned to Dad, seemingly wishing that he would take over, and he looked back reassuringly. Then tears came to Mom's eyes. "I'm sure she gave me a crumb or two, when she had one."

"I bet you would have done that for us," I said quickly.

"Can we talk about something else? This is making me sad," Gwyn said.

Having asked enough questions for one Sunday morning, I found myself wondering what it would have felt like to be Mom, at five years old, watching tanks roll past my kitchen window. I tried to imagine how I would feel if my home were invaded by an army of monsters.

"Rita, didn't you want to return that vacuum cleaner to Fedco this afternoon?" I heard my father ask. He could change the subject on a dime to break the tension in a room. When that didn't work, he would just walk out.

"What time is it?" Mom asked.

"It's almost noon."

"You're kidding. Where did the morning go?"

"You slept through it," I said, eager to validate my earlier assertion.

"No, I didn't. I'll get ready now, while you kids clear the table," Mom said. That was enough reminiscing for one breakfast.

ONCE WE ARRIVED at Fedco, our membership-based department store, we saw another side of Mom.

"Are you the manager?" she asked the gray-haired man behind the counter.

"Yes, ma'am," he said, smiling.

"Well, this vacuum is defective," Mom said. She was pointing to the box Dad had lugged in. "It makes a strange noise every time we turn it on."

The smile vanished from the manager's face as he realized he was not on the brink of another sale. "You can leave it with us, and we'll see if we can repair it," he said to Dad.

"Sir, this was a brand-new vacuum. It never worked right. My husband and I want another one today, or you can give us a refund," Mom said right away. In these moments, she displayed a tenacity that I admired, even if the manager was just doing his job.

"I'm afraid that's not our policy, ma'am."

"Rita, that's not their policy," Dad said gently to Mom. I looked away, wanting to melt into Fedco's gray linoleum floor, leaving only my baseball cap to mark my final humiliation.

"We're not standing for this," Mom said. Then she turned back to the manager. "I'm sorry, but this is not acceptable. If you don't give us a new vacuum, we will never shop here again. And I assure you, we are very good customers."

In a restaurant with a waiter, over the fence to a neighbor, or in some store up against a manager, there was always some right to be asserted. In the attic, Mom had been forbidden to express her feelings. In adulthood, she grew healthier by learning to speak her mind. As embarrassing as it was at the time, I was also taking careful notes. Mom got results. Sure enough, we walked out of Fedco with a new vacuum cleaner.

19

Time to Say "I Love You"

UNCLE NORMAN AND his wife, Helen, visited us in the early 1970s. I sat with them in the den, a sponge ready to absorb any drops of Mom's past that might spill out in the course of conversation. Mom's favorite uncle, graying and in his fifties, was doing well, personally and financially. It seemed that there was one question Mom was eager to ask him, because she brought it up out of nowhere: "Is there anything you remember about my mother?"

"I wish I could remember more," Uncle Norman said. "But I know that she was lovely, gentle, and generous. In the attic, it was a shame, she gave up her engagement ring for a sack of potatoes." That sounded odd to me. I could tell that Mom yearned to hear more, and I was disappointed for both of us that Uncle Norman had nothing more to add. But there was something else I wanted from my kind uncle—some attention.

"Uncle Norman, do you play baseball?" I asked hopefully. I always tried to lure guests outside to play catch with me.

"Baseball? I'm afraid not," he said. "But I did bring you a little gift." Aunt Helen reached into her handbag and retrieved a box of chocolates, which her husband then presented to me. I thanked them both and smiled shyly.

Wedding photo at Rita's half brother Sam's wedding, 1972, Chicago. Top row: Sandra Weiss (Rita's sister), Karen and Lauren Weiss (Rita's nieces), Pam and Sam Gamss (bride and groom), Frank, Leslie, Gwyn, David, and Rita Lurie. Bottom row, from left: Milton Weiss (Sandra's husband), Clara Gamss (Rita's stepmother), Isaac Gamss (Rita's father), Brad Gamss (Rita's younger half brother).

Uncle Norman seemed kind, but I could not see why Mom had loved spending so much time with him. Their special relationship was no longer evident. By this point they had lived far apart for nearly two decades. Each had families and competing demands on their attention. It seemed unlikely that Mom would ever recapture that long-ago bond with the magical uncle who had stepped in as a surrogate mother.

Of all Mom's relationships, the one that she had with Auntie Sandra seemed the most unfortunate. As far back as I could remember, it had been filled with unmet expectations and missed opportunities. After Leah's death, Mom longed to cast her sister, only fourteen months her senior, in the role of the nurturer. But Auntie Sandra resisted taking this part for which she had never auditioned. Growing up, many of my weekends were shadowed by their arguments.

One Sunday when I was eleven, we were waiting for Mom to get off the phone so we could finally leave on our family picnic. From the tense tone in her voice, it was obvious who she was talking to.

"It's Auntie Sandra, right? Why do they get into a fight whenever they talk to each other?" my brother, David, asked.

"Who knows," Dad said.

"Because they're sisters, and they have to work it out," I said.

"Not if they can't get along." Even at six, David resented complying with rules he found senseless.

"I haven't called you in weeks because you told me that you didn't want to hear from me," Mom was saying into the receiver, her voice raised a few decibels. Then she was quiet for a few seconds.

"No. That's not what I said."

We were not eavesdropping. This was not a hushed conversation.

Rita Lurie and her sister, Sandra Weiss, 1973.

As usual, the combatants were openly sparring, ostensibly over some hurtful comment or petty slight. In actuality, they were locked in a perpetual battle that neither of them seemed to understand.

"Then tell me, I want to hear," Mom was saying. She listened, her jaw tense and her hand clenching the phone.

"I was not bragging. I was sharing our joy. I'm just as proud of your girls."

Gwyn and I smiled at each other. Dad was pacing. "I just don't want to see Mom go through the hell she went through a couple months ago," he said.

Mom looked up and raised her index finger, indicating that she would be only another minute. But there was no end in sight. I felt bad for both her and my aunt. Auntie Sandra was the only person on earth who reminded me of Mom. Her difficult-to-pinpoint European accent, cautious demeanor, awkward sense of humor, and smooth, soft skin were almost identical to my mother's. She and her family had left Chicago to settle in Los Angeles a few years after Mom and Dad, and she was more or less the only relative of Mom's who had been a regular part of my childhood.

"That's not all I talk about!" Now Mom was yelling. Her eyes were focused and angry. She was a trial lawyer litigating her own case. "Hello? Hellooo?"

These arguments were punctuated by hang-ups and calls back. We listened, horrified and amused, to the anger, harsh words, passion, and familiarity of it all.

"And Mom hates it when *we* fight," Gwyn said to me.

"I wish we could just lock them in a room together until they make up," I said.

"They might never come out," Dad said. He was chuckling at his own quip.

A distressing thought occurred to me. *Now Karen and Lauren won't come next weekend.* The collateral casualties of Mom's and my aunt's unstable relationship were the children. Auntie Sandra's daughters, my cousins

Karen and Lauren, were my favorite playmates. Our mothers' arguments often portended months of silence, during which we too would not see each other, our communication limited to letters back and forth. The feuding in the background grew more intense. And then, I think it was Mom who hung up first.

"Okay, I'm ready. Let's go," she said. She sprang up off the couch and put on her sweater, ready to leave for the picnic. Just as we were walking out the door, the phone rang again. Mom paused momentarily but apparently thought better of turning back. As we climbed into the car, she said, "You kids are very lucky to have such healthy, loving relationships with each other."

MOM ALWAYS MADE it clear how important it was that my sister, brother, and I have a close bond—no doubt, what she had always longed for with her sister. With my brother, David, her wish was easily granted. As children, despite the five-year gap in our ages, we got along effortlessly. We played catch in the cul-de-sac and traded baseball cards in the den. I admired his independent spirit and appreciated his dry sense of humor. Much like me, David liked to stay close to home, and he looked out for Mom's feelings. Once as a teenager he went out for a run and tripped, cutting his upper lip. As he approached the door to the house, he called out, "I'm bleeding. Don't worry, Mom." Sometimes, *I* played the role of my brother's all-American mother. I rooted for him at his basketball games, spoke to his principal when he had a grievance, and later, when he entered college, used my relationships to help him get into a dorm. With David and me, Mom was able to imagine the close friendship she might have had with her younger brother, Nachum, had he survived.

If my relationship with my brother evokes images of *Ozzie and Harriet*, with my sister, think more along the lines of *The Simpsons*. My first memory of Gwyn was in her nursery, which just days before had been my bedroom. The animal-print curtains had been selected for me. So had the bassinet. Dad began the introduction by handing me a couple of wrapped presents. Mom jumped in before I opened the first one. "Leslie, we bought you a new set of watercolors and a diamond ring just like mine. And this is your new baby sister." Then she added, "She's too cute and tiny to call her Gwyn just yet, so let's nickname her Winnie, like Winnie the Pooh."

Maybe I began things on the wrong foot. As soon as Winnie was old enough to play, I decided that she would be the toy. I introduced her to the game of house. In our backyard I would mix dirt and water together, pretending to prepare delectable meals.

"Here, try this," I coaxed, spooning the mixture into my young sister's mouth.

"Yuck. This tastes like mud," she would say, spitting it out.

"No. It's pie, and it's good for you" (*but look out for that worm*).

Mom's shadow inevitably appeared. "Is that dirt in Winnie's mouth?"

"She was really hungry."

I actually enjoyed my sister's company back then, but at five or six, she began to assert herself. Suddenly we were like England and France, competing over property, territory, strength, and natural resources. Even eating dessert became a competitive sport.

My siblings and I loved Mom's warm tapioca pudding. Actually it was Jell-O brand's tapioca pudding to which Mom added milk before stirring it over the stove. Because it was so delicious, none of us wanted to be the first to finish. Sometimes one of us would pretend to devour the tapioca, hoping our unsuspecting siblings would follow suit. But secretly we would hold some in reserve. Eventually, we enacted a rule forbidding waiting for the others to finish first. It was always Gwyn or I who suspected the other of an infraction.

We bickered frequently throughout our childhoods, invoking all the standard-issue tactics—pulling hair, screaming, hitting, name-calling, and crying. With Mom, we tempered what we said; we knew that our angry words could injure her. But with each other, we felt free to fight, and we took full advantage.

Gwyn was charismatic, funny, and more daring than I. She spent nights at friends' houses and went to sleepaway camp (the ultimate litmus tests, for me, of childhood courage). Needless to say, I didn't. I was in awe and envious. Mom's past was not lost entirely on Gwyn, however. She had her own set of fears. When Gwyn first entered a room, for example, she scouted out the windows and doors to establish an escape route. And she took stairs rather than elevators where possible, insisting that her own legs were faster. I would ride up to the designated floor, to find Gwyn standing in front of me, panting, when the doors opened.

"See, it's faster to take the stairs," she would say, struggling to catch her breath. But we both knew the truth. To Gwyn, elevators were traps.

Gwyn sometimes felt shortchanged by me back then. She wished that I treated her the way her friends were treated by their big sisters. I was skeptical. *My* friends didn't have such perfect older sisters. Also, things were different in our home. As I saw it, Mom was my responsibility; Gwyn could fend for herself. She was talented, resourceful, and popular at school. Needless to say, I never articulated this rationale. I was quick to respond with, "I wish I had a different sister, too!"

For Gwyn and me, arguing was just a part of life. In retrospect, we were not actually competing over clothing, looks, or intelligence. We were in competition for the attention of one emotionally preoccupied mom. My strategy was to be the best child, to act responsibly, and to always put spending time with my family above all else. Gwyn took more chances. In most households of the 1970s, her behavior would not have raised an eyebrow. But in our House of No Risks, Gwyn was the daredevil child.

Inevitably, Gwyn and I settled our own disputes. We had good conflict resolution skills and a mutual love and respect. Even on days when we were furious with each other, I would often wander into my sister's room late at night and climb into her oversize waterbed. With exhaustion easing the senseless tension between us, we would promise to take care of each other if, God forbid, someday Mom was no longer around. Then just before we'd close our eyes, we always said, "I love you," just in case it was the last time we would have the opportunity.

20

A Word Game

THE HOLOCAUST, THE holidays, the outsider—my early associations with Judaism formed the basis for a complicated relationship. Mom often told me when I was growing up that she wished she were raising me in a more religious home. I assumed that meant Dad was the obstacle. It turned out that Mom, too, had ambivalent feelings about religion. We neither lit candles on Shabbos nor kept kosher. And while there was a mezuzah mounted on our doorpost, perhaps to protect us, we didn't regularly kiss it or say a prayer as we passed by. It was just a part of the door, like the hinges and the round bronze knob.

In our family, synagogue was mostly limited to the High Holidays. It never failed to impress me that Mom could read every prayer in Hebrew and recite so many of the songs. For me, synagogue was depressing. The numerous references to death throughout the High Holiday services were unbearable reminders that we were all going to perish, regardless of how well we fasted or obeyed the commandments.

In my teens I avoided going to services whenever possible. I would convince myself, if no one else, that I was too tired. I felt guilty when my family walked out the door; I disliked disappointing Mom, and I also had some trepidation about messing with God. But my concerns were usually quickly drowned out by the opening musical sequence of whatever sitcom happened to be on television. The laughs and friendly, familiar characters predictably raised my spirits higher than they had ever been elevated sitting in the temple of gloom's High Holiday services of my youth.

Religious school was even more of a struggle for me, in part because classes took place weekly rather than on an annual basis. I felt like a foreigner there as I watched my classmates regurgitating Bible stories and learning to read words in a language that none of us understood. To make matters worse, the teachers referred to me as rebellious! Didn't they realize how much I had already given to my religion? How much suffering my family and I had incurred as a result?

Aside from the Jewish obligation I keenly felt to help repair our broken world, the despair and anger that Mom's past evoked was, for me, the most sacred part of being a Jew. Had the Holocaust been a part of the curriculum, and the students been given an opportunity to grieve in the process for fallen family members, I might have better connected. Instead, we learned about Abraham's near-sacrifice of Isaac and Noah's ark, in addition to memorizing the Hebrew alphabet. I sat in class feeling alienated. How had this knowledge helped the six million Jews who were always in the back of my mind?

As far as I could tell, no one else in my class—not my friends with whom I passed notes, nor the teachers who bristled at my disrespect, nor the aloof elderly rabbi from whom I optimistically awaited words of wisdom that never arrived—could understand this. Eventually, when Dad was ill, bills were mounting, and Mom's time was stretched to the limit, my parents let me choose whether or not to remain in Hebrew school. I quit on the spot.

Conflicted feelings notwithstanding, I always felt proud to be Jewish. I appreciated the idea of sharing traditions and values with a people who preceded me by three thousand years and hopefully would live on in perpetuity. Moreover, I loved celebrating the Jewish holidays. For Passover, Rosh Hashanah, Yom Kippur, and Hanukkah, Mom created festive celebrations much like the ones she had enjoyed long ago. Her enthusiasm infused the atmosphere with an unusual levity.

"We'll be back in one hour," Mom said one December evening in 1971. I was watching *Laugh In* on television, but the excitement in her voice as she and Dad zipped up their jackets caught my attention.

"You're going Hanukkah shopping, right?" I asked. Mom loved to buy us gifts.

"Not necessarily," Mom said. She could never keep a secret.

"I still think we've bought enough already," I overheard Dad tell Mom as they headed for the door. "We'll have to rob Peter to pay Paul to pay for all these things."

"I want to be sure the kids each get exactly the same amount," Mom said, as the door slammed behind her.

By the eve of Hanukkah, the silver-wrapped gifts were out on the fireplace hearth in the den. We gazed at each one, and fantasized about its contents, as tantalizing and mysterious as the bonbons in a See's Candies box. Overhead, from the mantel, hung a blue and white "Happy Hanukkah" sign. When Dad finally got home from work, around five o'clock, we raced into the kitchen, where Mom was frying crispy latkes (potato pancakes). The aromas emanating from sizzling oil in the pan and brisket and onions in the oven heralded the arrival of the Festival of Lights. Atop the counter sat a simple turquoise-colored menorah in which one red candle and one yellow candle had been placed. Mom lit them, and we joined her in praising God for commanding us to celebrate the holiday.

"The brisket's delicious," Dad said. We had just sat down for dinner.

Mom looked over at his plate. It was already empty. "I'm taking my first bite, and you're finished? Frankie, it's much healthier to chew your food slowly."

"I know, honey."

I ate one or two latkes with applesauce and sour cream. The first bite was always the best. Once they cooled down, they tasted like soggy oatmeal. After rushing through dinner, we rushed back into the den, tingling with excitement.

"Mine's heavier," David boasted, lifting up his gift.

"Well, good things come in small packages," I shot back.

"You all got exactly the same amount," Mom said.

"I know what I'm getting. A brand-new bike," Gwyn said in dramatic fashion.

"This one is for you," Mom said, placing a sparkly blue present on my lap. Then she eagerly watched me tear off the paper and remove the box top. I lifted up the tissue inside to find a copper-colored suede vest with long graceful strips of fringe running down the back. It was the most exquisite article of clothing I had ever seen. As I held it up, visions of walking around school robed in its splendor as the other kids took note filled my imagination. Mom was so proud of her selection.

Just then, Dad wheeled in a shiny yellow bicycle with a bow tied around the white seat. "Winnie, this is for you," he said. He and Mom eagerly awaited her reaction.

"See, I knew it," she said gleefully. But then she examined the bike more closely. Her face fell in disappointment. "This isn't a Schwinn."

"So?" my father said.

"But all my friends have Schwinns. These handlebars aren't wrapped, and the seat's not the same."

"It's a Huffy," Mom said. "They're even better. But we can get the seat changed, right, honey?"

"Sure," Dad said, keeping up a brave front. I wished that my eight-year-old sister could just pretend to be happy. Wasn't it clear that we needed to make Mom feel good, so that things could be evened out for *her*?

My brother clearly had read that memo. "A CB radio! I love it!" David exclaimed. Caught up in the bicycle drama, no one had seen him open his present. Fortunately, he loved it so much he didn't notice.

Years later, he would tell me that he had in fact been so excited about this radio that his first thought after he opened it was, At least if the tanks invade tomorrow, something really good will already have happened to me. I was surprised to hear that my brother also savored his positive experiences in preparation for possible future famine.

On the last night of Hanukkah, Mom and Dad gave me a game called Scrabble.

"Is it fun?" I asked.

"It's supposed to be. It's a word game," Mom said.

After my siblings went to bed and Dad settled into his recliner in front of the television set, Mom and I sat hunched over the Scrabble board. From the beginning, we loved finding words to make sense of the disparate tiles. We were acquiring skills we would utilize years later, when we embarked on our memoir. That evening, I was surprised to discover that Mom had a competitive side. She actually seemed to care about winning, although maybe not as much as I did.

"Z-O-O," I said proudly, placing the "Z" deliberately on a double letter space.

"Q-U-O-T-E," Mom countered. "Look, it's on a triple word score!"

"Not anymore," I said, flipping the board over and sending the pieces flying.

Mom looked up at me in disbelief, apparently deliberating whether to laugh or be upset. "That's really not being a good sport," she finally said.

ON SOME LESS festive evenings, Mom would mysteriously disappear. The ensuing search often led me into the dark backyard. There I would find her alone, on a lounge chair by the swimming pool, staring up at the stars. One evening after dinner, when I was twelve years old, I sat down at the foot of her chaise.

"Why are you out here?" I asked, bracing myself for her response. I dreaded discovering that she was angry with Dad or worse, with me, and I also didn't want to hear that she was dejected.

"I just want to be by myself for a while," Mom said, in a far-off voice.

"What's wrong?"

"Nothing is wrong." The flat tone of her voice suggested otherwise.

"Then come inside, Mommy. It's cold out here."

"I will, soon."

"Then I'm staying out here, too," I said, flopping down on the other lounge chair and staring up at the oppressive, dark sky. I tried to stifle a shiver from the evening chill.

I came to learn decades later that this had been Mom's way of escaping. She would stretch out on the chaise longue and stare up at the stars and the airplanes, to vicariously travel beyond the confinement she felt as a wife and mother with few discretionary hours or resources. Perhaps in this respect Grandpa Isaac had not been so different from his daughter. He, too, might have looked to the heavens for relief from the pain and demands of his earthly life.

Someday I would find my own means of escape. I would be on those airplanes traveling as often as possible, and I would find countless local diversions as well. As for religion, I would come to see its beauty, and at least intellectually, appreciate the ideal of believing in an intangible being greater than ourselves. But the Holocaust and the holidays would be my primary connections to Judaism. In this respect, *I* would remain the outsider, peeking in.

21

Society of Overachieving Offspring of Holocaust Survivors

I WAS ANXIOUS about beginning junior high school. Being away from Mom was still challenging for me. Despite the ease of my situation relative to what she had endured as a youth, Mom never mentioned the contrast. Instead, she made me feel that my adjustment was nothing short of remarkable.

"Do you promise me I'll be safe?" I asked her the night before school started in September 1971. She was seated on the edge of my bed, brushing my hair, nurturing and empathetic.

"If I know you, you'll be the star of the school by the end of the semester."

"I don't care about being a star. I just want to be safe." I was not concerned about crossing intersections or keeping up in class, as Mom had been on her first day of school. But a rumor that the ninth-graders sometimes slipped LSD into the seventh-graders' lunches kept nagging at me. "Do you promise I will be?"

I believed Mom's promises, even when they defied logic, such as her assurance that I would live forever.

"Yes, I promise that you will be safe," Mom said at last. Then she added, "Just don't take any unnecessary risks. If someone asks you to do something you feel uncomfortable about, don't go along with it."

"Now you're scaring me even more."

"I just think you should keep your wits about you. That's all."

What did Mom mean by unnecessary risks? I lay wondering, after she had left the room. I pulled my blanket up tightly over my head, allowing in just enough air so as not to suffocate, and finally fell asleep.

At first my new school felt foreign and impersonal, with its sprawling beige single-story buildings, brownish green athletic field that always looked thirsty, and two thousand taller, mostly white, mostly middle-class kids. Within a short time, however, my apprehensions subsided. When my new best friend Shelley came over for the first time, Mom greeted us at the door.

"Mom, this is Shelley. Shelley, this is my mom," I said by way of introduction. "She's a Polack," I added, with a giggle. Since Shelley's father was also a Holocaust survivor, I assumed that she would appreciate the quip. And I hoped that Mom wouldn't mind my taking the opportunity to display my keen wit at her expense.

Mom smiled and opened the door wider. Then, as we walked past her into the house, she said, "And I'm not a Polack."

"Technically, you are," I said.

"No. The Poles didn't even consider us to be one of them," Mom said. I had no appreciation back then for the depth of her feelings on the matter.

Having long known that most of Mom's family were murdered as a result of an evil German leader, and later coming to suspect that the leaders of many other nations, including my own, sat passively by and tolerated the genocide, I *never* trusted that authority figures would protect me or do what was best. If adults were so wise or capable, why hadn't they spoken up all over the world? Why hadn't the adults in Mom's family better protected themselves? Or better taken care of Mom?

I didn't really even trust *Mom's* ability to protect me. In fact, I felt responsible for protecting her, at least from emotional upheaval. Had I rebelled against my parents, Mom would have been hurt and perhaps angry. I sensed that she would not recognize the importance of *my* struggle to become independent. Thus, I resorted instead to using the other figures of authority in my life, my teachers, as targets for rebellion.

I either loved or hated my teachers. Sometimes I loved and hated the same one. I needed to be liked by them, since they were in charge of my destiny—the commanders of the tanks. But, again, I did not trust them. And I longed to defy them in order to get even with the authority figures in Mom's past.

One day after school in the eighth grade, my friend Shelley and I were cleaning desks in our science room as punishment for talking in class. I noticed that our teacher, Mr. Livermore, had walked into the closet where skeletons were stored, leaving the door tantalizingly ajar. *Should I do it? No, don't. It will be funny. But he's nice, always proudly showing me pictures of his young daughter. It will be funny.* I raced across the room, swung the door shut, and stood against it. Within seconds, I felt the thuds of Mr. Livermore's fists pounding against the wood.

"I can't believe you did that!" Shelley said. She had light brown wavy hair parted down the middle like every other eighth-grader in 1972, and pretty green eyes that were locked on mine as she stood with her hand on the knob of the classroom door, poised to flee.

"It's funny," I said, trying to convince her and myself.

"Teachers never get mad at you. He'll blame me. I'm the one who always gets in trouble. Open the door," Shelley pleaded.

I did. Mr. Livermore stepped out. His face was red, and he looked right at me. "Leslie, sometimes you just go too far," he said, struggling to remain calm.

"I'm sorry." I was.

"And believe me, your parents will hear about this," he added.

Had Mr. Livermore phoned, the call would have been directed to Mom, the parent in charge of all school matters in our home, and she undoubtedly would have defended me. Mom disliked what she called "airing dirty laundry" in public. She rarely made a negative comment about any of her children outside of our immediate family. Even if she could see that I had done something wrong, she would not have let on to a teacher.

And she probably would not have viewed me as having done anything wrong. Mom associated criticism of me with an attack on her. Sometimes she was so blindly supportive of me that I found myself actually defending the person on the other side of the dispute. Not only were Mom and I on the same team, but from her perspective, we played the same position. Of all her accomplishments, Mom seemed proudest of being a successful mother. When I did something wrong, when any of her three children did, Mom was inclined to justify it so that her parenting reputation remained untarnished. She viewed her children through the rosiest-colored lenses, and if we locked our teachers in the closet, then we must have had very good reason.

For the most part, I tried to avoid putting Mom in situations where she had to defend me. I had no control over her past, but I was determined to be the kind of daughter who would bring her satisfaction in the present. I held on to the fantasy that if I were just a little nicer to her, or more sensitive to her feelings, I could actually expunge her pain from the record. In the meantime, Mr. Livermore never did call my parents. I was not called to task for the science escapade, further confirming my view that teachers were merely adult peers. The cost was that I doubted more than ever that they would be able to protect or even teach me very much.

I, myself, needed to become a commander of sorts rather than relying on others. By the age of thirteen I was elected student body president, was writing for the school newspaper, and was acquiring memberships in school clubs as rapidly as my classmates were amassing trendy Chemin de Fer jeans. The more positions of leadership I held, the more at ease I felt. Mom never seemed surprised by my accomplishments. She communicated to me, and those around her, a grandiose belief in my ability, which gave me confidence. I believed her when she said I could do anything I put my mind to, oblivious to the years I might spend later on doubting whether I was living up to my enormous potential.

By the ninth grade, I was well on my way to becoming a poster child for the "Society of Overachieving Offspring of Holocaust Survivors." The appeal of becoming a leader extended beyond issues of control. I was certainly aware by then that I had been born in the face of long odds. Most of the Jews in Poland had been killed in the Holocaust, including those who had gone into hiding; an even higher percentage of the Jewish *children* were killed. My birth seemed a miracle, which motivated me to make the most of it. I would strive to mend the damaged world I inhabited, to make it good and just again, not only so that I could feel safer but to add meaning to Mom's survival.

Like Mom, in junior high school I became enamored of a cute boy who, to my surprise, turned out to also be interested in me.

"Do you want to give it a try?" he asked me on the phone one Saturday night.

"Give what a try?"

"Us. Being boyfriend and girlfriend."

"Sure," I said, my heart racing. At school on Monday, he gave me his silver ID bracelet to seal the deal. When he came over to my house, Mom was unsure how to supervise us.

"I have to run to pick up Winnie," she said one afternoon. We were listening to Elton John's new record album in my bedroom.

"Okay," I said, more than happy to have her leave for a few minutes.

"While I'm gone, I'll need you to wash the mushrooms in the sink," Mom said.

"All of them?" I asked, embarrassed.

"Yes. When I get back, they better all be scrubbed," she said. "I want you both to keep busy while I'm away."

Mom and I had never had one of those coming-of-age, birds-and-bees talks. Occasionally she brought home pamphlets from the pediatrician's office about venereal disease or teenage pregnancy and tried to coax my sister and me into listening to her read them to us. After a few sentences, my sister would run out of the room, covering her ears. I was usually right behind her. Mom was so determined to protect us that she even made the topic of sex scary and its discussion embarrassing.

Another time, Mom put us to work for the business she had begun at home, rolling colorful fabric around metal containers.

"We have to wrap up trash cans?" I asked, laughing.

"They're decorative wastebaskets. What's so funny?"

"They're pretty, but who are you selling them to?"

The Lurie Family in 1972. Frank, Gwyn, Leslie, Rita, and David.

"A lot of people are interested. But I need them wrapped carefully in the plastic and stacked in the garage."

Nothing was going to happen between a fourteen-year-old boy and Mom's eldest daughter if Mom had anything to say about it.

Then one evening, after a few months of teenage bliss, the phone rang. "I think we should break up for now," my boyfriend said, or something to that effect.

"Really?" I was shocked.

"We're still cool, right?" he asked.

"I guess. But why?"

"I think I'm just not ready to have a girlfriend right now," was all he said.

When we hung up, tears streamed down my cheeks. I felt abandoned. But in that same moment I knew that I would be okay. Any obstacle that didn't involve death was surmountable. The following morning, I announced the news to my parents. Dad was up first. He gave me a sympathetic hug when I told him, and then he asked if I wanted to go with him to the car wash. Later, I found Mom, just getting out of bed.

"We broke up," I said, fighting back tears.

"You know, I had a feeling . . ."

I could feel myself getting annoyed. "Why did you have a feeling about it?"

"You're always awake when we get home, and last night you were asleep. I just knew that you were upset about something, and I had a hunch. Anyway, it's his loss, that's for sure," Mom said.

"No. I'm the one who's upset." And Mom was going to get the brunt of my anger.

"To be honest, Dad and I never understood what the attraction was. He hardly spoke to us. He is a nice boy, but you are much more mature."

"Mommy, you and Daddy don't know him like I do."

"Well, I can assure you, you will have boys tripping over themselves to be with you."

"Why can't you just say I'm sorry rather than trying to solve the problem?"

"I am sorry," she said, finally. "But it's his loss, I promise you that."

22

Team Leah

MY PARENTS NAMED me in memory of Grandma Leah, Mom's mother. In the Jewish religion, it is traditional to be named after a cherished deceased relative. Grandma Leah symbolized more than that to me, however. She was my grandmother who had died senselessly and tragically without ever knowing me, cuddling me, or spoiling me. My name carried a weighty obligation. I was living for three: my grandmother, my mother, and me—you could call it "Team Leah." As its self-appointed captain, I dedicated my high school days to piling up a winning record.

At sixteen, I attained my first coaching position. A local park director persuaded me to manage a youth baseball team. Since all of the other coaches in the league were men, generally fathers, I viewed the opportunity as a worthy challenge. From the beginning, I loved the kids and the competition. Even before I got out to the field after school, I would sit in class rearranging positions and batting orders, much the way I had done at home over the years with my baseball card collection. On the field, I was transformed—content, fearless, and focused on the present moment. Of course, I never entirely lost track of my responsibility at home.

Mom was eager to contribute to the household economy, which was suffering after Dad's illness. Having failed to find financial success in various entreprenurial ventures and a brief stint as a travel agent while still being a full-time mother, she had recently become licensed in cosmetology. For Mom, beauty symbolized health. She had begun representing cosmetic lines in department stores, but her goal was to ply her trade in the entertainment business. One day, on the baseball field, I overheard that the father of a player on the team worked in the movie industry. No, he wasn't Steven Spielberg. He supplied camera equipment to the productions, or something of that nature. Still, he was, as they say, "in the business."

"Should we invite them to dinner?" Mom asked when I mentioned the connection.

"Maybe."

"Since you like the family so much, and you spend time at their house, it would be nice to get to know them anyway."

I loved inviting friends over to dinner. Dad told jokes (during which he usually began laughing before delivering the punch line). I could count on Gwyn to place a piece of dark green vegetable on one of her front teeth and then wait until she caught the guest's eye to smile, giving the appearance that a front tooth was missing. David peppered the evening with wry observations. While Mom enjoyed all of this levity, she herself had never learned how to act silly. Still, when new friends came to dinner, I was proudest of all of Mom. She was young (for a mom), beautiful, and wise. Even strangers recognized in her a sympathetic, interested soul, and they readily embraced her. Nonetheless, as I told Mom, I had reservations about inviting this family to dinner for the primary purpose of advancing Mom's business.

"I don't want to put him on the spot. When I tell people you're talented, they don't believe me because they assume I can't be objective," I said.

"I disagree. Everyone knows that you need connections to get into the entertainment industry," Mom said. She knew better than to assume that good fortune would just fall into her lap. Sometimes pushiness was required.

Ultimately, I invited over the family of four, and Mom cooked a gourmet dinner. Over salad, I told the father, "My mother is a makeup artist."

"Aha," he said, smiling at Mom. Then he added, "Your daughter is an exceptional coach."

"I'm not surprised. She's outstanding at everything she puts her mind to. Needless to say, we're very proud of her. Did she tell you that she was just elected president of her whole school for next year?"

"No. She didn't."

"On top of all of her other accomplishments, like being the photographer *and* a writer on the school newspaper, and captain of the swim team."

"I'm not the captain," I said quickly.

"Oh, well, it seems like you are."

I glanced over at my sister and brother, who were rolling their eyes. Apparently Mom noticed, too, because she quickly added, "By the way, we also have two other very successful children. Winnie was just elected the seventh-grade representative, and David already wrote his own newspaper. He was on the news." God forbid any of her children should feel slighted.

By dessert, Mom still had not found the opening to talk about herself. She took the bull by the horns. "So Leslie tells me you're involved with making movies."

"I guess you can say that," he said cryptically.

"Do you happen to know of any openings for a makeup artist?"

"Not off the top of my head," he said. "But I'll give it some thought."

I felt that I was letting Mom down by not making a big pitch for how talented she was, but I didn't know what more to say. The following week at baseball practice, the father told me what a nice time his family had had at our dinner. But he never mentioned a job possibility.

Beyond coaching baseball, I loved playing. What I lacked in natural ability, I made up for in passion and determination. There was something so calming about this game played on a field in a park, without clocks or buzzers or timers. I relished the cracking sound of the bat on the ball and the sight of the players tossing the ball around, inning after inning. And of course, baseball was the all-American sport. What better way was there to distinguish myself from my European mother, and all of the sadness from which she came?

Athletic teams were different for me than those other "one for all and all for one" organizations. Here, my teammates and I worked together to attain a common goal, to be greater than the sum of our parts. Sometimes I felt lonely, deep in my own thoughts, even in the midst of my teammates. But oddly, I found this sensation to be comforting, an old friend coming for a visit. Whether I was swimming, bowling, or playing tennis or softball, my fears miraculously went into remission. I felt at peace, focused on immediate goals, anchored in the eye of the ever-threatening storm.

Dad often came to watch me compete, even though he was never a big sports fan. His immense pride, beaming down from the stands like a klieg light, brought meaning to my victories and comfort to my defeats. Mom also came to watch me when she could, but she never seemed involved with the competition at hand.

"When did you become such a jock?" she used to ask me.

"I like sports. I'm not 'a jock,' " I would respond, annoyed by her inability to distinguish the two.

"I don't need to be told how to say things. I know what I mean."

I knew what Mom meant, too. She did not understand why I took sports seriously. The sports she had casually taken up as an adult, such as bowling and tennis, she enjoyed. But she always looked slightly awkward in these settings. Although she clearly had a competitive side,

Mom had never learned *how* to compete. She had missed the opportunity to experiment when she was younger—to learn to win and still be liked by her opponents.

LIKE MOM, I also wanted empathy in high school. I had close, kind friends, but I sought deeper understanding from adults—namely, strong, smart grown-ups looking for work as surrogate parents, who didn't need too much emotional care from me. My high school dean of students fit the bill nicely. She was single, in her early thirties, and had a biting sense of humor. Sometimes we would talk on the phone until two in the morning. When I brought her home to dinner for the first time, she and Dad particularly hit it off. But as we watched her drive away afterward, Mom turned to me on the front porch and gave me a funny look.

"What?" I asked.

"Nothing. It's just that you manage to find a mother wherever you go," she said with a hint of amusement in her voice.

"No, I don't," I quickly said, not wanting to hurt her feelings.

"I'm not mad. It's just an observation."

I realized that Mom was right, and I was reminded how perceptive she could be. This way, I would never be left motherless. In high school I frequently wheedled my way out of class to sit in the offices of my surrogate guardians. Besides the dean, there was also the assistant principal. Sometimes I sat silently.

"Is anything wrong?" the dean would ask me.

Tell her how sad you are. Say something. "No."

"I can tell something is bothering you, but you don't have to tell me."

I wanted her to intuit my sorrow, imperceptible to the naked eye but always lurking. I wished that she could magically fill my sense of emptiness. I hoped that she would say something to coax my own words, jumbled and leaden in the pit of my stomach, to rise up past my lips.

"I'll go back to class," I would finally say.

She would give me a puzzled look, and let me go.

WHEN I TURNED sixteen, in 1976, and got my driver's license, I relished a first taste of freedom without fear. The panic of watching my parents drive away vanished. Now I could make my own way back home. And I could abandon them before they abandoned me.

Unfortunately, on the Senior Weekend trip, students had to ride the bus rather than drive themselves. I wanted to go. I knew my friends would all be together and that I would be missing out. It was almost unheard of not to attend, particularly for someone like me, who was so involved in school activities. But the anxiety of going away, of being unable to get back home if I wanted to, overshadowed everything else.

My parents neither discouraged me from going on the trip nor pushed me out the door. "Just trust your own judgment," Mom had said. For Mom, as long as I *had* friends, spending extra time with them was not the top priority. Safety was. And family. I took a deep breath and made the decision to stay home. I spent the weekend contentedly coaching my baseball team and going out to dinner with my parents.

I did attend the quintessential senior event, the prom, however, since it did not involve a sleepaway. That day, late in the afternoon, I walked into Mom's bedroom as she was making her bed. I took a deep breath.

"Could you put just a drop of makeup on me?" I asked. I had inherited little of Mom's interest in cosmetics.

Mom was eager to help me, but she played it cool. Prior experience had taught her that too much enthusiasm might cause me to reconsider. "Sure," she said, barely breaking a smile.

"Just a little," I emphasized, as I sat down onto the soft round swivel chair at Mom's vanity. "I want to look natural."

"I know, I know." She leaned in and stared intently at my face. With her lips slightly parted, she began decorating me with her various colored powders.

"Close your eyes, gently," Mom said, applying eye shadow, liner, and mascara.

"That feels like a lot of eye makeup," I protested.

"You look gorgeous," she said. "Not that you need any makeup at all, really."

When Mom paused for a moment too long, I stood up. "He's going to be here any minute. I still have to get dressed."

"Wait, just a little blush." Mom opened the cover of a shiny black container and applied a dab of pink to her fingers before rubbing it into my cheeks.

"I thought I didn't need any makeup at all," I teased.

She ignored me. "Now the important thing," she said, "is to blend it in from the center of the cheek outward, so it goes on evenly." Even though I was nervous as to the outcome, I liked being around the Mom who put makeup on me, the one who reached out to me without any neediness. Every stroke of her fingers against my skin felt gentle and loving.

"I'm late. We have to finish."

"Okay. Just a little more . . . to balance out . . . There! You look ravishing!"

The doorbell rang, and I jumped. "Thank you. I have to go," I said, giving her a quick kiss on the cheek. As I raced out of the bedroom, I couldn't resist stopping in the bathroom to look at my face one last time under the brighter lights. *Oh, no. Light blue eye shadow, and black liner? People will know I'm wearing makeup!* I frantically wet cotton balls and scrubbed off Mom's creation while my prom date waited in the den.

"I can't believe it," Mom said when I came out of the bathroom.

"It just wasn't me," I said.

"I think you looked magnificent," she said with surprising equanimity.

IN JULY OF that year, 1977, Mom turned forty. Knowing that she had been born around the Jewish holiday of Shavuot, she had deduced at some point that she had actually been born in June, but we continued to celebrate on July 6, and to pretend that this was her real birthday. Before the guests arrived for the party, I found Mom in her bedroom and gave her my gift.

"I don't need a present. You're my present," Mom said.

"I know. But open it anyway," I said. I couldn't wait to see her reaction.

She unwrapped the gift and lifted up the life-size baby doll from inside its box. She stared at it for a few seconds and then, just as I had hoped, smiled knowingly at me.

"It's perfect," she said, before kissing me almost on the lips. She understood my intention immediately.

"Did you ever have a doll growing up?" I asked.

"No. Maybe a rag one when I was very young. But this is my first real doll."

Days later, I awakened feeling as though there were a hole in my chest. I was about to embark on a ten-day trip to Hawaii with three friends. I had worked after school at a small, shabby law firm for months to finance the trip. It was too late to back out.

"Just be careful," Mom said as she and Dad waited to see me off at the airport.

"Okay."

"There are all kinds of people out there."

"I know, Mom."

"And don't forget to wear sunscreen. The sun is very strong over there."

I smiled.

"I'm not kidding," she said.

When it was time to board the plane, I willed my legs to follow my friends onto the plane. "I love you," I called to my parents one last time.

"We love you, too!"

During the flight, I tearfully read the bon voyage note Mom had slipped into my brown-bag lunch. My friend Shelley comforted me. "Don't worry. I'll be your mom on the trip," she said. Each day, I recalculated the number of days remaining. But despite keeping a constant eye on my plane ticket home, I went sailing with strangers we met on the beach and danced into the night with young guys whose names I never caught. Beneath the Hawaiian sun, I felt myself starting to grow into me, one separate person. I had an inkling that I could, at least briefly, stand on my own.

23

"Just Jump"

AT SEVENTEEN I entered college at UCLA, having determined that it was the best university I could commute to from home. I approached my studies with determination, knowing that strong grades would help me get into a good law school. As a lawyer, I would be able to seek the justice that was lacking in the world. I could also acquire the financial security that had thus far eluded my parents and had caused Mom such anxiety.

"Mom bought a fur coat today!" my sister announced in the middle of dinner one evening.

"What?" Dad said. He looked like he was going to pass out.

"We went to Bullock's, and Mom bought a gorgeous mink coat," my fourteen-year-old sister said, sounding ecstatic.

"You're kidding," Dad said to Mom.

"I would never wear a fur coat," I said with disdain, hoping to quickly put an end to Mom's infatuation with a luxury item we could not afford.

"Actually, we're not kidding," Mom said to Dad. "Winnie told me that I looked so beautiful in it that I had to buy it."

"You have to see it on her," my sister said.

"But don't worry, I can return it tomorrow," Mom said quickly.

"Mom," I said. "Think about the amazing things we have that money can't buy. We're healthy, and we love each other. Most people would trade their entire fortunes for that."

"And I thank God every day for these blessings. But someday, Leslie, you will realize why money matters so much."

I already understood its importance. I knew that Mom worried about making ends meet, and I couldn't bear for her to feel deprived, or for Dad to think he was disappointing her. That year, at least, we all had hopes that the new bed and bath shop they had recently opened would improve their prospects. Dad was still employed by the pillow manufacturer, but he also worked with Mom at the shop on the weekends, selling high-end comforters and decorative pillows. In the meantime, I vowed that I would always be able to support myself and my family.

Toward that end, at UCLA, I took on two majors and often studied all night long for finals. The frenzy of cramming for tests distracted me from my worries. Afterward, however, feelings of emptiness returned. The challenge for me was not in being educated, or in *being* anything; it was in the immersion of earning more badges, this time in the guise of As—conquering one challenge after the next.

IN JULY 1978, the summer following my freshman year, Mom would face another great challenge as well. Uncle Sam had called from Chicago early one morning to say that Grandpa Isaac had died. The funeral took place on a predictably warm Chicago summer day. Mom and Auntie Sandra were there, and so were Uncle Benny and Aunt Dora, even though Grandpa Isaac had never reconciled with them after the falling-out over the grocery business. Grandpa Isaac's other brothers, Max, Henry, and Norman, flew in from New York. Per Jewish custom, they had ripped their lapels, to indicate that their hearts were torn. After the funeral, they went straight back to the airport, to sit shivah, the seven-day period of mourning, in New York.

I was trapped in a summer-school English class on the morning of Grandpa Isaac's funeral, but I couldn't stop thinking about him. Tears burned the inside corners of my eyes. These tears were not for *my* loss of a grandfather. Grandpa Isaac had been only marginally a part of my life; I suspected he would not have recognized me if he had passed me on the street. Mostly, I felt regret. Regret that my grandfather, once a bright star in his family and village, had not continued to shine in America. Regret that he had died, at the age of seventy-six, far from his two daughters and a virtual stranger to their children. I felt bad for Mom. A satisfying relationship with the man whom she had so revered as a young child had eluded her. And I also regretted that now *I* would never get to know my grandfather. I thought about the distinct foreign voice I heard on the phone every once in a great while.

"Ah, hello, Leslie?"

"Hi, Grandpa," I would say, summoning the warmth and enthusiasm I imagined came naturally to other granddaughters when their grandparents called.

"How are you? How is the family?"

"We're all good. How is everything there?"

"Fine, thank God. Fine."

I had no idea what else to say to him. "Hold on for one second. I'll get my mom." Did I say, "I love you?" I hope so, but I don't recall.

Mom and her father would then talk briefly, almost entirely in Yiddish. I listened intently, hoping that this time things would be different; that Mom would sound relaxed and happy, chatting with her father. Instead, she inevitably sounded tense, and from what I could make out, stuck to surface conversation about her children. Their calls always ended sooner and more abruptly than I expected, or hoped.

LATER THAT SUMMER, maybe because Mom needed a distraction, our family went on a weeklong Hawaiian vacation. We toured the island, went out to dinner, lay on the beach, and swam. Well, most of us swam.

At home I had been a swim instructor for the past two summers. Along the way I had come across only one water-resistant student. That week in Hawaii, I practiced with her in the hotel pool.

"You're doing great, just kick your feet," I said to the tense forty-one-year-old woman who was gripping my hands with all her might.

"I'm doing it, I'm doing it," she said proudly, kicking her legs.

"But you have to let go of my hands," I said.

Mom continued to cling to me, like two socks fresh out of the dryer. She never could relax enough to allow herself to float.

At the end of the trip, en route to the airport, I uttered two words that would later haunt me. We had pulled off the road to take in a view of a waterfall. Mom had climbed up onto a three-foot stone ledge to get a good look. Then she was ready to get down.

"How do I get off of here?" she asked, looking around.

How easy it would have been for me to walk over and take her hand. I suppose anyone in our family could have. But I wanted for her to be self-sufficient.

"Just jump," I said. It looked so simple.

"I can't jump off here in these shoes," Mom said.

I glanced at the thin wedges beneath Mom's sandals before saying, "Mom, your shoes are fine. It's not that high. Just jump."

She jumped. Then she landed, twisting her ankle in the process. Her face turned white, and she collapsed in pain. Why did she listen to me? I wondered. When she looked up, she calmly said, "I told you I shouldn't jump."

When our plane touched down in Los Angeles a few hours later, Mom was taken off in a wheelchair. She had a bad sprain and would wear a soft cast for six weeks. I realized how much power my words had over her. Power, I felt, that I had not yet earned. I promised myself that in the future, I would be more careful of what I tried to convince Mom to do.

Back at UCLA, I immersed myself in extracurricular activities. Rather than socializing between classes, I operated much like the executives I would soon be exposed to, scheduling meetings or meals, often with an agenda. Apparently Grandpa Isaac's message to Mom had trickled down to me: having fun was frivolous.

I was soaring through my sophomore year, still balancing Mom and Grandma Leah on my wings. I knew I had to try flying solo, but the day my family helped march my few essential possessions from our ranch-style haven of nineteen years into my new apartment felt like a funeral. My new roommate, Diane, a friend from UCLA student government, was there to greet me. She had a tough exterior, but once you broke through it, she was warm and funny. She treated me like a younger sister.

"Don't worry, she won't starve," Diane told Mom, as we all stood in the living room.

"We're not worried," Mom said.

"In fact," Diane continued, "I'm making my specialty, moussaka, for dinner tonight. My boyfriend will be here, too." As she spoke, Diane gestured to the small adjoining kitchen just behind us.

I took a deep breath. "Actually, I'm going back home tonight," I said. "I still have a few things there to take care of before school tomorrow."

Diane stared at me. She probably was wondering what I needed to take care of that I couldn't have completed over the previous two decades. Then she said, "Leslie, you have to leave home sometime."

"I am. I'll be here tomorrow," I promised.

I rented the apartment for two years but slept there only a few nights a week. Home was still with my family. Both Gwyn and David were busy with their own high school lives by then. As was Mom. On one rainy morning, Mom rushed Gwyn to high school so she would not be late turning in an important health class report. Racing out of Mom's car, Gwyn tripped, and her report splashed into a puddle. She and

Mom both broke into tears. As they gathered up the soggy papers in the driving rain that morning, it seemed to Gwyn as if the two of them had merged into one.

Mom was always at her best, ironically, when we were most upset. No matter how widely I would come to spread my wings in the coming years, or how many loved ones I might be surrounded by, when I didn't feel well, I wanted Mom.

"I'll make you feel better," she would say, gently stroking my hair and scalp. At times like these, there was no longing, and no wariness, just overflowing love from her enormous heart. I would lie in bed and hold Mom's hand, not to make her feel good but because she made me feel so much better. No one else would ever take care of me so devotedly when I was sick. In those moments, I felt so at peace with her, curled up in the safety of her unguarded compassion.

MIDWAY THROUGH MY junior year at UCLA, one of my achievements catapulted me out of my cocoon. I was appointed student regent on the University of California Board of Regents. Upon receiving the news by telephone that I had been selected after an arduous interview process, I was perhaps more ecstatic than I had ever been. But even before the receiver was back in the cradle, a shadow crept in. I could not entirely trust anything this thrilling. Something ominous was bound to follow. What if I died before my term even began? Then I calmed down. Even if I did, I reasoned, it would not be so terrible. I had already lived a life filled with opportunity and rich experiences.

Having survived long enough to take office, at first I was out of my comfort zone as the student regent. Not only was I traveling to meetings in northern California, but I was working with leaders in the state, including the governor, who were more concerned with their own agendas than with helping me accomplish mine. Over lunch, a politically liberal regent named Stanley Sheinbaum, who would become a mentor and lifelong friend, offered me advice. "Don't worry so much about being liked," he said in his characteristically gruff yet warm manner.

"Okay," I responded, hoping he liked me.

"Just speak up for what you believe in, and you'll be fine," he said.

Now I wasn't just on good terms with those in charge. I was one of them. I was using my own position and voice to protect others. When it came time for the regents to decide whether the University of California would continue to operate nuclear weapons labs for the Department of Energy, I found myself in the midst of a highly charged political debate, and ultimately was one of only a few no votes. At one point in the discussion, as I was advocating my position, I thought about Mom, arguing with the manager in Fedco and the other gatekeepers along the way. I had a greater admiration for her unwillingness to back down from what she believed, and realized that I had incorporated some of that stubborn determination into my own playbook.

For Mom, there was no denying that I was on a slippery slope toward independence. I didn't realize it then, but this must have been a very difficult time for her. Perhaps in an attempt to assuage her apprehensions about my impending graduation from college, she took me to a spa in nearby Ojai the summer before my senior year. Out by the pool the first day I was reading *The Brethren*, Bob Woodward's book about the Supreme Court, when Mom walked over.

"I'm going to the aerobics session. You should come," she said.

"No, thanks. I think I'll just keep reading."

"Are you sure? It's supposed to be very strenuous, the way you like it."

Why doesn't she ever take no for an answer? "That's okay."

Mom studied my face. "You need to put some sunblock under your eyes."

"I will." *I won't.* I turned back to my book.

"Really. It's not good for that sensitive skin beneath your eyes to get burned over and over again."

As I watched Mom walk off toward her class, I wondered what accounted for the new, nagging tension between us. After our Spartan dinner we returned to our quarters, furnished with two twin beds, a small dresser, and a lamp. I felt crowded and annoyed, although I still could not pinpoint why. I was particularly aggravated with myself for my inexplicable bad mood.

"Do you have any interest in that cooking class tomorrow?" Mom ventured. She was sitting on her bed, with her back propped up against the wall behind her.

"I can't even eat this food. Why would I want to learn how to prepare it?" Why did I have to say that? I wondered, as soon as the words escaped my lips. *Just say you'll go.* I sat on my bed, staring at her across the canyon that separated us, mute.

"It was just a suggestion." She sounded hurt.

"Let's call Dad," I said, hoping a distraction would improve things.

I knew that we should be bonding, that we both had looked forward to this trip, and that I needed to be a nicer travel companion. But I fiercely needed to protect the distance I had struggled so hard to attain. It still felt as tenuous as the loss of a few pounds after a juice fast. I was sure it would evaporate if my thoughts escaped into Mom's consciousness, or perhaps if her thoughts leaked into mine. At least for me, a more successful trip was on the horizon.

As student regent, I was invited by UCLA's chancellor, Charles Young, to join a delegation that was heading to Japan to attend the Mirage Bowl, a football game that would be played between UCLA and Oregon State. Although Japan had been the one country that Dad always wanted to visit, I found myself scouring Tokyo jewelry shops for a pearl necklace for Mom. It weighed on me like a fettuccine Alfredo dinner that Mom was missing out on this experience.

Once I selected the necklace, however, I felt sure that Mom and I could both now be happy about my weeklong trip. I toured, met new lifelong friends, and felt strangely elated. I realized that the tremendous pressure I carried around had lightened when I left town and my family. This time the space that opened up between us was leaving room for me to breathe. The fear I had experienced before I left home, the same anticipatory separation anxiety I had always felt, had not been the portent of a bad adventure. Rather than worrying so much about Mom's independence, I needed to remind *myself*, more often, to "Just Jump."

24

It's Not That Kind of Thing

I WAS STUDYING for midterms during my senior year in college when the phone rang.

"Leslie? Ah, I'm a little confused."

"Mom? Where are you?" Her voice sounded distant, like she was talking into a soup can.

"I'm on a pay phone at a gas station. Can you come get me?"

Now I was confused. "Why?"

"I was driving to my therapist's appointment, but I think I got off at the wrong exit. I'm not sure I can drive myself home."

When I picked her up, she seemed oddly subdued. But by the time we returned home things seemed normal enough, and I wrote the incident off to a strange morning. Later the same week we gathered to celebrate my twenty-first birthday. Dad baked his famous lasagna. I was hurt. This was Gwyn's favorite meal, and his. I didn't particularly like lasagna. Mom had always asked me what I wanted her to cook for my family birthday dinner, but this time she hadn't. Adding insult to injury, she had been withdrawn throughout the evening, damping down the energy in the dining room like an empty glass over a candle. *Why wasn't she happy about my birthday? Is she mad at me?*

In the den after dinner, I was confronting Dad with my grievances when I heard something that sounded like sniffling. I looked across the room at the oddest sight. Mom was mechanically wiping the large coffee table in front of the sofa with a rag, back and forth, again and again. Tears rolled down her cheeks. In that instant I realized just how unusually she had been acting over the past week.

"Leslie, I'm sorry. I just didn't feel up to cooking tonight," she said, through inconsolable sobs. She rarely apologized. And I had never seen her break down crying like this. My hurt feelings instantaneously vanished.

For days afterward, Mom lay in bed crying. I didn't know how to help her. I didn't understand what was wrong. I wondered whether her state was tied to the challenges her store was facing. Five years after it opened, the large retail bed and bath chains that had come into vogue were giving her a serious run for her money. I usually knew the right thing to say to make Mom feel better, but now my words fell on deaf ears. Mom would tell me that she knew I had other things to do, that she didn't want to keep me from my life. But then, when I would get up to leave her bedside, she would tell me that she felt like a small child being abandoned.

Miraculously, within a few weeks Mom's despair lifted, and like a painful bout of stomach flu that disappears from memory as suddenly as it arrives, it quickly escaped my mind. Three years later, when I was ready to graduate from law school, Mom's depression resurfaced, hungrier and fiercer than before. She had suffered a few recent setbacks. She had been forced to finally close her store and was faced with the question of what to do next.

Convinced that she was meant to have a meaningful career in business or mental health, Mom had enrolled in community college courses. The turmoil she felt in high school, however, churned up again as soon as she stepped back in the classroom. Concurrently, Dad was unceremoniously let go after twenty-five years at his company, in order to create a position for the owner's son. Both of my parents took it very personally. For months, Dad pursued jobs by day and worried at night, until he joined his brother, Buddy, in a thriving video security business. This crisis churned up painful memories for Mom of all those years when Dad had been sick and when her own father had been treated poorly at work. And there was one more thing. Although I had remained at UCLA for law school, in love with the university and still hesitant to venture far away, there was no denying that my life was increasingly busy and less centered on home.

Day after day, Mom lay in bed, in tears, not asleep but not entirely awake either. She felt intensely deprived, she later revealed, just as she had as a child. She thought that she was slowly dying, that her sense of self was coming to an end. She didn't want her children to see her in this condition, but she also didn't want to be alone.

"Mom, let's go for a walk," I would say as I stood beside her bed. "Lying there all day would make anyone miserable."

"Maybe later, Leslie. Not now. I feel numb." She seemed powerless and could barely string her words together.

"You'll feel better if you just get out of bed."

"Leslie, it's not that kind of thing. I haven't slept. I can't think straight. I need to rest before I can go for a walk."

I felt like a schoolteacher clumsily struggling to motivate a troubled student. "Let's at least think of something positive. Something that will make you happy."

"Don't worry. I'll be fine. I just have to go through this."

I felt that if I could only find the right words, assemble the Scrabble tiles on my rack in the proper order, I could beat Mom's depression. But I couldn't. I was frustrated by my lack of cleverness. I wished I could magically extinguish her sorrow and we could both get back to real life. One afternoon, as I sat by her bed, I thought back a couple years, to my first semester in law school, when I decided to apply for a summer clerkship. The deadline had fast been approaching. I could not find the time to make follow-up calls while studying for my first set of finals.

"Do you need my help?" Mom had asked, sensing my frustration one evening.

At first I just shook my head. But she persisted.

"Really. I can make the calls for you," she said, confidently. "Maybe I'll get myself a job at the same time," she added, half joking.

"They're law firms, Mom. You're not a lawyer."

"Well, who knows," she said.

I had studied for finals while Mom placed the follow-up calls to law firms. She sounded uncharacteristically businesslike. Not only was *I* proud of her, but she was proud of herself. "We got a job!" she told Dad when I received a clerkship offer. Now, I looked at Mom, lying in bed. I could not believe that she couldn't will herself out of this state, the way she had three years earlier. And I found myself wishing that she had at least chosen a better time. I wondered whether she had subconsciously synced her breakdown to coincide with my bar exam studies in order to keep me with her for a while longer.

After sitting by her side in the dark master bedroom for a couple of hours, I convinced myself that I had to leave. I didn't have more time. Time was so precious to me, always. I had to get outside, disentangle myself from the webs of melancholy. *Besides, thank God, it's not like she has a terminal illness. She's sad, she's not dying.* Surviving was the ultimate goal. Mom was a survivor. I remained convinced that ultimately she would will herself back to health.

I bent down to hug her. "I have to go back to school," I said gently.

"I know. Don't worry," Mom said, forcing a pathetic smile.

"I promise you'll get better. I love you," I said, kissing her again before I left.

"I love you, too," she said in a barely audible voice.

I left home that afternoon in a fog, sucked into Mom's despondency. Each time I departed, I felt that I should have stayed longer, holding her hand and making her feel more comfortable. Mom would have done that for me, or for anyone in our family. Knowing that my sister and brother, by then undergraduates at UCLA, also were not at home did not make me feel any less guilty about departing. I recently asked my sister whether my intense relationship with Mom ever made her feel bad. To my surprise, Gwyn told me, "No, it's a relief." Gwyn, who at the time had been serving as UCLA's student body president, also thought about Mom much of the time. "But you're like me on steroids," she said. My constant devotion to Mom took the pressure off my sister and even allowed her, later on, to briefly live in other parts of the country and the world.

I regretted that Mom didn't share news of her illness with one or two friends. For Mom, there was always a distinction between friends and family. The time she spent with her friends was often confined to dinners out with spouses or an occasional lunch. She rarely revealed to them her personal problems or intimate confidences, at least as far as I could determine. Thus, our nuclear family made up her inner circle. And I felt like her best hope for a cure. Yet here I was, once again leaving her, going out to dinner with my boyfriend or back to the library to study. I fled to restaurants and libraries, where lights were on, air was circulating, and people were living, even laughing. The outside world was full of possibilities, at least for those who weren't constantly looking back.

Mom took pride in the fact that she was able to attend my law school graduation, even though she later said that she felt like she was going to collapse. As connected as I felt to her, I still had no idea of the extent of the torment she was experiencing.

In desperation, Mom had found a psychiatrist who specialized in psychopharmacology. Because of the trauma she had experienced, he told her she probably had a chemical imbalance that could be treated with an antidepressant containing serotonin. Mom disliked taking medicine, but she would have tried anything by that point. Dad convinced me to go ahead and take the post-bar-exam trip I had planned with my boyfriend. I called home every day, dreading the same news that Mom still had not improved. Then one day, Dad sounded different. The antidepressants had begun to take effect. On the telephone, from my shabby hotel room in some province of China, I took a deep breath. For the first time in weeks, air came to me easily. That was when I began my vacation in earnest.

Mom slowly began a new chapter in her life. She had been to hell and back but emerged stronger. She told Dad and me that she had been disappointed by our level of support and empathy during her weeks of desperation. We could deal with this. At least she was back, healthy and relatively happy. I was on reprieve, once again free to enjoy life. Still, Mom's depression would leave its mark. I had witnessed an agony that had enabled me to better imagine the horrors that had imprinted themselves on my mother's mind. I had seen firsthand how devastating depression could be. I would work even harder to stay busy, to be successful, to keep options open, to maintain friendships, and avoid any life choices that might contribute to Mom's next deep, dark descent.

25

Inside NBC

ONE OF MOM's life choices that I thought prudent to avoid was becoming a mother of three by the time she was in her midtwenties. I never doubted that she adored us and that we brought her great pride and comfort, yet she had seemed discontent much of the time. So motherhood was not on my top fifty "Things to Accomplish Before I Hit the Big 3-0."

After law school, I accepted a clerkship with a kind and politically like-minded Ninth Circuit Court of Appeals judge. Best of all, he was in Los Angeles. While working in an intellectually stimulating environment by day and socializing in the evenings, I could still keep an eye on Mom. By the end of my term, however, I was questioning whether I wanted to earn a living as a lawyer. Uncertain as to what I wanted to do next, I decided to take a breather from law firm interviews and latch on to Mom, Dad, and Gwyn's trip to Europe. They were planning to visit my brother, who was spending his undergraduate semester abroad in Austria, and then to drop my sister off at Oxford, where she would pursue graduate studies on a prestigious scholarship. Although both of my siblings would now be living away from home for a period of time, in a foreign country no less, I had no similar desire.

Mom had coordinated the trip. She decided to forgo making prior reservations to ensure maximum spontaneity, a fact I think she mentioned sometime during the flight to London. Had I known this ahead of time, I would have advocated that she take only one modest suitcase, rather than the many larger ones that Dad and I would be lugging on and off trains for the next three weeks. We landed in the morning. Weary, we grabbed a cab.

"The Grosvenor Hotel, please," Mom said to the driver. She and Dad had stayed there two years earlier, on their first trip to England.

"Yes, ma'am."

Then Dad said to Mom, "What's the backup plan if they're filled up?"

"It's such a big hotel, there won't be a problem," Mom said.

One thing about being in London is that the cabdriver usually understands English.

"I sure hope you folks have a reservation. There's not an empty room in the city with the conventions in town," he said.

We looked at one another. What conventions? If Mom was worried, she didn't let on. Rarely did she sweat the small stuff, particularly the small stuff that she created.

"Now what?" Dad asked. We were standing in the hotel lobby, having just been informed that the hotel was fully booked. Had Dad been in charge, the strategy might have been to head back home. He grew uneasy when he didn't have a solid travel itinerary.

"Why don't we spend the day in London, walking around," Mom proposed, "and tonight take the ferry to Paris?"

"I would do that," I said. As I had never been to Europe before, Paris sounded just as exciting as London.

Late that night, we took the Chunnel to France. Shortly after dawn, we found ourselves in the lobby of a small, quaint Parisian hotel. Dad, Gwyn, and I stood nearby, leaving Mom to approach the reception counter. She did so with complete assurance.

"Yes, hi. We have a reservation under Lurie," Mom said.

The clerk checked his ledger. "I'm sorry, madame, I don't see a reservation."

"Well, we made one," Mom said, without flinching.

"Yes, madame. Do you have your confirmation?"

"Confirmation? Let's see." Mom fumbled through her file, filled with a friend's hotel and restaurant recommendations. She was so convincing, I found myself expecting her to actually pull it out of the folder. "No. I don't think I received a confirmation. Maybe the travel agent never sent it to us." She was becoming perturbed.

"But that is impossible."

When the charade became unbearable to watch, I walked up to the counter and whispered to her, "Mom, let's go." We hadn't slept in two nights, and our patience was wearing thin.

"No. This isn't right," she said. She seemed to actually believe that *we* had been wronged. And after a few more minutes, she convinced the manager, too. He sent a bellman to investigate a possibility.

"Very well, madame. It does look as though I may have one suite available after all," the clerk said when the bellman returned. Mom looked over at us with a proud smile. A few days later, Mom talked our way into a hotel in Florence, too.

Mom seemed energized by Europe. She made the most of every day and was never too tired for any museum, restaurant, or shopping adventure. Not wanting to deprive herself, she stopped for ice cream and sweets as often as she felt she could without attracting a lecture from me about her weight or high cholesterol.

"Here, you have to taste this. It's delicious," she would say, pushing each treat on Dad, Gwyn, or me.

"No, thanks," we would usually say, having had plenty of our own.

"Really, it's out of this world. Just take one taste." Mom hated to enjoy anything without one of her family members sharing in the delight.

From Italy, we went to Austria to visit David, who was eager to take us walking along the Danube River and to his favorite tavern. At first Mom had bristled at the idea that David was going to spend a semester living in a German-speaking country, but David insisted that German was almost Yiddish.

From Austria, Dad headed back home with a toothache, and several of Mom's suitcases in tow. Mom, Gwyn, and I spent one more week together, during which Gwyn and I bickered constantly. We were still locked in a fierce, on-again-off-again irrational competition. Mom was so happy to be traveling, she barely raised an eyebrow.

Back in Los Angeles, I decided to pursue a job in the television industry. Television had been a loyal and comforting escape for me as a child, and I was willing to take a job at any level, or to volunteer, just to get in the door. I sought advice from everyone willing to talk to me, and called Dr. Diana Meehan, a generous and wise professor I had adopted back at UCLA. Her husband-to-be was a successful television producer, Gary David Goldberg, who had recently created the hit comedy series *Family Ties* for NBC. With the help of Diana's coaching, a well-placed call from Gary, and a strong endorsement from a college friend who had gone to work at NBC, I was offered a junior executive job at the network. Dad, in particular, had mixed reactions to the news. Did I really want to forgo a legal career to be a network executive? What *was* a network executive, anyway?

"Honey, if Leslie took the job, I'm sure it's a good opportunity," Mom told him. Her utter confidence in my judgment had only increased over the years.

"I don't think being a lawyer is such a bad thing, either," Dad said.

I reasoned that if television didn't work out, I could always go back to law. Meanwhile, I couldn't wait to begin. My job was in the comedy department, which I had some concerns about, since I wasn't very funny. Apparently, at the interview, I had managed to fool my future boss, Perry Simon. He had given me a problematic script to read and afterward asked me how I would comment on it to a successful producer who, he mentioned in passing, happened to be overweight. "We'll call him Mr. X," Perry concluded. "What would you say to him?"

I blurted out the first thing that occurred to me. "Can I get you something to eat first, Mr. X?"

Perry burst out laughing, and a few days later, I was offered the job. From the beginning, I knew that I had made the right decision. I felt at home in this new atmosphere, where people worked intensely but still laughed and had some freedom as to how to approach their jobs. To this environment I brought the self-assurance to stand up for my beliefs.

In the television industry, this was not always easy. Mostly, people only wanted to hear yes. As a young woman with more confidence than experience, I was an easy target for any disappointed writer, producer, or studio executive. Often I didn't even realize when I was putting my foot in my mouth, because in this world people often smiled and said one thing while feeling quite the opposite.

"Do you like this necklace?" a sitcom actress asked me on the set one morning, pointing to a strand of bright clunky beads reminiscent of something I had pulled out of a treasure chest in a children's dentist office years earlier. Being new to the job, I assumed that the actress would not have asked me my opinion if she herself had liked it. "I think you could do better," I said honestly.

"Oh, thank you," she said, with a huge, warm smile.

Minutes later, the producer appeared and told me not to give wardrobe notes to his cast. The actress was devastated that I had criticized her late grandmother's necklace.

Inside NBC, however, I managed to garner more approval. By twenty-eight, I was a vice president, overseeing the development of new half-hour television series for the network. I was fortunate to have as my mentor the president of NBC, Brandon Tartikoff. He could be demanding and critical, but he was always fair. I deeply admired his combination of brilliance, charisma, and compassion. By taking the word *determination* to a whole other level, he taught me to work even harder to achieve my goals. And work I did, day and night. The line between my social and professional life became blurry because most breakfasts, lunches, and evenings involved colleagues in the business. There probably was not a better career in which to distract oneself from a prior generation's demons—or anything else, for that matter.

Dad eventually shook off his early reservations about my job choice. But I felt guilty. My life was so different from Mom's. I lived in a part of town where she had never lived. I had a job she could not describe, and I was out at fancy restaurants and glamorous-sounding events until late most nights. As I became more successful, I instinctively tempered my enthusiasm out of concern that Mom would feel she was missing out.

"Was it fun?" Mom asked the day after the Emmy Awards.

"It was okay," I said, sounding more like I had returned from a double shift at the garment factory than an awards show. "But it was cold in the auditorium, and we couldn't eat or get up to walk around. I wish I could have watched it at home, like you."

26

The Most Beautiful Woman
in the Attic

I HAD GOTTEN into the habit of jogging around a local country club several times a week with a television producer friend of mine. Early on one such morning in the summer of 1987, I was wrestling with a decision I needed to make quickly.

"My cousin Debbie, who lives in New York, is going to film a documentary in Poland about our mothers' Holocaust experiences. My sister and some of my New York cousins are going along, and they want me to come, too. I doubt I will, but I can't quite bring myself to say no," I said.

"Aha." He was twenty years my senior and not Jewish, so I assumed that he would not voice a strong opinion one way or the other. But comedy writers, I had come to learn, often had insightful and unique ways of viewing the world, so I thought his perspective might be interesting. Besides, our run would likely be the only time I'd have that day to think about this.

"What does 'aha' mean?" I asked.

"It means you're going to go," he said.

"No. I probably won't. But I wanted to know whether you had an opinion."

"My opinion is that you should go."

"Why?" I am five foot four, and he was over six feet tall. I quickened my pace to keep up with his longer strides.

"Because one day you'll want to talk to your children about your mother's history, and this is how you'll learn more about it."

Up until then, the thought had not crossed my mind that I might someday have children who would be affected by what had taken place in their grandmother's life in another world and time. His words changed everything. "So when is this trip, by the way?" he was asking.

"Next week, believe it or not."

"We better pick up the pace, or you'll miss your flight."

At twenty-seven, I still felt that tinge of sadness when I left on a trip. The night before we flew to Poland, my sister and I were walking on the Upper West Side of Manhattan when the melancholy crept in. I turned to her and asked straight out, "Do you promise you'll be nice to me in Poland?" In that moment, I wanted her to be Mom. I needed to trust entirely that she would always be there for me. I knew that I would always be there for her. Gwyn looked at me like I was crazy.

"What do you mean, 'be nice'?"

"Just in case I'm sad." The pathetic nature of the comment was not lost on either of us. But the beauty of having a close sister is that in her presence an adult, socially successful and at the peak of her career, can act like a three-year-old on occasion, and afterward not have to pretend that she has been misunderstood.

"Okay," Gwyn said. She added, "Then you have to be nice to me, too."

Twenty-four hours later we were in Warsaw. Along with my sister I was traveling with four of my cousins, Debbie, Cheryl, Jack, and Leslie, whose mothers had hidden in the attic with Mom. We each were in our mid-to-late twenties, single, and working after graduate school. My

Poland, 1987. From left, Gwyn Lurie, Debbie Goodstein, Sheryl Silver, Leslie Lurie, Sally Frishberg, Leslie Frishberg.

mother's first cousin Sally also came along, with her husband, Kenny. Tsivia and Libish's eldest daughter was in her mid-fifties, with short gray curly hair, a warm, friendly face, and a compact, sturdy build. She was a retired teacher who, in addition to managing real estate properties, worked as a volunteer speaking about the Holocaust. Up until this trip I had spent very little time with these New York relatives, and I was surprised by how comfortable I immediately felt with the entire group.

On the first few days of our journey we toured Warsaw and then Kraków. We spent a very somber afternoon at Auschwitz, where I found myself grateful that this hellhole was one horror that members of our family had not had to endure. Then we made our way to the southeast of Poland, where we drove out to Przeworsk to see the home of our great-grandparents, Aharon and Paya Neshe. Cousin Sally directed our driver to the spot where, long ago, the family had gathered each week.

"Could it be farther up the road?" the driver asked, slowing down.

"No. I'm certain. This was the place," Cousin Sally insisted.

The bus stopped, but nobody stood up. We stayed glued to our seats and stared out the window at a barren, grassy hill. Somehow it seemed that if we concentrated intensely enough, the family home that once stood proudly on that spot would materialize.

"It's not here," Sally finally said. Apparently her grandparents' home had burned down, turning to ash our hopes of finding any sense of family spirit that still lingered in that place. I thought about the patriarch of the Gamss family, my mother's grandfather, Aharon, born eighty-three years before me. In other circumstances, I might have known him, albeit as a very old man. Grandpa Isaac or Mom at least could have told me stories about him, his world, and his idiosyncrasies. Instead, he was as distant to me as the biblical Abraham or Isaac.

A short distance away was my mother's hometown of Urzejowice. As we rolled into the small village, one of my cousins began singing "The Circle Game," by Joni Mitchell. We all joined in to sing about the child who came out to wander and grew fearful when the sky filled with thunder. The melancholy lyrics seemed to resonate with what we all were feeling. As we got to the chorus about the seasons going round and round, Cousin Sally shouted over our voices to the tour guide, "There is only one church in the town. Once you find the church, I'm home." We stopped singing and resumed our lookout positions, staring through the windows.

"Mom! There it is! There's the church!" my cousin, coincidentally also named Leslie, cried out, pointing to a small building just ahead, with a cross on its roof. Sally's daughter Leslie had curly brown shoulder-length hair, pretty blue eyes, and a loud, infectious laugh.

"Yes, there it is," Cousin Sally said.

Leaving the bus behind, we walked down an unpaved road until we arrived at Sally's childhood home. The wooden structure was in poor condition, with red tiles missing from the roof and its windows boarded up.

Poland, 1987. Sally Frishberg (left) speaks to childhood friends.

"Are you sure this is it?" Cousin Leslie asked her mother. Then, with a hint of a smile, she added, "Because this is not the way you described it."

"Yes. I am absolutely positive," Sally said, staring grimly at the home she remembered as having been so beautiful.

Two plump women in cotton print dresses happened to be passing by. Sally approached them and in rapid Polish said, "Excuse me. Do you remember Tsivia Engleberg?"

The women looked at her and then broke into smiles, nodding their heads.

"I'm her daughter," Sally said.

"Her daughter. Oh, my God. I remember you as a little girl. Sally Engleberg!" one woman said.

"I was your neighbor, Tselka," the other woman interjected triumphantly. Tselka had wavy blond-gray hair that she wore pulled back in a loose bun, and pale blue eyes. I was not surprised when Sally later mentioned that Tselka, who never married, had been a pretty girl. The Polish women were now hugging Sally as if she was their long-lost best friend.

As they conversed, I tried to get a sense of Mom's childhood village. Everything we had seen thus far seemed just as I imagined it had been a half century earlier. Elderly men and women dressed in caps, sweaters, and cotton dresses, occasionally with cows and other large beasts in tow, ambled slowly down the unpaved roads past aging cottages. But there was one eerie difference, I realized. At the beginning of the war, Jews constituted more than one-third of the small town's population. Now, there were none. I wondered how Cousin Sally's former playmates viewed the disappearance of the Jews. Where were they when Sally, her sisters, and her cousins came back home and were forced to leave again? Of course, they had been only adolescent girls themselves

Poland, 1987. Sally Frishberg points out the type of haystack in which her family hid out in the spring and summer of 1942.

at the time, just a bit older than Sally. Later I would learn that Tselka's mother was the woman who during the war had balked at returning Aunt Tsivia's fur coat until her priest encouraged her to do so.

When I turned my attention back to the reunion, Sally was saying how disappointed she was to find her home in such poor condition. The neighbors explained that the dilapidated building was now used to store vegetables. Sally shook her head sadly. I then noticed Tselka's friend whispering something in her ear. The interpreter translated that the friend wanted to introduce *me* to her son, a student at the University of Kraków. I politely declined, but found myself smiling as I imagined Mom's reaction if I came back from the trip with a Polish boyfriend. Then Tselka said to Sally, "I remember a song we used to sing about you and your sisters."

"Really?" Sally asked, her eyes growing wide. "Can you tell us the words?"

Tselka looked over at her friend, and together, they began chanting.

> *In the middle of a village,*
> *In the corner of a barn . . .*

"I remember the ending," Sally interrupted, bursting into song with them.

> *In the middle of a village,*
> *In the corner of a barn,*
> *The Engleberg girls will yet do a dance.*

They laughed and reminisced a while longer. Then we bid farewell to Sally's former neighbors and continued up the road, searching for Mom's former home. Two boys and a girl, probably nine- or ten-year-olds, rode by on old bicycles. Eyeing us carefully, one of the boys shouted,

"Heil Hitler!"

"Did he say what I think he said?" my cousin Leslie asked.

"Yes. I heard it, too," Cousin Sally said.

"They probably just wanted to get our attention," I said. Not only did I instinctively look for the good in every child, but I was concerned that the encounter might upset Sally. Fortunately, when I glanced over at her, she seemed fine.

"*They* might not have known what the words meant, but I'm sure whomever they learned them from did," Gwyn said.

The anti-Semitic slur reverberated in my mind. I felt bruised by it, and I continued to wonder whether we had heard correctly. I also felt for the first time just an inkling of the anguish my mother, Cousin Sally, and the rest of their family must have experienced during the war, when their familiar world turned against them, spewing venom and hatred.

The Polish children rode out of sight, off into the distance, and we continued on. We had to get directions once or twice along the way, but we soon arrived at a low chain-link fence and found ourselves staring over it at a modest but charming cottage. It was off-white, with bright green trim. I wanted to absorb every detail so that I could carry my impression back to Mom. The roof was corrugated steel, the windows metal, and the construction stucco over cinder block. Between the fence and the front of the house was a garden brimming with golden wild-flowers, much as Mom had remembered it.

"It's so small," I said to my sister. We were standing slightly apart from the others. A chill swept through my body.

"Can you believe that this is it? That Mom used to live here?" Gwyn asked.

"I'm sorry she's not here now," I said, suddenly feeling that this was an experience we should be sharing with her.

"It's not like we didn't invite her," Gwyn said.

"I know, but I should have been more persistent." The truth is, I had

Poland, 1987. Leslie and Gwyn Lurie outside Rita Lurie's original home.

been ambivalent, and I now regretted it. If I hadn't been worried about feeling responsible for Mom's emotional and physical well-being on the trip, perhaps I could have convinced her.

"If she had been ready for it, she would have found a way to be here," Gwyn insisted.

I was impressed by my sister's ability to appreciate the moment without worrying that Mom was missing out.

We walked through the front garden and knocked on the door. A petite elderly woman answered. "Yes?" she asked, tentatively clutching the door.

We smiled and tried to look amiable. "Hi. Our mother lived in this house as a young girl," I said, with the aid of our Polish interpreter.

"Yes?" She seemed neither shocked nor particularly welcoming.

"Would you mind if we came inside and looked around for a minute or two?"

"Oh. It would be all right. I'm sorry it's not very clean," she said. We walked into a small country kitchen with peach-colored wallpaper and painted cabinets. White lace curtains hung in the windows.

"It's cute," I said to Gwyn.

"And so neat," my sister said. "If this woman thinks this isn't very clean, I wonder what she would think of my apartment."

"Or mine," I said, picturing the piles of newspapers and scripts on my nightstand and the clothes I had left strewn about my bedroom in my race to get out of town.

In this small kitchen that seemed straight out of an antique doll-house catalog, I had a hard time imagining Grandma Leah preparing her elaborate Shabbos dinners.

"How long have you lived here?" I asked.

"I just recently moved in and renovated it," she said. Perhaps she wanted to make clear that she had not confiscated Mom's home. Did she know about its history? I wondered. Had she heard of the Gamss family? I suspected that she had, given that so many of the family's former neighbors still seemed to reside in the small village. But she was not letting on, and we were grateful for the chance to have a look around.

"Can we take a quick peek at the rest of the house?" I asked.

"It's not very large, but I suppose."

We self-consciously poked our heads into two small, sparsely furnished bedrooms, and then a modest master bedroom. Each had wooden floors, lace curtains, crosses on the walls, and all of the charm of a Motel 6 garden-view room. The biggest disappointment was that the home contained no sign that Mom's family had ever lived there. They seemed to have been the proverbial trees that fell in the forest with nobody to hear them.

AND YET THERE we were, in Urzejowice. From Mom's first home we walked past the small railroad station to which, in 1942, her family had been ordered to report. Nearby, we encountered an elderly man dressed in a black leather cap and white button-down shirt. I felt as if I was dreaming when he said that I looked like Isaac, my grandfather, and my sister looked like a mix between Isaac and Leah. Another villager along the way matter-of-factly told Sally that a redheaded cousin of my grandfather's named Moishe had been shot by Nazis right where we were standing. I got the impression that he had witnessed the murder. Ready to return to the bus, Sally remembered a shortcut back through the center of town. Taking it, we passed a stately building where the wealthy Kapetsky family had lived before fleeing in 1942. Afterward, it became an SS headquarters. When we stopped for one last glance at the boarded-up facade of Cousin Sally's childhood home, we noticed a black swastika on the front wall.

"It's definitely new. It wasn't here this morning," one of my cousins commented.

Poland, 1987. Sally Frishberg and Maria Grajolski (the Polish farmer who, along with her husband, kept Rita Lurie's family hidden in her attic for two years).

We studied the jerky lines, which suggested the work of children. "They didn't even draw it correctly," Cousin Sally said. She chuckled sadly.

We were unnerved, once again. Most of the Poles we had met were so kind and friendly to us. We wanted to believe that they were mortified by the actions of many of their countrymen during the war and that the world had become a much better, safer place. But now we were uncertain about whom we could trust.

The following day we drove out to the nearby town of Mushanka to meet Maria Grajolski, the woman in whose attic Mom had spent two years of her childhood. Maria's kind husband, Stashik, had passed away years earlier. As we approached the dark green farmhouse, a petite elderly woman with her hair pulled back under a bright pink and orange scarf walked toward us. She was wearing a blue denim shirtdress, with an apron tied around her waist. Cousin Sally quickened her stride to greet her.

"*Panye* Grajolski, do you know who I am?" Cousin Sally asked, reaching her hand out to the Polish woman.

"Yes?" the woman asked.

"It's Sally. We wrote to your daughter and told her that we would be coming from America. I survived because of you, and I brought my family to meet you."

The two women hugged. Maria then stepped back and smiled shyly at Sally. She adjusted her scarf self-consciously. "I was just in the field," she said. "I did not understand that you would be arriving today. But please, come inside."

"Do you still work at your age?" Sally asked.

"Yes, but it's difficult."

Maria led us up cinder-block steps, through the pinewood front door of her home, into a small, musty-smelling anteroom. In the intimate space, she noticed the cameraman we had brought with us. She pulled off her scarf, revealing severe tan lines down the centers of her cheeks, and began combing her shoulder-length gray hair. At eighty-two years old, with skin weathered by wind and sun, she resembled one of those dried apple dolls we created as children.

"It's harvest time now," Maria said. "That's why I'm dressed like this." She came across as modest and sharp as a tack.

"Tell her we think she's beautiful," one of my cousins said to our interpreter.

We wanted to make our Polish hostess feel comfortable. We wanted her to like us, as if to justify the enormous risk she had long ago undertaken when she agreed to harbor our family in the attic. In any event, she seemed interested in knowing from whom each of us was descended.

"I am Tsivia's daughter, and this is my husband," Sally said, pointing to Ken. "This is my daughter, Leslie [my cousin], and hiding somewhere over there is my son, Jack," she said proudly, pointing to my only male cousin. She then introduced the rest of us. "Remember Isaac?" she asked, when she got to my sister and me.

Maria nodded.

"Those are his granddaughters."

The woman studied my face and remarked, "You look just like your grandfather."

"Thank you." I was flattered. Until the previous day, when we encountered the elderly man in the road, no one had ever compared me to my grandfather Isaac. My mother had mentioned on occasion that I had the "Gamss family eyes." But no one I knew, outside of my family, had ever even met my grandfather Isaac.

"How is Nachum?" Mrs. Grajolski asked Sally at the first opportunity, inquiring about her youngest uncle, Norman.

"Norman is fine. He remembers you very well," Sally told her.

"He's the only one who wrote to me. And I wrote him back that it was by God's grace alone that you all survived."

"He's the only one who wrote you because his wife speaks Polish," Sally said.

"You're Polish people," Mrs. Grajolski said. "You can't write to us?"

"I never learned to write in Polish. I wasn't allowed to go to school," Sally said.

"Ah, that was that time," Maria said.

I wondered whether she could possibly have forgotten what time that had been. "Mrs. Grajolski, do you remember Leah, my grandmother?" I decided to ask instead.

"Yes. Your grandmother was the most beautiful woman in the attic," she replied, looking directly at my sister and me. I felt proud. Later, my sister and I joked with our cousins that our grandmother Leah was "Miss Attic," while their grandmother Tsivia was the runner-up, who would serve if our grandma could not fulfill her responsibilities.

"Do your friends know that you are a hero?" my sister asked next.

"No. We never revealed the secret, afraid of how our neighbors would respond."

None of us knew what to say. One of my cousins interrupted the awkward silence with the million-dollar question. "Can we see the attic now?"

"Yes, of course." We followed our eighty-two-year-old hostess through a hallway and up a narrow ladder, which she seemed more adept at climbing than the rest of us. "Now you will see it authentically," she said.

Actually, this was not exactly the case. The original house had been razed a few years earlier, due to some sort of fungus. "But the reconstructed building is virtually identical. The new attic is just two meters wider and slightly taller," the elderly woman assured us, as she crouched low to lead the way in.

The dark, confined space was twenty-five feet long, twenty-one feet wide (compared to approximately fifteen feet originally), and still under five feet high. I took a deep breath as I sat down on a bale of hay. I could not believe we were actually inside *the attic*, site of the horror and deprivation that had haunted me all my life. My sepia-toned mental image was suddenly awash with color. This was as close as I would ever come

Poland, 1987. Gwyn Lurie climbs upstairs to the attic, where Rita Lurie and her family hid from 1942 to 1944.

to seeing for myself what my mother had endured. Even though it was a bright August day, my teeth were chattering, and I hunched over to keep warm.

"Can you believe our moms spent two years inside here?" Gwyn asked. "I already feel claustrophobic." None of us could imagine.

I looked around, wondering where my mother had slept, and peeked out the tiny round window through which I assumed she had glimpsed the outside world.

"No. We couldn't look out that large hole," Cousin Sally said. "We might have been seen. We could only peek through the cracks in the wall." I looked over at the thin crevices through which small rays of sunlight were shining.

"Everyone had his own crack. Through there we saw the world," Sally said.

When I peeked through, I realized how little they could see—how truly in the dark they had been while in hiding. Mrs. Grajolski sat on a narrow ledge against the wall, off to one side. "Late at night, when my children were asleep, I would bring soup up to the attic," she told us. "But sometimes there was nothing to feed everyone."

I imagined my mother as a scared young girl, starving; not allowed to speak; sleeping apart from her own mother, wondering why she couldn't be lying beside her. The attic had become very still. I wished the cameraman and sound technician accompanying us would leave. I wished Maria Grajolski would leave. I wanted to be up there alone, with my relatives, and the spirits of our family.

EN ROUTE BACK to the hotel that afternoon, we stopped at an old Jewish cemetery in a nearby town called Kanczuga. To get there, we had to park down below and hike up a steep hill through brown, overgrown foliage. Once at the top, we were eager to find the spot where

Poland, 1987. Maria Grajolski and Sally Frishberg speak in the dark attic.

our great-grandmother Paya Neshe had been buried before her family went into hiding. Cousin Sally also hoped to locate the gravestone of her sister Feigla, the baby who had been taken to a church when she had grown so sick in the attic. Apparently a couple had brought her home and baptized her, but she died shortly thereafter. Alas, we were disappointed to discover that most of the gravestones had long ago been destroyed or knocked over. The only small solace came from finding one with the family name, Schiffman, the maiden name of my great-grandmother Paya Neshe, but once again, there was virtually no trace of Mom's family.

The next afternoon, we returned to Maria Grajolski's farm. She was waiting outside, wearing an attractive black-and-white-plaid dress and a paisley scarf on her head.

"Please, come in," the wrinkled old woman said, appearing more at ease than on the previous day. We were surprised that she was inviting us back into her home, having planned to simply pick her up on the way to meet one of her (now grown) children.

This time, Maria led us into a small living room with gold-painted walls, a white ceiling, and a pretty brown-and-cream-colored couch. A folding table was covered with a white linen cloth. Two glass pastry dishes full of éclairs and homemade apple cakes had been set on top, along with a bottle of vodka.

"This is to apologize for my failure as a hostess on your visit yesterday, when you caught me off guard," the elderly woman explained.

"You didn't have to do this," Cousin Sally protested.

As I looked around the room, wondering whether this was where the Grajolskis had dined while my mother and her family starved in the attic up above, a stocky, bespectacled woman in her early sixties entered with a man of about the same age and a teenage boy in tow. Maria introduced them to us as her daughter, son-in-law, and grandson. I didn't catch their names.

"You must be proud of your parents," I said to the daughter.

"Yes, of course. Very proud."

The fifty-something daughter explained that they lived there, in Maria's home. Her youngest brother lived there as well, after recently suffering a stroke. Then she began pouring the vodka into small glasses for us. "Please, drink some."

I noticed a book about Auschwitz on the bookshelf and asked why they had it.

"I picked it up on a tour there," Maria's daughter said.

"All schoolchildren are required to visit a concentration camp," the grandson clarified. "They want us to know what happened so history does not repeat itself."

I was heartened to hear this, always relieved to find evidence of some logic and sanity in the world.

"But why did you want to meet us?" the teenager asked.

"We've heard about your grandparents for our whole lives. We probably would not have been born if it were not for them," my cousin Debbie said. Tall and lanky, Debbie had dark, wavy hair, a wry sense of humor, and a tendency to imagine the worst when plagued with a minor ailment. As the producer and director of the film we were making, she was the de facto leader of our Poland trip.

The teenager nodded seriously.

"Do you ever wonder why your parents would have risked their lives to save our family?" I asked Maria's daughter.

"No," she answered. "Those who had good hearts took in another person."

As we prepared to leave after an hour or so, the daughter brought out gifts for us—blouses, tablecloths, and glassware.

"You've already given my family the greatest gift. We should be giving you more," Cousin Sally said. We felt worse when we learned that this woman, and her husband, had taken the day off from work to prepare for our visit. Maria then escorted us to the home of another daughter. This one sewed for a living, and her husband played the organ at church. They appeared to be fairly well-to-do, judging by their well-decorated home. Over borscht, sweets, and more vodka, we delved deeper into the past.

"When the children in the attic cried, our parents would hit one of us," our new hostess explained. "Our shrieks concealed the noises above." The Grajolski children clearly had sensed the anguish upstairs, and yet nothing had been explained to them. Everyone in that home must have been suffering in one way or another.

This couple's twenty-four-year-old son and eighteen-year-old daughter dropped by to meet us. They were very proud of their grandparents and emphasized that they believed people were people, regardless of their religious beliefs. Our conversation was interrupted by the sound of a fork clinking against glass.

"I would like to propose a toast," my cousin Leslie announced from across the room. With more vodka and food, we were losing our earlier inhibitions. We raised our glasses and toasted to Maria and Stashik Grajolski's "incredible act of heroism." Because of them, we calculated that sixty-nine members of our family were now alive.

In what was shaping up to be some sort of Polish progressive dinner, at which every home served the same courses—vodka, desserts, and an entree—we next visited a third daughter of Maria's named Zosha. Zosha had briefly lived in New York, working as a housekeeper for Sally's sister Lola, in order to send money back to her family in Poland. Spurred on by exhaustion and too much alcohol, we put on dark glasses and broke into song, in an attempt to amuse ourselves, entertain our hostess, and convey our gratitude. Before long, Maria Grajolski was wearing the silly dark glasses, too, as she listened to us belting out the lyrics to Carole King's "You've Got a Friend."

When we boarded the van, weary from all of the meals and conversation, I was sure I misunderstood our interpreter when he announced, "We will visit one last home." I craned my neck to look at Maria Grajolski, in the seat behind me. The octogenarian seemed to be in high spirits. To change the itinerary was unthinkable. Soon we were walking into the home of her youngest daughter. Two clean-cut teenage grand-sons met us at the door. Two tables were beautifully set for dinner. Fortunately, we never ran out of questions.

"When our family was in the attic, did you suspect that there were people up there?" my sister asked our latest Grajolski daughter-hostess. Like her sisters, she appeared to be in her mid-to-late fifties. She was neither attractive nor unattractive, neither thin nor fat. With her short blond hair, gold button-down dress, and ruddy complexion, she looked a bit like a human sunset.

"Yes. But we weren't curious," she said. "We knew not to talk about it. We only said to our father, 'There's someone up there.' If we were more curious, we would have ended it by asking more directly what was going on above us." Surprisingly, the Grajolski children had even been allowed to have friends over to the house during the war.

Although we had been eating for hours, we found ourselves enjoying a delicious stuffed cabbage dish as we conversed with our hostess and her family. Besides her two sons, a daughter had stopped by with her fiancé, who was studying to become a pilot. Around midnight, the evening drew to a close. As we bid Maria Grajolski farewell, we presented her with feeble gestures of our deep gratitude—money, coffee, and the cigarettes she had requested.

"You suffered a lot," the old woman told Cousin Sally. "Now you are doing very well for yourself," she added, stealing a glance at her diamond ring.

Cousin Sally was doing well. But she was still suffering. In the van once again, heading back to our hotel, we drove past the wheat fields, which she said made her sad. Upon hearing the word *sad*, we went into the rescue mode we knew so well. Almost in unison we resumed singing the song we had cut short the previous day on the way into town. We confused some of the words, but we all knew the chorus. We related well to feeling captive to time, the challeges of looking back in history while not being able to go back, and seasons endlessly going round.

Back in Los Angeles, Gwyn and I were eager to describe our journey to Mom. She herself had become more interested in rediscovering her past as of late. With a new lease on life after her depression, she had joined an organization called Child Survivors of the Holocaust. Members shared stories and met kindred spirits who were also still struggling to overcome the demons of their past. Mom had become particularly close to six women in the group. Together, they had begun studying at a local synagogue to become *b'not mitzvah*, the ceremony in which more than one person becomes bat or bar mitzvah together. This seemed to be a perfect time in Mom's life for her to hear about our visit to Poland.

Sitting with Mom and Dad on the couch in their den the day after we returned, I could not wait to describe every detail of our trip and show them the photographs we had taken. It was as though we possessed the missing evidence to support Mom's claims as to where she had been born and what she had experienced. Upon examining one photo, Mom commented, "The kitchen looks completely different from the way it had been."

"You remember how your kitchen looked when you were five?" Dad asked.

"Of course. I remember it pot for pot."

Then she focused on a picture we had taken inside a small bedroom. "Also, this bedroom over here had not been completed when we lived there. It was being built for my sister and me," she said, with a rueful tone.

Surprisingly, Mom did not ask many questions. I had fantasized that our detailed descriptions would provide longed-for answers. Perhaps Mom instinctively knew then what it would take me another decade to discover: I would never be able to answer the questions that most plagued her—what her mother had thought about her, why exactly she died, and how this horrible tragedy could have occurred in the first place. In the meantime, she would continue to move forward in her life. And in the coming few years, she would have many things to celebrate.

I WAS THIRTY on the sunny June day in 1990 when I sat in temple, gazing up at my fifty-three-year-old Mom on the bimah. She had missed out on so much, and lo and behold, she was participating in a rite of passage she never could have as a young girl in Poland. In her family's Orthodox Jewish world, girls had been prohibited from becoming bat mitzvah. Mom looked elated, reading from the Torah and being celebrated in front of her friends and family. She wanted her children to be proud of her, and we were. With joy in her heart, she was celebrating being a survivor.

Rita Lurie on her bat mitzvah day, 1990.

27

Water Your Garden

WITH ALL I had to celebrate in my own life, I felt that I should be happier. Perhaps I was choosing to operate at a cautious, steady emotional state to help cushion future blows. The consistent low-dose sadness that trickled through my veins seemed to act as a vaccine, immunizing me against future, deeper pain; it was the small tremor that staved off the devastating quake. The potential side effect was that if someday a chilly winter actually did set in, I would have no warm reserves. I went to see a therapist, although I was skeptical that he could ease my mind. Experts with impenetrable boundaries and forty-five-minute attention spans, whom I could not convert into peers, made me uneasy. Moreover, in order to help me, he would have to convince me that, despite all I knew to the contrary, the world was a safe place.

As I had suspected, the therapist did little to change the way I viewed the world. During one session, however, he did introduce a provocative word into my vocabulary: *enmeshed*. I was telling him that Mom felt excluded when my sister and I spent time together without her, when he matter-of-factly said, "You obviously have an enmeshed family." I found myself shaking my head in agreement, although actually I had never heard the term *enmeshed* before. It just sounded like an apt description of my family. None of the high-achieving children had left the city for college. We saw each other multiple times a week. My brother David, in fact, had recently moved into my apartment.

A few days after this therapy session, over dinner with Mom and Dad at a local Italian restaurant, I floated the concept. "We're an enmeshed family," I calmly mentioned. I watched carefully for their reaction. Dad didn't have one. He continued twirling pasta onto his spoon before inhaling it. Mom, in contrast, bristled.

"We're not any more enmeshed than any other close family," she said, setting down her fork so she could gesture with her hands. "Besides, you make it sound like it's a bad thing," she added. Mom can be a moving target in these disagreements. If she feels criticized, she will take my statements and, without hearing what I am actually trying to communicate, project her fears onto them. This keeps us from talking things through and coming to deeper levels of understanding. Consequently, Mom, my model for speaking one's mind, doesn't really allow me to do this with her. When it came to discussing our relationship, I, too, sometimes felt that a pillow was placed over my mouth.

"I'm just saying that's what the therapist thinks. It's an interesting idea."

My new knowledge helped me to move forward. Maybe I would never feel that the larger world was a safe place, but mine was a friendly and enjoyable one in any event, and I would continue to make the most of it. At thirty, I purchased my first home. Then I fell in love with Cliff, twelve years after he had been my teaching assistant at UCLA. Boyishly handsome, with a warm, gentle voice and a slight gap between his front teeth, he had come across as smart and funny. The fact that he was my teacher, an authority figure to level, undoubtedly added to the initial attraction. As I sat in his First Amendment class, back in 1978, the thought had crossed my mind that someday, if I met a man like him, I might actually leave home and get married. I lingered after class to ask questions and make (what I hoped were) witty remarks, and while, unfortunately, Cliff never displayed any signs of romantic interest in me, we had developed what turned out to be a lasting friendship by semester's end.

After that, once a year or so we would catch up over a lunch or dinner. When I was in law school, Cliff got married. My new boyfriend, whom I had met while summer clerking, and I were guests at the wedding.

Seven years later, in the fall of 1990, Cliff told me that he and his wife had separated. By then he was an entertainment lawyer, and our paths had crossed professionally from time to time. Our ensuing dinner at a local French bistro seemed surreal. Cliff and I talked easily about work and travel and his four-year-old son, Christopher.

"Let me ask you something," Cliff said toward the end of dinner. "Are there men you wish you dated but never did?"

Was he saying he had noticed me all those years ago? "Are there women you wish you had dated?" I responded.

He looked up at me and smiled shyly. Without ever answering the question, he left me wondering, Could I have been right, all those years ago, about him being the kind of man I could marry?

Cliff came by my home the next day, with Christopher in tow. The beautiful boy with straight black hair and clear olive skin brought me a flower, and we looked at my baseball cards together. A series of dates followed, and then a romantic weekend getaway, over which we slowly got to know each other after twelve years of sporadic conversations.

By this time in my life I had endured countless dates during which men speculated as to why I did not want to rush into relationships—"I can see you're a workaholic"; "You obviously have fears of commitment"; "My sister is gay. I bet someday you'll realize that you are, too"; "Who's the other guy?" I would smile; I would laugh; I would nod sympathetically. But I couldn't wait to get back home from my date, alone. I liked befriending a man first, even pursuing him, before he began maneuvering around boundary lines that I had carefully constructed decades earlier in self-defense.

Cliff and I had begun dating in September. By the time January rolled around, we were officially a couple. One evening, I hosted a salon of sorts on contemporary spiritual issues. The moderator was a rabbi, Laura Geller, whom I had met through a liberal Hollywood women's political organization. Fifteen or so friends had come over that evening, as had my parents. Cliff was there, too, but less out of interest in the topic at hand than to be supportive, and to meet my parents for the first time.

"So what did you think of my mom and dad?" I asked Cliff as soon as everyone left.

"I didn't get to talk to them much, but they seem very nice. I liked them." He was helping me push chairs back into place.

"That's it? No other observations?"

"Well, your dad seemed very helpful. I noticed he carried all the trash bags outside afterward."

"He always does that. He's the nicest man. Did you talk to my mom at all?"

"Not really. But I could tell she is interesting and has a lot of opinions."

I had not worried about their first encounter. Cliff and my sister, then a feature film executive, had already become fast friends, and Cliff had also gotten the green light from my brother, who recently had moved up to San Francisco. I assumed all would go just as smoothly between Cliff and my parents. Had things not gone well, however, it probably would not have boded well for our long-term relationship. Not only would I have questioned Cliff's judgment if he had been critical of my parents, but the risk of having to choose between a man and my parents would have been too threatening.

"Your parents seem to have a good relationship," Cliff then added.

"Yeah, I guess they do." Actually, I had never thought that my parents were perfectly suited for each other. Mom enjoyed going to the theater, reading novels, dining on gourmet foods, preferably in exotic locations, and making up for a lost childhood by experiencing as much as possible. Dad loved being surrounded by our family, either out at a favorite restaurant or at home. He was in his element eating spaghetti with canned tomatoes, developing photographs in his darkroom, and reclining on the Barcalounger watching television. Mom was wise, intuitive, and edgy; Dad, pragmatic and logical, yet accepting. Mom asked how we were feeling, while Dad focused on what we were doing. Mom also looked for opportunities to express her feelings, regardless of the argument that might ensue, while Dad preferred resolving disputes quickly and painlessly, if they didn't just disappear on their own. Their differences were numerous, and yet they stuck together like stamps on an envelope. Their bond of deep love and friendship was a testament to the potential in marriage for the sum to become greater than the parts.

The next morning, I called Mom first thing, on my way to work. "So?"

"So what?" she said. I could hear the amusement in her voice.

"You know. What did you think?"

"He seems very nice. And he's handsome. He's obviously very smart."

"What else?"

"What else do you want me to say? Are you serious about him?"

"I don't know. Maybe. But I wanted to hear your impressions."

"Dad and I liked him. That was our impression," she said, laughing.

I was relieved to have my parents' approval. Over the next few months, I came to adore Cliff. We shared so many interests, we had so much fun together, and he was such a good person. His happy, passionate disposition was a good balance for mine, which tended to be more contemplative and rational. Particularly after a failed marriage, Cliff valued putting effort into maintaining a strong relationship. He accepted my family, and never acted as if he was in competition with them for my affection. Cliff loved children, and I adored his son, Christopher. Cliff was also respectful of boundaries. He never pressed me for details about men in my past, some of whom he was likely to have heard rumors about in the insular, gossipy entertainment world. I felt more at home with him than I ever had in a romantic relationship. In Cliff, I finally found the organization I wanted to join. So I should have been ecstatic on that midsummer evening in 1991 when Cliff asked me to marry him.

From the outset, his behavior was unusual. He hadn't wanted me to invite friends to join us, and he had brought his own bottle of champagne to the elegant restaurant. As we conversed in the intimate dining room, he seemed preoccupied. I tried to convince myself that I was imagining things. *But what if I'm not? Please don't ask me. Not yet. Not tonight.* Then he reached into his pocket and withdrew a small box, which he placed in front of me. Everything slowed down and became a little fuzzy.

"Liesl?" Cliff had a nickname for everyone, and mine was Liesl, the name of the eldest daughter in *The Sound of Music.* Cliff said I reminded him of her, particularly with my family history. In any event, our names were similar. "Will you marry me?" he asked.

As I gazed into his soft, hazel-brown eyes and smiled back, my mind began to race. Was Cliff really asking me to marry him? This was the moment I had been hoping for. I opened the box and stared at the deep blue sapphire, set in a gold band. It sparkled before me, seductive and confident, eager for me to behold its beauty. It was too good to be true, and yet I sat, still and quiet. How could I get married? I already had a family. How could I love anyone else as much? How could I handle being needed by anyone else as much? For Mom, marriage had offered the hope of escape from her family problems. For me, it conjured up a spirit of confinement. I had worked so hard to become independent. I wanted to remain that way. Yet I loved this man. How could I say no? Were it the other way around and he turned me down, I'd be devastated.

After one of those moments in which you pack all of your inadequate wisdom into the pause between question and response, I heard myself tell Cliff, "I love you. I think I want to marry you" (or maybe I whispered "think"—or said it to myself). "But . . . I don't feel like I'm ready to actually wear this ring, to wake up tomorrow morning officially engaged."

I looked into his eyes, hoping he wasn't crushed. Or angry. He was actually pulling something else out of his jacket pocket. And to my great relief, he was smiling.

"I thought you might feel this way," he said. "So I had a contingency plan." He set another box, this one long and narrow, in front of me. "Open it," he said.

I found a delicate sapphire tennis bracelet inside. "Put it on," he told me. I did. "Every time you look at it, remember that I want to marry you." I could not have hoped for a more loving response. As he helped clasp the bracelet, I summoned the nerve to ask, "What about the ring?"

"Put it away until you're ready to wear it," he said. I loved him even more.

At home, wanting to keep the ring that did not yet feel officially mine in a safe place, I wrapped it in a sweat sock and hid it inside the carved wooden Chinese trunk that sat at the foot of my bed. Every once in a while I took it out to show a friend, or just to admire. I began to watch Cliff carefully, with an eye to how my life would change if I were to marry him.

Over Labor Day weekend, Cliff, Christopher, and I traveled to Maine to visit my best friend from law school, Barbara, and her family, and then to Vermont, where we stayed with my guardian angels, Diana Meehan and Gary Goldberg. Everyone got along famously. Back in Los Angeles on Tuesday morning, six or seven weeks after Cliff had popped the question, I awakened at peace with a decision. I knew that my friends would not disappear, my parents would survive, and Grandmother Leah would remain a part of me. As Cliff and I left my home that morning to go for a jog, I stopped at the white picket fence that bordered my front yard and turned to face him.

"Look, we're engaged," I said, holding up my left hand to display the sapphire ring I had slipped on moments earlier.

"We are?" he asked, caught off guard.

"Yes. I love you."

From the first moment, I knew it was the right decision. After returning home from our jog, we immediately called our parents, all of whom were very excited. In fact, mine were ecstatic, although not weepy. Mom and I had never shared a teary moment of unadulterated happiness. We contained our tears, like camels carrying water in the desert, knowing we might need them in the future.

"Can we take you to lunch to celebrate?" Dad asked.

"Sure, Franco," Cliff said, invoking his nickname for Dad and laughing because he had anticipated the proposition. The two had already become great friends and looked forward to celebrating every occasion with a festive meal. They also, I imagine, recognized in each other a respect for the complicated women in their lives. These intense women seemed to complement their own, less angst-ridden approaches to life.

Cliff and I were married four months later, on a Saturday night in January. At the ceremony beforehand, where we signed our *ketubah*, or Jewish marriage contract, in the presence of our parents, siblings, Christopher, and a best friend apiece, Rabbi Geller asked if anyone had advice for us. Mom spoke up first.

"Cliff and Leslie, my advice to you is to water your garden often." Everyone nodded in agreement and chuckled, wondering precisely what Mom had in mind. In the ensuing years, Cliff and I would come to fully appreciate the wisdom in her comment. We surprised ourselves

*Leslie, Cliff, and Christopher in wedding
photograph, 1992.*

by how many times, with Mom's words hanging in the air, we reminded
ourselves to take a break from work or children and, at least for the
evening, focus on each other and on watering our garden.

As the string quartet played Vivaldi's *Four Seasons*, I walked down
the aisle between my parents. How comforting that was. How secure I
felt entering my new phase of life. How different from what Mom had
experienced thirty-four years earlier. I glanced sideways down the rows
of chairs and noticed Cliff's friends and family, and all of mine, whom
I had felt free to invite. I smiled at Dad's brother, Uncle Buddy, and
Mom's siblings, Auntie Sandra, Uncle Sam, and Uncle Brad, as I glided

by. Clara was there, too, still part of my family. I looked up ahead and saw my sister and brother, my maids of honor, and my bridesmaids—my cousins Karen and Lauren, and seven of my closest friends. Although I rarely spent as much time with any one of them as I would have liked, each made my life better, and I took comfort in their numbers. At least I would never feel utterly alone, as Mom had felt. Finally I stood beside Cliff, under the chuppah, and I knew everything was right.

At the reception afterward, Mom seemed to have the most fun of anyone. She truly appreciated life's celebrations. Gwyn, on the other hand, was uncharacteristically subdued. She feared losing her only sister to Cliff, or, as she called him, her BIL (brother-in-law). I spent the evening on task, circulating from table to table, greeting our nearly three hundred guests. I looked forward to attending someone else's wedding in the near future, so Cliff and I could finally have an uninterrupted dance together.

28

The Present I Needed to Appreciate

MUCH TO MY relief, marriage barely altered my relationship with my parents. If anything, Cliff served as a welcome buffer between Mom and me. When Mom brought up some perceived slight, or I overreacted to her, Cliff helped me to step back and view things less emotionally.

In the beginning, I safeguarded the cornerstones of my premarital life. Cliff moved into the bright, cozy home I had purchased just before we began dating. I maintained an amiable, uncomplicated relationship with my new in-laws, Gil and Helen, who blessedly demanded nothing more. Beyond wanting Mom to know that her role would not be usurped, I had neither the time nor the energy to devote to a new mother the way I did to my original one. Fortunately, over time, my mother-in-law and I would develop our own special (yet never all-devouring) relationship, and I would come to love Cliff's siblings and their families as well. Finally, to keep the bonds with my "first" family intact, and also to defy what I viewed as a sexist assumption that the wife should necessarily be the spouse to change her name, I held on to mine, Lurie. Then Cliff and I discovered that our family would be expanding, and overnight everything changed.

It began with the house. My beloved first home had agreeably accommodated my new husband and stepson, but it was questionable where a nursery would fit in. For six months we searched for a roomier place. One evening, we drove with a real estate broker to a small community on the outskirts of Los Angeles County. I was immediately struck by the charm of the rural streets, lively with pedestrians, horseback riders, and kids on bikes. The backyards were large and green. *Little House on the Prairie* could have been filmed in a few of them.

"The drive to work would be torture from here," Cliff said as we toured one of the homes. "Even without traffic I bet it would take me forty minutes in the mornings."

I cringed, imagining the similar drive to my office. Then I remembered something I had heard in passing. "What's the rattlesnake situation like here?" I asked the broker.

"Well, this town is not for the faint of heart," she said with a chuckle. "It's country living. But it *is* the safest city in California."

My heart went pitter-pat. "What do you mean by the safest city?"

"There's virtually no crime. We're remote, and we're gated."

Cliff, busy tapping on the walls and inspecting the infrastructure, had missed this comment. I knew on the spot, however, that I wanted to move out there. Yes, we would live far from our work and friends, and the community's gates felt exclusionary. But I would be safe there—at least when the doors were locked, the alarm set, and our hard hats tucked under the beds in case of an earthquake.

We moved in a month before our baby was born. First thing, we nailed a mezuzah by the front door. Hopefully ours, beautifully designed in the shape of a cello, would protect our family better than Mom's family's had done back in Poland. In keeping with Jewish superstition, I was reluctant to decorate the baby's room until he was born, even though we had already learned we were expecting a healthy boy. I didn't take any future happiness for granted.

Actually, I did take something good for granted. I assumed that my children would inherit few, if any, of the apprehensions that plagued me growing up. Not only was there Cliff, whom I had come to refer to as "the happiest place on earth," to dilute my mother's gene pool, but even I was far more relaxed than Mom had been as an expectant mother. Whereas Mom had extreme trepidations about bringing a baby into the world, I was confident. While Mom had found herself wondering whether she would still get to be a child, I had never ceased being her child. Cliff and I even spent occasional nights sleeping over at my parents' home, in my childhood room. I was certain that our children would grow up proud of their family, basking in laughter, ideas, and great adventure. We would encourage them to take reasonable risks—intellectually, creatively, and even physically—so that they could grow strong. I had no anxiety about being a good parent, and I could not wait to meet my son, God willing.

Gabriel was born in July of 1993. We chose our favorite name that began with a *G* to honor my father's late mother, Gertrude, and for all the Gamss family members who died in the Holocaust. Only a name that linked our infant son to Mom's deceased family members seemed meaningful enough to me. As for why we placed the Holocaust legacy on the tiny shoulders of a third generation, it never occurred to me that my son would feel anything but pride in representing such a connection. As of this writing, fifteen years later, he seems not to have given it too much thought.

I lay in my hospital bed, with my newborn son on top of me. He looked like an angel, with his pink lips, large, dark eyes, and perfectly formed head. Cliff sat in a chair by my side, as did my brother, David, still in his pajamas after flying down from San Francisco at the crack of dawn to witness his nephew's arrival. Of course, my parents were there, too. In fact, Mom had been so excited to get to the hospital that she backed her car off the driveway into a set of rosebushes. Once the gardeners had pushed her car back onto the road, she was on her way. Now Mom sat in the rocking chair as Cliff transferred her newborn grandson from my arms into hers.

"Look, look," she said proudly. "He's staring straight at me. Look." She was beaming. "I love you," she kept telling Gabriel. "Grandma loves you."

My first four weeks with Gabriel passed in a magical flurry of naps, strolls, and infant massages. Then it was time to return to work. Along with my close friend Vicki Horwits, I was now running a production company at NBC under the banner of Lurie-Horwits Productions, charged with creating television programming for the network. I held Gabriel in my arms that morning, savoring his cuddly warmth and delicious, sweet scent. I hugged him as he cooed calmly. I willed myself to hand him to the stranger hovering over us, his warm and adoring baby nurse. As I drove to work, I wiped away tears. What kind of mother am I? I asked myself. Why can't I just enjoy this time with my baby?

In the following weeks and months, my doubts persisted. I thought about how I would have felt as a small child if Mom had left me to go to work. I felt fortunate that *I* had Mom as a mother, rather than me. Even at age thirty-three, I was able to return to work so quickly because my parents, the two people with whom I had always felt safest, were so involved with Gabriel. Still, it bothered me that Mom was not more supportive of my going to work. She made it clear that she felt bad for my baby. I promised myself that within the year, when my deal with NBC came up for renewal, I would choose to stay home with Gabriel and make up for lost time.

Time flew by. As Gabe's first birthday approached, I considered my vow. My career did not seem meaningful enough to justify the long hours apart from my son. Had I been working to eradicate cancer or bring peace to the Middle East, or, I confess, managing the Dodgers, I might have felt differently. Similarly, if my income were necessary to support our family, I would have kept working. Instead, my only reservation was whether I would *later* have regrets. Always focused either ahead on the next challenge or back a generation or two, I rarely appreciated what I had at the present. To do so, I imagined, one had to become more comfortable with loss, since the present was always changing. Like Mom, I was not even on remotely good terms with loss. Still, I reminded myself that I could get another job in the future, whereas I wouldn't have a second chance with Gabriel. He was the present I needed to appreciate.

At home, living in the present, I began writing a screenplay about a youth baseball team during a major-league strike. I also began investigating local preschools. One at the nearby Conservative synagogue came highly recommended. Even though Cliff and I were Reform Jews, we joined. To my surprise, the temple environment no longer felt like an itchy wool sweater. I was more comfortable there now.

In terms of God, I continued to wrestle. I wanted to believe absolutely. Perhaps if I possessed the unshakable faith of my grandfather Isaac, my fears would diminish. Yet I couldn't help but assume that if Grandpa Isaac had shared my skepticism, he and his family might have fled Poland before it was too late. I liked how J.B., the title character in Archibald MacLeish's play of the same name, so eloquently expressed the paradox: "If God is God He is not good, if God is good, He is not God." A good and all-powerful God, in other words, would not have created a world with evil. Parenthetically, some thinkers believe that God was not to blame for the Holocaust. Rather, they ask, where was man? They point to the indifference that the international community, particularly the United States and England, showed the Jewish refugees during and after the war.

I trusted neither God nor man entirely. But still, I had come to admire Mom's indomitable faith, despite all she had endured. Mom's faith in her family, in her own self-worth, and in God carried her through the greatest challenges. So I prayed each night as I had done since I was a child, hedging my bets, and I enrolled my son in a synagogue preschool.

On Rosh Hashanah, Mom and I went to services together. Cliff, having come the night before, opted to stay home with Gabriel. Dad had eagerly volunteered to keep them company. In synagogue, once again I envied the ease with which Mom recited the prayers and songs in Hebrew. Although I had chosen to forgo Hebrew school, I was now frustrated by my limited ability to participate in the service. Once again, I couldn't help but feel like an outside observer. And as an observer, I also noticed all of the other husbands, lovingly sitting beside their wives and families.

I described these romantic images to Cliff as soon as I got back home. Clearly he just had not understood how important it was to me for him to come.

"You can ask me to go to temple only once a holiday," he insisted. He had been napping with Gabriel asleep on top of him. They looked very cute, but I still felt hurt.

"It's a two-day holiday. And today is even more important than last night." I tried to get Cliff to recall how many premieres, events, and business dinners I went to just because they mattered to him.

"Religion is different," he insisted. "Sitting in temple is not the way I experience spirituality."

It was bad enough that Cliff didn't love to play baseball or Scrabble. Now he disliked High Holiday services, too? "Why didn't I know this about you?" I asked.

"About me? Since when is going to temple so important to *you*?"

Up until then, I hadn't realized that it was—how instilled my Jewish identity was. But now, while wholly illogically, I felt that Cliff was belittling all Mom had endured. And I was fighting on her behalf. He sensed my disappointment and reached out for my hand.

"It's not that bad. At least I believe in God."

I could not change his mind. And I wasn't positive that I wanted to. Had Cliff been more religious, I probably would have run the other way. I needed the freedom to negotiate religion on my own terms. Cliff didn't try to control me. He was a constant source of love, devotion, and support. Like Dad, he was a voice of calm in the stressful aftermath of the storm. He gave me the space I needed to think, to act, and to believe.

TAKING TO HEART Mom's wedding-night advice to "water our garden," Cliff and I celebrated our third anniversary at the nearby Hotel Bel-Air. Gabriel was a year and a half old by then, and I was five months pregnant. We were enjoying a candlelit dinner in our room when Cliff said, "Liesl, I think we should have the same last name."

My heart began racing. *Slow down. Change up ahead.* I invoked a delay tactic. "Are you upset that the bellboy just called you Mr. Lurie?" I asked.

"No. I couldn't love you more, or be happier. I've been thinking we should hyphenate our names for our anniversary."

Cliff was offering to break with tradition and risk the inevitable ribbing from his friends, family, and colleagues to share a name with me. I had always thought that I would merge our names if he wanted to, particularly since we had hyphenated Gabriel's last name. But at the moment of truth I felt that familiar anxiety at being pulled one tug farther away from my parents. I also wondered how my stepson, Chris, would feel, not having the same name as his father.

Cliff reasoned that in our home, Chris would be considered a Gilbert-Lurie, too, just like the rest of us. As for my parents, I realized that now I was married. I had a child. I was playing on an expansion team, with new teammates to consider. Of course we would merge our names.

"A toast to the Gilbert-Luries," Cliff said, lifting his champagne flute. We clinked glasses in celebration of our hyphenated status. Then we kissed to bolster our confidence in the decision.

Late one morning in May 1995, I looked up at Cliff, beaming by one side of me, and at Mom, so happy, on the other. Then I focused on the tiny being on top of me, whose heart still beat in concert with mine. Moments before, Mikaela had been born. I cried tears of joy, perhaps for the first time in my life, as it dawned on me that I was bringing into the world another generation of Weltz/Gamss/Lurie women. To memorialize the link, we selected Wynne as her middle name, in memory of Grandma Leah, whose maiden name was Weltz. As with Gabriel, I had high hopes that she would grow up to be kind, intelligent, strong, and free from the fears and torment of the generations before her. Free of the worries I had inherited. In his first two years, Gabe's calm and cheerful demeanor served to bolster my belief that a brand-new day had come for the Gamss offspring, and the future looked bright.

In the nursery, dappled by the eastern sun, I rocked my sweet baby daughter before taking my young son to the neighborhood Mommy and Me class. On the weekends, nine-year-old Chris would join us, and I coached his baseball team. I loved practically every minute I spent with my children, and yet I felt a vague unease. I had an eerie premonition that I was turning into my mother. I began to wonder whether I would become sad, too, staying home day after day. Before these irrational thoughts took deep root, I received a call from Perry Simon, my first boss at NBC, telling me that he had the perfect job for me.

There was a new chief of programming at USA Networks who wanted me to come on board as a "creative consultant." I could work limited hours, giving advice on their television series, and I would rarely have to leave home. I said yes.

A few days later, Los Angeles County supervisor Zev Yaroslavsky, a good friend with whom I had worked in politics since my college days on the board of regents, offered to appoint me to the county's board of education. There I could work on behalf of the high-risk children in Los Angeles, children who, like Mom, had been dealt weaker hands. I agreed to that position, too.

While still at NBC, I had found time to help form a nonprofit legal organization dedicated to serving indigent children. But now I also became the president of its board of directors. I began to amass commitments as enthusiastically as I had once earned badges.

I wanted to make a difference. I needed to make the world a fairer place, in which underdogs could thrive. Mom's experiences taught me that even one individual, acting alone, could be powerful. In Nazi-occupied Europe, only 7 percent of Jewish children survived, compared to 33 percent of the Jews overall. Since the annihilation of children was a particular goal of Hitler's, most of those who survived were hidden. Mom's life was spared by the kindness of one farmer whose goodness overcame his very real fears. It was also saved, in part, by a Nazi soldier who tipped off her uncle over games of chess, by her father and uncles who foraged for food, and by the Italian nuns who nursed her back to health. I didn't know all this at the time, but I did know not to assume that if I didn't help those in need, somebody else would.

Ironically, however, while Mom's struggles were informing my mission, tensions between the two of us were actually multiplying. Mom and I had never argued very much, until I had children. That's probably when I became an adult in her eyes—a demographic she had come to distrust early on. She seemed to be particularly wary of Cliff's and my ability to protect her grandchildren. I knew that we were not the

Rita Lurie, with her grandchildren, Gabriel and Mikaela Gilbert-Lurie, and her children, David and Gwyn Lurie, 1996.

first mother and daughter to encounter such a struggle, but boundaries had never been easy for Mom to navigate, ever since those days in the attic when they were obliterated for the sake of survival. Now this difficulty was compromising my ability to raise my children without being constantly second-guessed.

One evening, driving from a board of education meeting out to dinner, I called Mom to check in and see how she was doing.

"Leslie or Gwyn?" Mom asked when she answered the phone. It always took her a few seconds to distinguish our similar voices.

"It's Gwyn," I said.

"No, it's Leslie. I knew it was you. Anyway, I'm glad you're on your way home to the children."

I felt my neck tensing. "Actually, we have a business dinner, which I'll leave early." I mentioned leaving early, and business, for Mom's benefit.

"Oh," she said. I could hear the concern in her voice, before she changed the subject. "I just had a wonderful conversation with the children."

"Good. Anyway, I wanted to see how you guys were doing today."

"Well, we're okay, but actually, I'm a little concerned," she said.

"Why?" *It's something about the children.*

"Why? Oh, well, the children haven't eaten dinner yet."

"I know. I just talked to them. I said they could watch a video before they ate."

"You know, I just don't think it's the best idea, do you?" Mom persisted.

I had begun to notice that when I mentioned plans to Mom that did not include my children or her, she would say something like, "Oh." Not, "Oh, you'll love that restaurant," or "Oh, have a great time." Just, "Oh." Which I took to mean, "It's a shame you're not going to be with your children, or with Dad and me." I wondered whether my busy life made hers feel emptier. Maybe when I had left NBC, Mom had anticipated me being mostly at home, cooking dinners or hosting play dates, as she had done. Perhaps this would have made her feel better about all the years she had dedicated to caring for my siblings and me. Whatever her feelings may have been, they were beginning to grate on me.

"Mom, my children don't need another mother!" I finally said.

"But I love them so much that I often have to remind myself that I am the grandma and not the mother. Especially when I go crazy with worry that Gabie is putting dirty hands in his mouth or Mikaela is being carried too much by the nanny. When they're in pain, I'm in pain. They need me."

"Yes. As a grandmother. But I still need you as a mother. You barely take the time to ask me anything about myself these days. You're always worried about my children, who by the way don't need to be worried about, because I take good care of them."

"I don't see how we can have a close relationship if I can't speak from my heart about what's best for my grandchildren," Mom said.

"We'll be closer if you trust me to be a parent," I responded.

To my surprise, Mom was not so defensive. "I know you are a very good mother. I always tell you that. And I love you very much," she said.

She loves me. My heart melted like a Hershey's kiss in the sun. The next day, Mom seemed genuinely interested in how I was rather than just marking time until she could ask about her grandchildren. Hope springs eternal.

PART III

A Joint Venture

(1997–2008)

29

Maybe I Should Write It

"MAYBE IT'S JUST not meant to be," Mom was saying, with a hint of disappointment in her voice. We were sitting in the kitchen of her Malibu townhouse, talking about the book Mom wanted to write. "I don't know if I can work on this with a stranger," she added.

I pointed out that the woman with whom Mom had begun to collaborate was hardly a stranger. They had been friends for several years.

"But she's not family."

I opened the refrigerator in search of a snack, briefly fantasizing that it would be filled with fruits, vegetables, and leftovers, as it always had been when I was growing up. But instead it was bare, save for a couple of sad tomatoes that had not been chosen for a previous day's salad, and some soy milk. It still surprised me to see how little food my parents stocked now that it was just the two of them.

"Maybe you should write the book yourself. Tell your own story."

Mom chuckled. "First of all, I'm not a computer person."

"You don't have to use a computer. You can write with a pen and paper."

"No, I've tried. I've written pages and pages."

"That's good. Why don't you start with those?"

"I can't. I tore them up. It's too hard to write by myself. I need feedback."

It occurred to me that perhaps I could help Mom write her memoir. I still wanted to learn more about her past, and maybe in the process discover how her troubles had passed down to me—why I seemed to teeter on the edge of a lake of sorrow, fed by streams that originated beyond my own experiences or disappointments. Also I felt bad that I never went out to lunch or shopping just with Mom. I knew that we should spend time together while we had the chance, and a mutual project, particularly one so personal, seemed a good way for us to do so.

"Maybe I should write it," I told her.

"Really? Would you have time?"

I was surprised that Mom really wanted *me* to write her story. Had she forgotten that I had never written a book?

"I'm just not sure I'm the best person—"

Before I could finish my sentence, Mom said, "It's a great idea. It feels right to me."

Wait a minute! Did I really say I would write her book?

Perhaps sensing my ambivalence, Mom reiterated why this was so important to her. She had wanted to honor her parents and leave a legacy of knowledge about her past. Recent remarks in the news by some Holocaust deniers had made her particularly angry, and eager to clear up misperceptions. Moreover, in schools, synagogues, and churches, Mom had been speaking frequently to students, who constantly told her how inspiring she was to them. She hoped that in book form, her message of surviving well would reach a larger audience. Then she looked directly at me. "When should we start?"

I got the feeling we already had.

The following week, Mom walked into my small home office, munching on an apple, ready to officially begin. "Where are the kiddies?" she asked.

"They're at school. They'll be home soon." I looked up from my desk.

"I hope they brought coats," Mom said. "It's freezing outside." Then she looked down at her apple. "I had to grab a fruit on the way in. I haven't eaten anything since the few bites of oatmeal I had this morning."

My V-shaped desk was built into one corner of the office. Mom scooted the extra chair right next to me, as if the two of us would be sharing my one pen and pad of paper. I felt a familiar sense of confinement.

"Wouldn't you be more comfortable sitting over there?" I asked, pointing to the soft chenille couch against the other wall.

"Okay." Mom moved to the couch. "You know," she said, "the more I've been thinking about this, the more I believe this is going to be a good bonding experience for us."

The word *bonding* made me cringe. I hoped that Mom would treat this as an arm's-length writing partnership. I wondered why she always wanted to get closer to me, as if I were a thin blanket she needed to wrap increasingly tightly around her on a chilly night. We seemed as close as a mother and daughter should be.

Mom smiled. At sixty-two, she still exuded a style and grace that was more European than American. Her peaches-and-cream skin was virtually unaltered by the years. Still, the subtle tension in her eyes and jaw never vanished entirely, and her shoulders appeared burdened without actually stooping.

"Yes. I really hope that this will be liberating for both of us," she told me, gesturing with her hands to emphasize "us." As a child I had not heard her distinct yet untraceable accent. Now I clearly detected the way she stressed her *t*'s and *d*'s in words like "Reet-tah" or "good."

"I hope so, too," I said.

Mom was unusually focused as she began to recount her life story. In between our sessions, I devoured relevant books, articles, and films to help me better place her words into historical context. Mom told me about her early childhood, much of which I had never heard. Her dark days in the attic followed, and then her recovery in Italy. But as Mom geared up to describe her arrival in America, I still longed to know even more about her life as a child, and about her family. I wondered why my religious grandfather, Isaac, had not married until he was in his thirties, exactly how long Mom's family had hidden in the attic, and whether Grandma Leah had been a lot like Mom or like me. I wondered whether Mom's relatives might be able to shed any additional light.

Of Mom's eleven relatives who had survived the war, five were no longer alive. In the decade following Grandpa Isaac's death in 1978, three of his siblings, Uncle Benny, Uncle Norman, and Aunt Tsivia, along with her husband, Libish, passed away. The remaining relatives were in New York, except for Mom's sister, Auntie Sandra. I first went to interview her at her home in Los Angeles.

Over tea and almonds, Auntie Sandra tried to recall her early days. As she reflected, I studied her face, noting the similarities between Mom and her. They both had beautiful, pale skin, dark eyes, and a youthful appearance. Even more striking was the familiarity of Auntie Sandra's indecisive smile, seriousness of some indescribable purpose, and similar though less pronounced accent. Her mannerisms underlined the sisterly connection.

Cousin Sally had once mentioned to me that as a child, Auntie Sandra had never complained. She had loved that about her cousin. My sense was that all of Auntie Sandra's relatives had appreciated this trait. Yet Auntie Sandra had had many of her own demons to deal with during the years she was raising her children. As an adult she seemed to express her sadness, aches, and frustrations no more or less than my own mother.

In her home on this day, Auntie Sandra recalled being scalded by her mother's chicken soup and having been fearful of dogs after a near encounter back in Poland. She also remembered a relative once telling her, "Your mother could live anywhere as long as your father was there." Auntie Sandra had relished hearing about the love Grandma Leah had for Grandpa Isaac, and I, too, got teary when she recounted these words. Finally, she shared many of Mom's observations about Clara, her stepmother. Beyond this, my aunt could not broaden my perspective. She had forgotten or repressed much of her early life. Still, like Mom, Auntie Sandra possessed extraordinary strength. I would soon come to recognize this strength in Mom's New York survivor relatives as well, when we flew east the following month on a fact-finding mission.

"Don't worry, I'll take good care of her," I told Dad at the airport in Los Angeles.

"We'll look out for each other," Mom said, squeezing my hand with the same gentle firmness she had used when I was six years old and we were crossing the street.

"You have your ticket, right?" Dad asked Mom, as if she were the daughter he was reluctantly sending off to college.

"Ah, let's see, do I have my ticket?" Mom said in a way that did not instill confidence. She began rummaging through her purse.

"I handed it to you this morning, and I said to put it somewhere safe," Dad said, beginning to sound anxious.

"Then I'm sure I have it, honey." She continued to shift around pieces of Kleenex, her vitamin dispenser and wallet, and who knows what else in her purse.

"Dad, if you gave it to her, I'm sure it's in there," I said.

"Ah, here it is," Mom said, triumphantly pulling the ticket out. "I knew I had it."

With the crisis averted, a small cloud rolled in. *Maybe we shouldn't go.* I became aware of a hollow feeling in my chest; a sense of leaving behind a part of me. Although I had traveled extensively by this point, personally and professionally, every parting continued to feel potentially final.

I still possessed the Hansel and Gretel complex, the apprehension that I would not find my way back home.

I pictured Gabriel and Mikaela, their huge dark eyes conveying trust in my promise to return the day after tomorrow. I worried what it would do to them if my vow was broken—if I died in a plane crash on the way. Mikaela, in particular, had seemed solemn in Cliff's arms, watching me drive away early that morning. While Gabriel had cheerfully hugged me good-bye and confirmed he would see me soon, I could have sworn I recognized a look of distress in my nearly two-and-a-half-year-old daughter's eyes. But maybe, hopefully, I was just projecting my own anxieties onto her. I knew that things would seem different to me once I just got on the plane. I had learned over the years that by the time we reached cruising altitude, I would usually feel something between relieved and elated, my concerns vanishing into the clouds. Whether I could feel carefree traveling with Mom as my partner, however, remained an open question.

Mom's cousin Sally had generously offered to host a gathering at her home in Brooklyn. I wanted most to talk with the oldest survivors, like Uncle Max, who had bravely foraged for food during the years in the attic, and his quietest brother, Uncle Henry. I suspected they might remember more than the others, who were only children at the time. After Mom moved to Chicago, she had seen these uncles very infrequently. As Grandpa Isaac and Clara had harbored resentment toward them, Mom had taken this on as well. For me, until this project Uncle Max and Uncle Henry had simply been part of an undifferentiated mass of religious relatives, remote relics with whom I'd exchanged the briefest of pleasantries at one or two family celebrations.

Mom and I arrived first. Cousin Sally urged us to not have high expectations. "I recommend that you tread lightly. Max and Henry might not want to talk about the war. I must tell you that trauma hits hardest when we're old or weak." She enunciated each word in her distinct Brooklyn dialect. As I was coming to learn, Cousin Sally had a habit of warning loved ones not to set their hopes too high, lest they be disappointed. Perhaps this was her way of coming to terms with her tremendous early letdowns.

I would have preferred to meet with each relative individually, but Cousin Sally suggested that they would find comfort in numbers. Apparently not enough comfort for quiet Uncle Henry, however. As soon as Sally finished cautioning us, he called to say he would be unable to attend because he had a bad cold. Never one for excess conversation, from what I had heard, Uncle Henry had spent his adult years working hard in manual-labor factory jobs like pressing and packing. Now retired, in his late seventies, he was still married to the woman about whom my grandfather had provided an unrequested opinion fifty years earlier. I had known him only by reputation as the uncle with the three beautiful daughters. But now he also had seven grandchildren and several great-grandchildren as well.

I feared that Uncle Max would be the next to cancel, particularly because he had recently suffered a heart attack, and his wife, Aunt Sonia, didn't want him to become agitated. But I underestimated him. He and Aunt Sonia arrived with the middle of their three sons, Benny, a kind-looking family man in his midforties. They greeted Mom with hugs and kisses, and then turned their attention to me.

"Hello, Leslie," Uncle Max said. He sounded wary, as if I might begin interrogating him on the spot.

"Thank you so much for coming," I said, hugging him and his wife. They sat down in the two seats closest to the door and looked like matched bookends—short, smartly dressed, and relatively youthful. Uncle Max in particular appeared younger than his eighty-six years. With a trim build, gray-black hair, and deep-set dark eyes, he looked much the way I remembered his eldest brother, my grandpa Isaac, whom I had last seen on our one family visit to Chicago, for my uncle Sam's wedding, when I was thirteen, a quarter of a century earlier. Aunt Sonia reached out for my arm and pulled me in close.

"My husband will not be discussing the Holocaust this evening," she whispered. "In a few weeks, *I'll* call and tell you what you want to know."

At least they came tonight, I thought, trying not to be disappointed.

Sally's sisters, Lola and Miriam, were there by now, with their husbands. Finally, Uncle Norman's widow, Helen, arrived with her three grown children. Norman had died nine years earlier, in his late sixties, following angioplasty surgery.

"Okay, let's get started! Why doesn't everyone take their seats?" Cousin Sally was announcing to the group. True to her firstborn status, she took charge. We shifted our chairs into a circle, and I briefly described our project. My relatives nodded their heads encouragingly.

"I have a question." Mom got right to the point. "Does anyone remember my mother, Leah?"

"Yes," Sally said. "Your mother did me a great kindness."

"Really? What?"

Cousin Sally spoke directly to Mom. "At the age of four, I had not known that a boy's basic anatomy was different than a girl's. One day, when your mother, Leah, was changing your brother Nachum's diaper, she noticed that I was staring at him."

"Aha," Mom said tentatively, bracing for what her cousin was about to say.

" 'Sally, come over here and help me,' my Aunt Leah had said. Then she proceeded to explain the basic anatomical differences between a boy and a girl. Those few moments made a lifelong impression on me."

"I never knew this," Mom said, a tempered excitement in her voice.

"After that," Sally continued, "I would forever think of Aunt Leah as a strong lady who was in my corner. And I want to tell you something else."

She had our full attention.

"Your mother was more affectionate than mine. I remember thinking that she hugged and kissed her children, while my own mother didn't." Cousin Sally's mother, Aunt Tsivia, had died in 1981, after undergoing cardiac bypass surgery, and her father, Uncle Libish, had died a few years after that.

"I'm so glad to hear that my mother was affectionate," Mom said. Her upper torso now inclined slightly forward, as if a weight had been lifted from her shoulders. "Because I can't remember whether my mother hugged and kissed me."

I hoped that Sally could clarify another matter. My mother and Auntie Sandra had not recalled their family members having worn Jewish stars prior to going into hiding. Yet everything I had read suggested that as of 1940, all Polish Jews over sixteen years of age had been required to wear armbands with the Stars of David. When I asked her, Sally said, "Oh, yes. Not the children, but the adults were required to wear them."

"Are you sure?" Mom asked.

"Absolutely. They were white with two blue lines in the middle, and a Star of David. My mother made them for the whole family according to very precise instructions. They had to be worn above the wrists and below the elbow."

"Were the adults upset about wearing them?" I wanted to know.

"Yes. There was a great deal of fear attached to the obligation. The family had wanted to look just like their Catholic neighbors. The armbands added to the anxiety that they'd be picked up and taken away."

Apparently, this jogged Cousin Miriam's memory. Sally's middle sister was a petite woman with short, curly brown hair. She was an accountant, and with her husband, Herbie, had two married daughters, Sheryl and Lori, with children of their own. Lori lived nearby, while Sheryl, who had been part of our documentary group in Poland, was working as a lawyer in Israel. Cousin Miriam looked directly at Mom and said, "I remember in the attic that you wore a white shirt

and a dark skirt with *shelkis* [straps or suspenders attached to the skirt].
They were always falling down, which drove *our* daddy crazy. Do you
remember that?" Miriam asked, in the same Brooklyn accent as her
sister Sally.

At the mention of Miriam's father, Libish, Mom gave me a knowing
glance. Clearly Miriam and her sisters had adored their father, whom
they remembered as having been kind and loving. But Mom still felt
wounded by his criticisms of her in the attic and afterward, in Europe. I
quickly turned back to the conversation, not wanting to take the chance
that Mom's reaction would hurt her cousins' feelings. The youngest of
her cousins, Lola, was now speaking.

"In a small pocket of my sundress, I saved beans from the soup that
Maria Grajolski brought up for us so that I could share them with the
others." Lola was sixty, like Mom. She had taught, briefly, and now
spent a good deal of time fund-raising for Jewish causes. With her husband, Mike, she had two daughters, the ages of my sister and me. Her
older daughter, Barbara, had earned an MBA and worked in the banking field, and her younger daughter, Debbie, had also earned a master's,
from film school, before filming the documentary *Voices from the Attic*,
which featured our trip to Poland. The award-winning film had received strong critical acclaim.

"One more thing," Miriam added, looking intently at Mom. "Do
you remember the night when your father [Isaac] left the attic to get
water? He dropped the cup, and we all were afraid that the neighbors
would hear."

"That sounds vaguely familiar," Mom said, furrowing her brow.

"Let me tell you something." To my delight, the heavily East
European–accented words were emanating from eighty-six-year-
old Uncle Max. "Some people say that the Holocaust did not occur.
I myself cannot believe it took place. In Poland, we were six years
under Hitler's occupation. But because we came from farms, for a
long time the Nazis left us alone, and the Poles didn't betray us."

Every word from Uncle Max's lips felt precious. He went on to explain how when Germany bombed Poland in 1939, he was serving in the Polish army. He was captured by the Germans and locked inside a stable with three hundred other soldiers. "To escape, I pulled out a piece of wood from the wall, slipped through the crack, and ran back home." There he resumed working with his father and brothers until the summer of 1942, when *Juden Frei* ("Free of Jews") signs were posted in their village, and the family went into hiding.

Everyone was listening intently to the clear train of thought emanating from the quiet voice. "I had many friends in our village," Uncle Max said proudly, "including Stashik Grajolski. While we had grown up near each other, we became good friends in the army. That's why, when he agreed to hide my brother's and sister's families, he asked me to come as well, to act as a liaison."

"Mordche, tell her how you were the breadwinner in the attic," Aunt Sonia prompted. She still called her husband by his Yiddish name.

"Okay," Uncle Max said, looking at me. "I spent my days and nights in the attic worrying about how to feed my beautiful family . . ." He drifted back in time, recalling how he foraged for food.

"You and I are the only ones who know the gentiles in the community," Uncle Max had told his eldest brother, Isaac. "Since I am single, I should be the one to sneak out."

To avoid being seen, Uncle Max picked the darkest nights, with the worst weather. From time to time, neighbors prepared small bundles of food that they either left out for him on their doorstep, or handed him when he tapped on the door.

"Here's some beans and bread," a kind neighbor would whisper, opening the door just wide enough to pass the package through.

"This is for the children," another villager told Uncle Max, handing him a bag with bread and fruit. "We pray for you each night," he added.

"Once, a friend gave me a ham sandwich, but I couldn't eat it because it was not kosher," Uncle Max said. I wondered whether my grandmother Leah would have eaten the sandwich, or shared it with her sick young son, Nachum, to save their lives.

Mom leaned into me and whispered, "I absolutely remember my father going out for food, too."

"Okay," I quickly said, not wanting to miss one of Uncle Max's words.

"Tell her about finding food in the winter," Aunt Sonia was urging her husband.

"Oh, you want to hear how I found food in the winter? Okay, I'll tell you. The fruits and vegetables were less plentiful then, so there was not much to eat. My brother-in-law, Libish, and my brother Iche [Grandpa Isaac] fought over an apple one morning. When I went out in the snow for food, my boots froze to my feet. This made it difficult, afterward, to climb back into the attic. Sometimes, once I got up there, I would sleep on a pack of straw, in my boots, because they wouldn't come off. Can you believe?"

"No." I couldn't.

As Uncle Max described his ordeal, he wondered aloud, "How did I manage to lug that heavy sack of food, through bitter weather, up the ladder and into the attic? An angel must have helped me." Then he added, "I believe these years with no toothpaste, poor nutrition, carrying backbreaking loads in the bitter cold, permanently harmed my health."

"But you're in your eighties. And you look great," I said.

"My strength was depleted by those awful years," he insisted.

He looked closely at his fellow surviving attic-mates—Sally, Miriam, Lola, and Mom. Perhaps he was picturing them as children, because he began reflecting on how difficult it had been for them in the attic. He said that the family *had* brought a few quilts and pillows with them, but these were not sufficient to keep the children from freezing in winter. One bitterly cold night, Uncle Max said, Stashik noticed the children shivering, and he took pity on them. He carried them down, one by one, to sleep in a small, warmer room, where pigs were kept. Later, I asked Mom whether she remembered this.

"Come to think of it, I have had dreams about wallowing with pigs, chasing them around in the mud. But I'm sure I didn't spend much time there, or I would have clearer memories." I was struck with the realization that at night, when Mom finally managed to fall asleep, the horrors of her childhood never failed to reassert themselves.

As the war dragged on and Stashik grew impatient, Mom's family eventually ran out of bribes. "So I got rough," Uncle Max said. "I told him I belonged to a partisan group."

"Are you threatening me?" Stashik had angrily whispered.

"I'm just telling you the facts, Stashik. If I am unable to deliver my messages, or if something happens to any one of us, your family will be killed or your house burned."

"How could you threaten the man who hid you?" Aunt Sonia blurted out.

"It was him or me," Uncle Max told his wife. "We had little hope by then that we would survive, but we were determined not to end up in German hands."

"What about my brother, Nachum, do you remember when he died?" Mom asked.

"Yes, of course," Uncle Max said. "I carried the boy down from the attic and buried him in a field, about two kilometers away."

"Do you know why he died?" I asked my great-uncle.

"The child died because he had cried so much. Stashik would knock on the door to get us to keep him quiet. The smart, beautiful child was always covered up, deprived of enough food and everything else, even though we fed him all we could. A child his age should have been running around and playing."

Could Mom's brother have been smothered because he was making too much noise? Had this occurred to Mom? When I looked over at her, she didn't seem shocked. Maybe she hadn't heard Uncle Max clearly. Hopefully I hadn't. But Uncle Max was already dropping another bombshell—"Leah died two or three weeks after her son's death. Maybe her heart gave out from the pain. She wasn't sick," Uncle Max emphasized. "She just lost the will to live."

Again, I checked Mom's reaction. She had longed to learn more about her mother's life, but Uncle Max was describing her death, and perhaps corroborating Mom's worst fear—that she had not been incentive enough for her mother to live. Mom's hands were clenching the edge of her chair, but she nodded her head from time to time, stoically absorbing the information.

There was a break in the tension when one of Uncle Norman's sons, Josh, joined the conversation. He mentioned that the only thing that kept *his* late father alive in the attic was dreaming of his mother's (Grandma Paya Neshe's) gefilte fish. In his midforties and boyishly handsome, Josh was yet another high-achieving child in our family. He was an Orthodox rabbi and medical doctor with a wife and five children. His kind, gentle demeanor was much like that of his late father.

Josh's brother, Arthur, wanted to tell me that he had heard that my grandfather Isaac had been the leader in the attic. Uncle Max's son, Benny, added that my grandfather had been very handsome.

Uncle Max jumped back in. "He was considered very cosmopolitan. But once his wife and son died, he was a broken man. Never the same," he said, sadly. Then he recalled one morning, in the final weeks in the attic, when he himself had opened his eyes and couldn't see anything.

"Benny, wake up, I am blind," Max had said, shaking his next younger brother out of a doze.

"Stay calm," Benny said. "Tonight I will take you for help."

That night, Benny guided Max to the home of a smart Catholic friend. "You have chicken blindness," the friend told Max, pulling the brothers inside.

"Chicken blindness? You're making a joke, right?" Benny asked.

"No. It's an affliction caused by lack of exposure to sunlight. Peek outside for a few minutes each day, and your sight will return."

The advice worked. But everyone's life seemed to hang in the balance by this point. "If we had stayed another two months there, many more of us would have died," Uncle Max concluded. Since Mom had been the most ill, I was fairly certain that my uncle was including her. My own existence suddenly felt more miraculous.

Uncle Max's reference to the end of the war reminded me that I still did not know exactly when the family had left the attic. He knew immediately. The family left the attic on July 24, 1944, two years to the day after they had gone into hiding.

"Did you hear that, Mom?" I asked, thrilled to obtain such an important item of information. She was in the midst of a side conversation but looked up. "Uncle Max says you hid in the attic for exactly two years, July to July."

"Oh. I thought we left home in September. But maybe he's right," she said.

Suddenly, I heard Aunt Sonia saying, "Mordche, either calm down or we'll have to leave." I looked over to see Uncle Max in tears.

"Okay. I'm okay," he said.

"See, Leslie dear?" Aunt Sonia was saying to me, "We're still half broken. Even today when we talk about the past, it puts us in a state of numbness. Horrible feelings return." I had grown up believing that almost any problem could be solved by talking it through, by finding the right words. Surrounded by five Holocaust survivors that evening, however, I began to wonder. Like Humpty Dumpty in the nursery rhyme, they were all partially broken, and perhaps all of the understanding, love, and forgiveness anyone could muster would not be enough to make them whole again.

I looked intently at my elderly great-aunt and -uncle. They were insightful, intelligent, and funny. They also were part of a large, loving family. Yet I felt regret for them. Like Grandpa Isaac, they had lived most of their lives in foreign countries. They had been adults when they immigrated to the United States, which made it more difficult for them to assimilate. Their English never became perfect. They had come with high hopes that their dreadful memories would be washed away. But they never were. Nor were those of my mother and her other cosurvivors. Consequently, my cousins, my siblings, and I grew up well acquainted with our parents' demons. Haunted, but at least not marginalized. We had the freedom, the health, the education, the confidence, the language, the irreverence, and the drive to attempt to make things right again.

By this time in the evening, the orderly conversation at Sally's was breaking down. Cousins wanted to say things to Mom individually. Aunt Sonia sat down beside me with an album on her lap. "I have photographs to show you," she whispered.

"I would love to see them." That was an understatement.

Aunt Sonia began turning the pages of the album. I glanced at the faces of Old World strangers, wishing that I recognized more of them. She stopped and pointed to one particular photograph. It looked like it had been taken not long after the war, in one of the displaced persons camps. "This was your mom."

"Oh?" I said, trying to reconcile the image of the frail, serious eight-year-old girl in the picture with my mother, sitting nearby. "She was pretty," I said.

"She was very cute, but not well," Aunt Sonia said. "She played with the other children, but she needed a lot of attention, and she kvetched." Of course she kvetched, I thought. She was sick and had lost her mother. Who wouldn't complain under those circumstances? Then, perhaps sensing my discomfort, Aunt Sonia added, "She was okay anyway, though, and we all loved her."

Mom, noticing the photo albums, had walked over. Apparently she had overheard Aunt Sonia's remarks. "I was not okay," she said. "I always felt sick, and I had tuberculosis and rickets. Some call it kvetching. I was trying to express my pain and discomfort."

"Well, of course," Aunt Sonia said. "But at the time, we did not understand the needs of the children. Here, let's look at the rest of the album," she suggested, continuing to flip through pages. I glanced at each passing photograph. How I longed to savor the ones of Mom and my other relatives, to set them in silver frames so I could stare at them, uninterrupted. But none were offered to us.

By midnight, the guests were leaving. The evening had exceeded my expectations. We had found so many missing pieces. Everyone had been so warm and kind. Then I realized that Mom was less thrilled.

"Why? What didn't you like?" I asked, sitting on my bed in the hotel room while she washed her face. I had forgotten about her lengthy bedtime cleansing ritual, but now that I was older, it was less perplexing to me than it had been as a child.

"I wanted to ask more questions about my mother. But I didn't want to upset anyone," she said.

"Weren't you happy to hear that your mother was affectionate? I loved hearing that."

"Yes. But I wanted to hear more. Also, I had hoped to learn about my grandparents."

"I'm going to call Aunt Sonia and Uncle Max and ask more questions," I said. She still looked unsettled. "What?" I asked her.

"I don't think Max was right that my mother lost the will to live. I know that she was also suffering from grave physical ailments. Otherwise, she would have wanted to remain with her daughters and husband."

"I'm sure you're right. But don't you still feel that we learned a lot?"

"It's just that buttons still get pushed."

"What buttons?"

"Did you notice that Sonia did not offer to give us the photographs of my sister and me?" Mom asked.

"I'm sure she'll send us copies."

"I wouldn't count on it," Mom said. Then she sighed. "I guess I still have this hope that my relatives would go out of their way to help heal my wounds. Why do you think we haven't had more of a relationship with them all of these years?"

I had no answer, but I still wished that Mom would not be upset. For the time being, I decided that I would be her ambassador to the extended family. I would interact with them in the way I wanted her to, see the good in them and not take the bad so personally. Perhaps I could succeed in creating the larger family she still wished for—and I always longed to have. My eyes were closing as Mom was in the final phases of applying moisturizer.

"Good night, Mom, I love you." No one in our family ever went to sleep without saying "I love you," lest it be the last time we ever saw one another.

"I love you, too," she said.

30

Feelings of a Deprived Child

BUOYED BY OUR evening in New York, I wondered what other pieces of the puzzle still lay dormant, in the hearts and memories of my other relatives. Mom mentioned a cousin to me, David Seitelbach, the one whose sister and father had been shot that winter day in 1943, outside the attic. Mom had not spoken to him since she was a teenager in Chicago, but she heard through the grapevine that he was living in Canada, and she was willing to call him with me. David, now a seventy-something cabdriver, sounded happy to hear from Mom. I may have been more excited than either one of them. Regardless of the fact that he had little information to share, I loved talking to one more of the handful of people on earth who had known Mom as a young girl.

David could not recall anything of significance about his aunt, Grandma Leah, since he had only been a boy himself before the war. He did share some memories, however, of returning to Grandpa Isaac's home after hiding, which we would weave into the fabric of the memoir. What I was most struck by, in our conversation, was David's final question to Mom. He wanted to know why she had not invited him to her wedding. Had she been mad at him? Mom sounded surprised to hear that she hadn't invited him. But she quickly added that she had asked

almost no one to her wedding, including her best friend from high
school. It was unfortunate but somehow sweet that for nearly fifty years
this man had been harboring these feelings of rejection.

In the following months, I interviewed my siblings, Gwyn and
David, my cousins Karen and Lauren, Mom's half brothers, Sam and
Brad, and even Marilyn, her best friend from high school. Each spoke
to me at length and without hesitation, adding to my understanding of
Mom and her family.

With respect to my uncles, Sam and Brad, I had always hoped that
Mom would develop a closer relationship with them. The small amount
of time I had spent with these uncles over the years, in Los Angeles and
Chicago, I had thoroughly enjoyed. They were warm and funny and
always made me feel like we were close family. Sam was now in his
fifties and working in the commercial real estate business. He was married with grown twin children and a grandchild. Brad, a jeweler in his
late forties, was also married with a teenage son and two grown step-
children. I found it mildly amusing that my mother's youngest brother
was the exact same age as my husband. Mom told me that she, too,
wished that she and her half brothers were closer, but sometimes, their
past got in the way.

"We didn't grow up together in a happy, healthy family, and we
don't have a foundation of common experiences," she said. "Also, you,
Leslie, feel deserving of all the love you receive. I don't. I felt replaced
by my stepbrothers. For me, doing the right thing is not necessarily the
healthiest thing." Mom explained that being with her brothers risked
being drawn into conversations about Clara, which evoked bitterly
painful memories. I knew that Mom was a loving sister who longed to
be loved by her brothers. But she had not yet managed to get past their
shared history to allow for a more involved relationship with them.

Sometimes, even with me, Mom's past made its ugly way into the
present. We were celebrating Mikaela's sixth birthday at one of those
Japanese restaurants where the chefs cook the dinners at long *teppan*

dining tables, and every few minutes the waitstaff congregates to sing "Happy Birthday" in Japanese. Mom wound up on the opposite end of the table from my sister and me. Right away, I noticed that she was unusually quiet. My head started to hurt, and the butterflies began fluttering lightly in my stomach. Could she be mad at me? I wondered.

"What's wrong with Mom?" I asked my sister.

"I think she's mad at me," Gwyn said, in a solemn tone.

"Why?"

"I have no idea."

As the chef flipped shrimp shells from the grill over his head, catching them in a bowl, and Mikaela engaged in animated conversation with her former nanny, seated beside her, I grew increasingly alarmed by Mom's stony silence. I could not stand for her to be mad at me.

"Do you think she is upset that Mikaela's paying more attention to your nanny than to her?" Gwyn asked.

"Then why would she be mad at *us*?" From down the table, I asked Mom, "Is anything wrong?" She looked away.

Gwyn turned to me and whispered, "I wonder if when Mom looks at Mikaela, she remembers how happy *she* had been before the war."

That thought had crossed my mind, too. Mom's world included constant reminders of all the rites of passages she had been deprived of: happy children celebrating birthdays, teens heading off to college, middle-aged women having lunch with their elderly mothers. But that evening, Mom was not just unhappy, she was angry. And as the meal progressed she became quieter and quieter. By the end of dinner, we parted without a word.

The following day came and went without us speaking, as did the day after. It took all my willpower to resist picking up the phone. A discussion with Mom, when she was hurt or upset, rarely remained confined to the issue at hand. All of her pent-up hurt and fury came into play, entangling huge past disappointments with minor present ones.

Finally I called Dad, who sounded miserable, too. "I really don't know what's going on," he said. When Mom was upset with someone in the family, it was no picnic for him either. Her happiness was central to his. Dad didn't have buddies with whom he went to blow off steam or huge hobbies to distract him. He was a family man, a loyal, loving, and ever-present grandfather and father, and first and foremost a Rock of Gibraltar for Mom.

"Here's Mom," he said, as quickly as possible.

Mom got on the phone. "Hello," she said in a cool and distant tone that scared and angered me as soon as I heard the *H* in "Hello."

"Why are you mad at me?" I asked.

"I'm just very upset," the foreign, cold voice said.

My heart was racing as if I had been called into a radiologist's office to discuss the results of a mammogram. I so dreaded what she would say next that I went on the offensive. "Do you know that you ruined Mikaela's birthday dinner for me?" I asked. "Rather than celebrating, I was focused on what you were upset about."

"Did you call just to induce guilt, you bitch?" Mom said. "David's not around, and you and Gwyn think you're above everyone. You treat me like a poor stepchild."

Even though I had determined that I would stay calm, I couldn't. I was already in tears. How could she say this to me? She disdained name calling and never cursed. I was glad she called me an outrageous name, because it validated the hatred I was feeling toward her.

"I can't believe you called me a bitch!" I sobbed. At some point, Mom hung up on me. Cliff had come into the room and caught the last exchange. He gave me a supportive hug and asked what was going on. I couldn't answer. I didn't want him to think less of Mom, though he probably would not have anyway. He instinctively knew that between Mom and me, there wasn't really a side I wanted him to be on.

At that moment, however, I was furious. Mom, whose daughters meant so much to her, went two more days without speaking to us—

days that felt gray and lifeless to those of us waiting for the phone to ring. I appealed to my six-year-old daughter for help.

"McKay, would you please call Grandma?"

"And say what?"

"Just tell her that you love her."

"You love her, too, Mommy."

Mikaela left a message on Mom and Dad's answering machine, and minutes later Dad called back. Sounding like the weight of the world had lifted from his shoulders, he said, "Yeah, hi, Leslie. I just want to say how much we loved Mikaela's beautiful message."

"Good . . . ," I said tentatively.

"Here's Mom."

"Hi, Leslie," Mom said, sounding calm.

Immediately, I began breathing easier. Still, I debated how to respond. *Be cool and distant? Make her grovel? Who am I kidding? I can't take another minute of this. Tell her whatever she wants to hear.*

"Hi," I said, in as neutral a tone as I could muster.

"I want you to know that I love you."

The tide had turned. Mom was back. My real mom, not the alien who had been inhabiting her body for the past few days. I couldn't resist asking why she had been so mad.

"I guess I felt excluded at the restaurant," Mom said.

"You weren't excluded."

"When I'm feeling well, Leslie, I'm thrilled for you. But when I'm down, I revert to feeling like a deprived child. I hope you'll remember the good when I'm like that."

"It would be easier to remember the good if you wouldn't get so angry with me."

"I guess my rejection buttons were pushed when I was not given a place of honor at the dinner."

"Mom, I didn't *give* anyone a particular place. Everyone just sat down. Look at me, I was on the other end of the table."

"On top of that, Mikaela and Gabriel teased me that evening, for which there was no reprimand from their parents. And even my daughters were throwing daggers at me."

I began to get annoyed all over again. I never could understand how, at these times, Mom could so suddenly lose all faith in me and in my love for her. It was as though a wounded part of her personality emerged and took over. But since things were back on track, I decided to leave well enough alone. "I'm sorry your feelings were hurt, and I hope next time we can avoid a fight," I said.

"I hope so too. I love you."

"I love you, too."

I hung up exhausted. And angry, too. Angry at a maniacal tyrant whose anti-Semitic underlings murdered my relatives, stole my mom's childhood, and ran her out of her own country. I would always be angry. But not at Mom—at least not for long. Some readers will feel this is dishonest. They may see me as being too protective of my mother, or perhaps ignorant of the possibility that my guilt is by-product of repressed anger. But at the risk of protesting too much, I simply say that I am grateful that Mom did her best; that she did it with grace, intelligence, and all of her heart. I only hope that my children grow up to be as proud of me.

31

I Tried My Best

"ARE YOU ALMOST finished, Mom?" Mikaela asked one day when she was eight.

"Soon," I said, pecking away at the keyboard.

"Can we go on our picnic now? I already packed our lunch." She was dressed in her red skirt and sparkly shoes (think Dorothy trying to get back to Kansas), holding a basket that she had piled high with her favorite foods.

"I just have to make one phone call for my book first."

"I'm just saying *when* we go, do I need a jacket?"

How would Mikaela have been changed by life in that attic? I wondered. How many months would it have taken to crush her vibrant spirit? Thank God, this had not been her fate, or that of Gabriel and Christopher, my son and stepson. But how would they be influenced by their grandmother's past? There was no way of hiding it from them. Here I was, every day at home, writing about it. My office was filled with books that had "Holocaust" or "World War II" in the title.

As my children were getting older, I wondered how I would discuss Mom's past with them without inducing guilt or angst. I wanted my children to inherit Mom's wisdom but not her apprehensions. I wanted them to understand that her life had been action-packed, even heroic, but not easy, and that their lives were a gift. And yet how could they know all these things without inheriting *my* fears? Mikaela already had a difficult time separating from me. I often had to persuade her to go to the birthday parties of even her closest friends. At home, on the other hand, there was no end to the get-togethers my daughter enjoyed hosting. I did not give this behavior much thought or push her too strongly, given how similar I had been and how young she still was, but I was certainly wary about intensifying any innate fears she might have.

"Yes, you should bring a jacket. I'll come get you downstairs as soon as I'm done."

"Okay, but hurry up." Mikaela left my office and closed the door behind me.

I took a deep breath and picked up the phone, determined to procrastinate no longer. I would call Mom's stepmother, Clara, for the first time ever. At ninety years old, Clara was still going strong. She was living in a Chicago area retirement home near her sons, Sam and Brad. While the phone rang, I studied the framed photograph in my office taken of Clara five years earlier, when she came to Los Angeles for my cousin's bat mitzvah. Surrounded by Mom, Dad, Sam, Brad, me, and other family members, Clara is short and somewhat stout, with permed hair dyed light brown, and glasses. She is wearing a bright floral-print skirt, a blue short-sleeved blouse, and a tentative smile.

I was on the tenth ring when Clara answered the phone. I took a deep breath. Although I had cleared the call ahead of time with Uncle Brad, not wanting to upset his elderly mother, I was nervous nonetheless.

"Leslie? Oh my God in heaven, I cannot believe it!" she said excitedly.

"Hi, Grandma, how are you?" I said, thrusting the word *Grandma* off my tongue like the shell of a sunflower seed, and already feeling like I was betraying Mom.

Los Angeles, 1999. Back row: Rita Lurie, Brad Gamss (Rita's half brother), Nancy Gamss (Brad's wife), Gwyn Lurie, Leslie Lurie, Mike Gamss (Sam and Pam's son), Pam Gamss (Sam's wife), Sam Gamss (Rita's half brother), and Frank Lurie. Front row: Clara Gamss, Ryan Gamss (Brad and Nancy's son), and Karen Gamss (Sam and Pam's daughter).

"Thank God, not so bad," Clara said.

We briefly chitchatted, and then I asked if she was ready for a few questions.

"Sure. I'll tell you what I can. Oy vey, I'm so glad you called. You know, I love you," Clara said, with a great deal of passion.

"I love you, too," I said, swept up in the moment.

"So Leslie dear, why does your mother never call me?" Clara asked, before I could say anything. I was caught off guard.

"It's complicated for her. I wish the two of you would talk."

"But she doesn't call," Clara lamented.

"Why don't you call her?" I suggested.

"Does she want to hear from me?" My stepgrandmother was sharp as a tack.

No. "I'll ask her," I said. Eventually, I steered the conversation to the war.

"How am I still alive after all I survived?" Clara asked rhetorically. "Did you know that in my early twenties I was taken to Auschwitz?"

"Yes, I did."

"No, really. Have you heard of Dr. Mengele?"

"Yes, sure, the infamous doctor at Auschwitz."

"Exactly. So you do know. Soon after we got to Auschwitz, there was a lady who came into my barracks. She said, 'Today is the day we decide who will live.' Then she brought me before Dr. Mengele. He put me straight to work. Leslie dear, Dr. Mengele saved my life."

"That was a miracle."

"Yes. But he sent my sister and her children to the ovens. I've never recovered."

Clara then explained that after the war, she had returned to Czechoslovakia without any resources. She had come from a poor family to begin with. A friend of her late father suggested that she go to Bucharest, Romania, because they were "giving away money there." Clara could afford one item of clothing, so she bought a coat to cover the rags she wore. In Romania, she met Dora, the fiancée of Mom's uncle Benny. Dora then introduced her to her future brother-in-law, my grandfather Isaac.

"Was it love at first sight?" I asked.

"Almost, Leslie dear, for your grandfather. After I played the violin for him, he proposed to me," Clara said. "I swear to God. But I cried, because I was afraid to marry a man with two children."

Grandpa Isaac's sister, Aunt Tsivia, along with Dora, changed Clara's mind.

"Isaac's daughters are beautiful, and soon they will grow up," Tsivia told Clara.

"And Isaac himself is a handsome, religious man with a lot of money," Dora added, embellishing the financial picture more than a little.

"We're all waiting for visas to the United States, and you'll be left behind if you don't marry him," Tsivia threw in for good measure.

To clinch the deal, Isaac himself paid Clara. "He gave me two thousand dollars," my stepgrandmother said matter-of-factly. "Did I have a choice?"

"Well . . ."

"Of course not," she said quickly. By their wedding day, Clara had grown to love her fiancé, so she refunded the payment. Apparently, Isaac was happy, too. "Ten times a day he would ask if I loved him," Clara said.

I braced myself, and asked Clara what she recalled about Mom in those days. She said, "I tell you the truth, Leslie dear, I saved her life. I swear to God."

"How?" I was doubtful.

"Your mother was so sick when we got married. Whatever I gave her to eat, she threw up. So *I* took her to the doctor," Clara said. She apparently sensed my skepticism and added, "I am also the one who brought her to the hospital after the doctor ordered her to go there."

"She doesn't remember that," I said, trying to ascertain her veracity.

"I swear to God. I used to walk to the hospital twice a day to feed your mom."

"Huh."

"I can prove it," Clara said, still sensing my doubt. "Your mom slept in Crib 23 for the eight months she was in the hospital."

I wished I could verify this, but the hospital and its records no longer existed. Clara insisted that the other children even became jealous of all the attention that she had bestowed upon Mom. One afternoon, for example, when she brought homemade soup to Mom and began to feed her in front of the other children, the nun told her that it was not a good idea.

"Ruchaleh, come with me," Clara urged, helping Mom out of bed.

"Where are we going?" nine-year-old Mom allegedly had asked.

"To the washroom."

Clara recalled that in the washroom, out of view of the others, she fed Mom. "I only wish she appreciated what I did for her," she lamented. She added that after Mom left the hospital, and the doctor prescribed fresh cow's milk, it was *she* who walked six kilometers a day to acquire it. "I'm very happy I saved her life," Clara said. She sounded alert and energetic, but still, she was ninety; before she grew too tired, I wanted to ask her the question that was weighing on my mind.

"Why do *you* think you and my mother had such a difficult relationship?"

"Your mom was difficult to raise," Clara said. "She loved her own mother and was jealous of me. I don't blame her, since she lost her mother when she was too young. But I had not understood this back then. I only knew that I was not the one who killed her mother."

"Did my mom ever talk to you about her mother?" I asked.

"No. You see, my husband was very sensitive to my feelings, so no one spoke of your grandma in front of me." Still, Clara's transition into marriage had not been easy. "Do you know that I did not sleep with my husband for the first three months?"

"No."

"When I married Isaac, your mother and your aunt Sandy said to me, 'You are not going to sleep with our daddy. We sleep with our daddy.' So each night, my husband left me and went to sleep with his daughters. I'm not a selfish person, but each night, I would cry."

"I would have done that for my children, and I'm sure you would have done the same for your sons," I said. I had determined that Clara deserved to hear my frank reaction. She clearly still cared about her relationship with Mom, and I still held out hope that the two of them could reach an understanding and live at least happier ever after.

"Probably," Clara admitted. "It was very difficult for everyone. Leslie dear, I did the best I could. I gave the girls what I didn't have. I made them beautiful clothes and arranged their hair in neat styles.

When I met them, they each had only one little cotton dress. Afterward, they looked like dolls. They were the best-dressed girls in the camps. I wish they appreciated that."

Before we hung up, Clara repeated her wish that Mom call her.

"I'll tell her you said so," I promised.

"I tried my best," she repeated.

A FEW DAYS later, my parents came over for a Mother's Day barbecue. After dinner, Mom seemed happy and relaxed.

"Do you want to hear about my conversation with Clara?" I tentatively asked.

"Not that I care, but what?" I was struck by how tense Mom became whenever she heard Clara's name. I quickly gave her the highlights.

Mom listened, but her face tightened. "She lied. Only my father came to the hospital regularly."

"How can you be sure?"

"I remember that time clearly," she insisted with utter certainty. "Maybe Clara came a few times at the beginning, but I would know if she had visited me often."

"She wants you to call her."

"I'm not going to call her. I still remember the terrible names she called me."

I heard the mounting strain in her voice. I wished I could leave it alone. But I couldn't. "Like what?" I asked.

"Like *oysvurf* ('outcast'), *groiser pisk* ('bigmouth'), and 'nemesis of my life.' "

After Mom left, I felt bad that I had upset her. But I still believed that if Mom had closure in her relationship with Clara, she would feel more at peace. If she could be at peace with her past, so could I, which meant that I could focus better on my present life. Also, Clara was not entirely unsympathetic. Although she had been an unfortunate choice for Mom's stepmother, she, too, had been a victim. I picked up the phone to call my mother.

"Can I just ask you one more question?"

"Sure," Mom responded, in a voice that said, *Don't you dare bring up Clara again.*

"Can't you just have one conversation with Clara?"

"No." Mom was not going to budge.

32

Ma of the Grand

GABE'S LANGUAGE ARTS teacher was on the other end of the line when I answered the phone. My heart started to beat more rapidly. *Was Gabe joking around too much in class? Turning in assignments late?*

"Gabe mentioned that his grandmother is a Holocaust survivor," the teacher said.

"Ohh." I quietly sighed, relieved. "Yes. She is."

"Would she be interested in coming to speak to the seventh-graders about her experience?" The students were learning about the Holocaust as part of a unit on tolerance.

Mom readily agreed. In addition to the lure of having her cherished grandson in the audience, Mom enjoyed spending time in schools speaking about her Holocaust experience. She knew that it was through the children that its lessons would be passed down.

On the arranged day, I tagged along and introduced her to the class.

Mom walked up behind the small wooden lectern, looked around at the eager faces, took a deep breath, and said, "Let me see, where should I begin?" Mom never prepared speeches ahead of time, or wedding toasts, come to think of it, insisting on speaking extemporaneously. She began this time by describing her pastoral early childhood, and then moved to the attic. The main message she tried to communicate was that while life was rarely perfect, individuals had the strength inside to overcome setbacks, to love instead of hate, and to influence others to be better human beings. Mom urged the students not to go along with what they knew was mean, wrong, or destructive to themselves or others.

The administrators, teachers, and eighty or so students listened intently. When Mom got teary or tongue-tied, I read excerpts from our still-unfinished book so she could pause to regain her composure. The students smiled at Mom compassionately. When she finished with her family's climb down from the attic, the hands sprung up.

"Yes." She pointed to a girl in the front row.

"How do you look so young when the war happened so long ago?" she asked.

Mom smiled. She loved this question. "I was just a little girl at the time. Younger than you. But thank you." She called on a boy next, who asked what they used for a toilet in the attic.

"We used barrels that were emptied at night. The farmer who owned the home didn't have indoor plumbing either. Even his family used an outhouse."

Some of Gabriel's classmates seemed unsure whether certain topics were off-limits. As usual, however, a few students worked up the courage to probe deeper about the deaths in the attic and who took care of Mom afterward. When class ended, virtually everyone lined up to tell Mom how much her story had touched and inspired them. They revealed things about their own home lives. Mom's audiences, particularly the children, always seemed captivated by her courage and lack of pretense. Gabriel's pride was evident in the thank-you note he wrote afterward.

Dear Ma of the Grand (Grandma),

Thank you for coming to speak to my class. I know it probably took a lot out of you to get up and tell that heartbreaking story in front of eighty-some kids who you don't know. I know you made a big impression on them and they will remember what you said for the rest of their lives. Believe it or not, you made an impression on me too. I love you grandma and I want you to know that what you did for my grade and me was fabulous.

> Love,
> Gabriel Gilbert-Lurie

I knew that my parents would be involved grandparents. They adored our children and the children adored them. They stayed with them when we left town, helped shuttle them to various classes, and took interest in every aspect of their development. I was so grateful that on Cliff's side of the family as well as mine, my children had what I had missed—loving, supportive, involved grandparents. Mom's grandmother status also continued to present occasional unexpected challenges, however.

I was writing upstairs and Mom was in our family room one afternoon when Gabriel stormed in through the front door, with a neighbor in tow.

"Hi, Gabriel!" I heard Mom eagerly call out.

"Hi, Grandma," he responded affably, before disappearing from sight.

"Where's my hug?" she called.

"I'll give you one later." He was already in his room, without any trace of the guilt I would have felt if I were in his shoes.

I cringed, knowing that this would upset Mom, and pried myself away from my desk. "He has a friend over," I said, making my way downstairs to assuage her feelings.

Mom shook her head like it was no big deal, but then added, "I just think he needs to be taught that it's disrespectful not to greet his grandmother with a kiss."

Now it was my fault. I was sorry I had intervened. "Mom, you should find the right time to tell him. The two of you have your own relationship."

"I think *you* need to teach him."

Mom had very idealized notions of grandparent-grandchild relationships. She recalled her own grandparents, Aharon and Paya Neshe, having been treated with reverence. But, courtesy of the Nazis, they died before their grandchildren were old enough to have come into conflict with them, assuming that coming into conflict with a grandparent was even heard of in her religious East European culture. Mom rarely felt as adored by her grandchildren as she believed the grandparents of her fleeting youth had been by theirs.

Gabriel, who began calling himself Gabe on the day he realized that it entailed writing fewer letters, walked into my bedroom one morning when he was twelve years old. In my sleep, I heard him loudly say, "Hi, Mom."

I tried to remain asleep.

"I hope Grandma doesn't have dreams like the one I had last night," he said. Mission accomplished: I was awake.

"Like the one you just had?" I asked.

"I'll tell you about it, okay? But I know you'll hate it."

"I'm prepared."

Gabriel sat down on my bed and began speaking rapidly. "Some friends came to my house and asked if I wanted to go and shoot Nazis. But they really were neo-Nazis, because the dream took place today."

"Aha."

"I went to Auntie Gwynnie's house to borrow guns. But she gave me really pathetic ones. When I went outside to shoot the Nazis with them, there were only animals in sight. But I knew that the animals were really Nazis, so I started shooting at them. Only my guns kept jamming. Suddenly, real neo-Nazis jumped from a plane and took me prisoner, forcing me onto a bus. Jack Black was the head Nazi."

"Didn't you tell me that you reminded one of your friends of Jack Black?" I asked.

Gabe just stared at me. "Anyway, I still had a pistol. I put one last piece of ammo in and I killed the neo-Nazis just as their bus crashed."

"Wow . . ."

Gabe was now pacing back and forth. "But Mom, Jack Black was still alive. He was standing right in front of me, and I was desperate. I looked up and saw my whole family out in front of my house, but it didn't look like our house. Anyway, I ran inside and slammed the door. Then someone started knocking, so I raced up to get a shotgun." Gabe, knowing my distaste for guns, took the opportunity to demonstrate how he held the weapon and kicked in a door. "Then Jack Black stormed in. He said, 'Now you die, Gabe.' And I woke up."

After Gabe recounted his dream, I felt bad. I was sorry for the graphic, violent way that his impressions of the Holocaust collided with his present-day worries and heroic fantasies, exploding inside his head in the wee hours of the night.

"What's wrong, Mom?" Gabe could be so brash, but he was highly attuned to my reactions.

"Nothing."

"No, really. You look sad. Oh, I know, it's because I was talking about guns, right? It wasn't my fault, it was a dream. Right?"

"I just feel bad that you had such a scary dream. I'm not mad at you."

"Oh, good." Gabe's biggest concern when I looked troubled was that I might be mad at him. He didn't have my need to shield his mother from all unhappiness. "I'll meet you downstairs for breakfast."

In an instant he was gone. But I continued to wonder about the impact that Mom's trauma might have on him, either directly or indirectly through me. I reassured myself that Gabe was not afraid to sleep away from home or of bogeymen in the night. He was much more adventurous than I had been. Maybe it was a good thing, I decided, that he worked out his apprehensions in his dreams. They might be scary from time to time, but they did not appear to be holding him back. Then my thoughts turned to Mikaela, whose fears of being apart from me had all at once become overwhelming.

33

A Deluxe Buffet

THREE MONTHS EARLIER, in Washington, D.C., Mikaela had begged me to bring her home early from the leadership conference, to release her from the sentence she felt she was serving for the brief lapse of judgment she had displayed when she had first opened the invitation and jumped up and down in excitement. "Yes, I definitely want to go," she had shrieked. It would be months between that decision and the actual start date of the conference, but in the interim, Mikaela hadn't second-guessed her decision—that is, until she arrived.

Having vowed not to repeat my parents' mistakes, and vividly recalling all the times that my friends' children had begged to be retrieved early from sleepaway adventures only to wind up staying and having the times of their lives, I had refused to come get her. Throughout the week, from her hot pink cell phone, which I wished had been banned, Mikaela relentlessly called me, begging for a reprieve. I assumed that things would turn around, and she would thank me when she returned home. I fantasized about that moment, wondering whether I would be able to resist saying, "I told you so." But I never had the chance.

Things did not return to normal when Mikaela came home. Not only did she remain steadfast in her insistence that she had not enjoyed one minute of the trip, but she was suddenly afraid to leave me, even to go to school. This was the same school she had been attending for six years, since kindergarten. Now, when I dropped her off, she refused to get out of the car. In the blink of an eye, my daughter had become a frightened, clinging child, and I, already sensitive to confinement, had become a mother yearning to break free. It was a dangerous combination, and our previously sunny relationship was now approaching hurricane conditions.

"Mommy, I can't leave you. I just want to stay with you forever," my eleven-year-old daughter would say. I wanted to hold her in my arms to calm her, as I had when she was a baby. I tried to reason with her and, I confess, even to bribe her with little treats to look forward to at the end of the day. My words seemed to fall on deaf ears. The only ones she would have responded to were, "Let's go home." There was desperation, and a grim determination, in the way in which she locked her arms around my waist, reminding me of the blood-pressure cuff that tightened with each pump of the nurse's hand during a physical exam. Only there was no release. The tension intensified week after week.

Each morning, as we stood facing each other on the school campus, I would grow more insistent that she had to go in to school, raising my voice in frustration. She would dig in her heels, as tears poured down her cheeks. I wondered what the teachers were thinking as they rushed by on their way to class. Here was one of their students, well liked and highly accomplished, acting as if she had never seen the inside of a classroom before. They, too, seemed at a loss as to how to console her. And I cringed to think what the other parents were imagining I had done to put my daughter in this state. Most of all I worried that her friends would judge her negatively, just as my cousins and friends had judged me when I couldn't bring myself to stick out a sleepover, and as the adults of Mom's youth had judged her when she complained more than they would have liked.

· Was Mikaela simply trying to punish me for not bringing her home from Washington, D.C., when she asked? I wondered. All I knew was that my daughter was suffering. Although she was poised, friendly, and a natural leader, she had clearly inherited a fear of separation from the two generations of women who had gone just before her. Even before the leadership conference in Washington, when I went out, Mikaela had needed to know where I was going and precisely when I would be home. If I was a few minutes late and neglected to call, she would mount an all-out search effort, resourcefully leaving urgent messages with every nearby relative and family friend she could think of. At night, when I sat on her bed and brushed the knots out of her hair, we would talk.

"When I couldn't reach you, Mama, I sat on the front porch and thought about what I would do if you died and I didn't have a mother," she explained one time.

"Why did you think I had died?" I asked.

"I know there are some bad people in the world, so I couldn't help but worry."

Up until the leadership conference, Mikaela's behavior had not worried me. She reminded me of myself at her age, and what had not destroyed me ultimately made me stronger. Much of what I had missed out on as a child—the social events and adventures— I had made up for with a vengeance as an adult. My only real regret was not having gone away to college, and even with that, I attributed much of what was good in my life, including meeting my husband, to having been a student at UCLA. But now I was growing concerned about Mikaela.

Beyond not wanting to go to school, Mikaela did not want me to go anywhere without her. Even when Cliff and I were just going out to dinner, she would chase us down the driveway, crying hysterically. She was so unlike the funny, life-affirming daughter I had always known. And something else was odd. I would hear her describe her sadness in words that I had heard Mom use, and I began to suspect she had over-heard one or two of Mom's private phone conversations.

I brought Mikaela to speak to a therapist, hoping he would give her some tools to help her better cope. Toward the end of the first session, the psychologist asked me to join them. I sat down beside my daughter on the couch and braced myself.

"Mikaela has a question for you," he said.

My daughter nodded solemnly.

"Go ahead, Mikaela," he said. Suddenly, a virtual stranger was urging *my* daughter to talk to *me*.

"Why do you have to go to a hundred stupid board meetings?" she asked.

"A: They're not stupid. B: I'm on seven boards, not one hundred. And C: I like helping children who are not as fortunate as you." *I rest my case.*

She stared at me, unconvinced. I looked to the therapist, hoping he would referee. He turned to Mikaela. "I think that your mother is the kind of person who has to do a lot of things, or she won't be happy," he said, to my enormous relief.

In that moment, I flashed upon the Yiddish proverb Mom had fre-quently invoked to me over the past years: "M'ken nicht tantzen oif tzvei khasenes mit ein tokhes," which basically means, "You can't dance at every wedding at the same time with only one *tuches* [behind]." I sud-denly wished I had taken that advice to heart, and had not become involved in so many endeavors at the same time. Even though I did not believe for a minute that my hectic schedule had caused Mikaela's sepa-ration anxiety, it might have exacerbated it. All the good I was trying to do in the world was perhaps not doing so much good for my daughter.

My life felt like a groaning plate at a deluxe buffet. I had piled on so many engagements and commitments that I could not fully enjoy any of them. As I grew older, I became increasingly aware of how little time I had to right the world's wrongs. My plate kept getting fuller. No career, hobby, or number of loving friends and family was enough, so I pushed myself to make the most of every hour, and I encouraged my children to do the same. My saving grace, I told myself, was that at least I wasn't a perfectionist. I loved that we all were in the game, trying our hardest. We did not have to hit home runs each time for me to appreciate the miracle of having had the chance to play.

Meanwhile, I promised Mikaela that I would reexamine my commitments with an eye to spending extra time with her in the coming weeks. The therapist was doubtful, however, that this would cure Mikaela's separation anxiety. He explained that it would probably come and go throughout her childhood. But in the ensuing months, as I became familiar with the research that had been conducted on Holocaust survivors indicating that posttraumatic stress disorder, or the effects of a severe trauma, could be transmitted from generation to generation, I realized that this could be precisely what Mikaela had been suffering from.

Perhaps I had always sensed that I, too, had this predisposition, which is why I had remained braced for an unanticipated catastrophe, to proactively avoid being overwhelmed by any extreme stress. For Mikaela, the Washington trip may have been enough to trigger a posttraumatic reaction, leaving her feeling as though her life were truly endangered.

There were some suggestions in the research that the transmission of trauma could be mitigated in Holocaust families by involving a child in activities outside of the home, or referring to the Holocaust survivor in heroic terms rather than as a victim. Mikaela certainly participated in many outside activities and had constant exposure to friends and teachers outside our family. She also knew she had descended from a resourceful, strong-minded survivor. Perhaps these mitigating factors had contributed to her being so vital and successful, so much of the time. Yet at least thus far, there were no magic bullets. I, too, had been involved in countless outside activities and had always viewed my mother as a hero, and yet her trauma had still seeped through. We would always carry it around with us, my daughter and I, and our challenge was to carry it well, to be stronger as a result.

As for me, I continued to feel guilty about having an easier life than Mom's. When Cliff and I took the children on vacation without her and Dad, I felt bad. When I bought a purse, I felt selfish that I was not getting one for Mom, too. When we were invited to a friend's Fourth of July party and my parents weren't, I worried what they would be doing. To be clear, I enjoyed taking family vacations with my parents, and I loved surprising Mom with gifts like purses. But I also knew that almost anything I did or acquired would elicit within Mom feelings of her deprivation, and in me, feelings of regret about her deprivation. If, God forbid, Mom died tomorrow, aside from the fact that I would miss her with every ounce of my being, I would primarily feel terrible for all she had been cheated of, for all she had missed.

In the dark of night, ghosts of the Holocaust still haunted me. When I climbed into bed and turned out the lights, I heard the attic door slam shut. I was trapped with my apprehensions. Hadn't Mom's family life been good before the war? Hadn't the lives of many European Jews? But then the unimaginable occurred, so why couldn't it happen again in my lifetime?

Mostly, I worried about death. What would life be like without my parents? Without Cliff? Without my sister, brother, or children? Or what if I were dying? I couldn't shake a feeling of complete vulnerability. I worried about toxins in the soil. I vowed to remind Cliff to wear sunscreen, and Chris to schedule a doctor's checkup. At the first sign of glorious morning light, the attic door swung open and I was free again, excited about beginning a new day.

Despite this constant vigilance, I didn't let my fears get in the way of making the most out of each new day. I have flown in helicopters to get to remote regions in the world, taken walking safaris in African forests teeming with wild animals (of course, with an armed ranger), and rappelled from the heights of the jungle canopy of Costa Rica. Each time, afterward, I felt the elation and power of defying not death but a dark destiny of fear. I remained confident that Mikaela also would ultimately develop the coping skills she needed. She, too, would grow strong, gain some distance from me, and face down her own legacy of fear. Until that time, there would be more painful episodes of separation, and more missed opportunities. But I would be there to support her and gently steer her in the right direction. Just as Mom had done for me.

34

Mikaela: Different from Other Kids My Age

STEERING MIKAELA IN any particular direction was no easy feat. Within her comfort zone she had never ceased being a confident, articulate, and charming girl. By twelve years old she had a strong sense of self, an articulate voice, and a desire to speak for herself.

I don't know when I first heard the word *Holocaust* or learned what it meant. Maybe I always knew, but chose not to understand. I do remember that when my teacher first mentioned it in the fifth grade, I seemed to know more about it than the other kids in my class. I knew that when you take a power-hungry man with unfortunate facial hair like Adolf Hitler, and give him someone or something to blame his troubles on like the Jews, you get the Holocaust.

Since then, I have learned more. I know that Germany was in an economic depression when Hitler came to power and told people that their problems were the fault of the Jews and other people who were different. Through propaganda

Mikaela Gilbert-Lurie, 2008.

in newspapers and posters, Hitler compared Jews to creatures such as rats. At group meetings, he convinced large masses of Germans that they would have more money and that their economy would flourish if they got rid of these people. All Hitler needed was a group of mindless but loyal followers to do his dirty work. The Nazis were created, and for the Jews, it all went downhill from there.

The Nazis erected concentration camps like Auschwitz and other less famous ones, where millions of Jews were sent to die. They marched the Jews into showers to kill them efficiently by flipping a switch and waiting for their lungs to be filled up with toxic vapors. Other Jews were just shot or stabbed to death; even people who helped Jews would be killed if they were caught. There also was Dr. Mengele at Auschwitz. He experimented with prisoners, particularly twins. And of course, there was Grandma Rita's family. They were very happy until the Holocaust came and they had to hide in a small attic for two years.

What I will never be able to fully grasp is the moral aspect of the Holocaust. These people, who were doing hateful and cruel things to my family, still had hearts, souls, and supposedly, moral compasses. Somewhere inside they must have known right from wrong. So what happened? For a child I know a lot about the Holocaust, but I still don't quite comprehend what the Holocaust means for both its perpetrators and victims, and maybe I never will.

So how does this all relate to the rest of my life, to a twelve-year-old girl, born and raised in the suburbs of Los Angeles, who loves to cook and shop? When my grandmother's mom died right in front of her eyes, it affected her. Because of that, my own mother was always afraid to sleep away from her mom for fear that something would happen to her. Even now, two generations later, I am too scared to go to sleepaway camp, or even to sleep over at friends' houses. I feel the most safe when I am at home, but even there, I worry whenever my mom leaves the house without me. If something were to ever happen to her, I would feel one hundred percent responsible for it. Even though I am probably not strong enough to defend her, I somehow feel as if my presence protects her from the evil in this world. Of course I know it isn't true, but I still feel this way.

My mother and I are both very smart and very cautious. Why are we cautious? Because we don't want to die. Ever. We both like good food, clothes, winning, and helping other people. We dislike mean people. We also both have the same soft pajamas with lambs on them. I think that because of my grandmother's Holocaust experience, my mother is more loving to her own children. She also taught us more about staying healthy. At other people's houses they eat potato chips and cookies for snacks, but ever since I was four years old I ate whole-wheat snacks and drank nonfat milk. My mother and I are both pretty happy people, despite our fears.

Although I see the world as a warm, welcoming place, and I surround myself with kind people, I still seem to be afraid of nearly everything. I told my mom this, and she said that wasn't true. "You're not afraid of strawberries," she said to prove her point. But I told her that I am, if they're not washed. I do not see the world as being a very safe place. People can turn around and shoot you, or an animal can maul you, or a car can hit you.

My biggest fear is of my mom dying. I don't think I could be happy without her. No one talks to me the way she does. She's the only person who understands why I miss her so much. My other two big fears are that *I* will die, and (let me be blunt about it) throwing up. Three days ago one of my closest friends slept over. At about midnight, she woke up and told me that she felt sick to her stomach, and instantly I went into I-love-her-but-I-need-to-do-whatever-I-can-do-to-get-her-out-of-this-house mode. I ran upstairs to wake my dad, since my mother is as afraid of throwing up as I am. It's too violent and out of control for us. Grandma Rita does not have this fear. But she and I have many other traits in common.

Grandma Rita and I both like to care for people and make sure that everyone is happy. We both cook well, and we have the same soft skin. I think she and I also like to feel special and be surrounded by luxurious things. My grandma acts happy around me, but it would not surprise me to learn that she is not so happy, since I hear sometimes that she isn't.

After what my grandmother endured, I believe I can over-come anything and be whatever I want to be. I look around, and I think I have a good life. I have good health and a happy, healthy, and loving family. I know that everyone has fears about something, even if they don't have mine. I have no idea how I will prevent my own children, someday, from having my same fears. But for sure, I will be understanding. I will know that their fears are real to them, even if I do not share the same ones.

I'm not sure whether my grandmother's Holocaust experience makes me different from other kids my age, but I feel that I am different. I am more cautious. Also, I think of things more abstractly, or more conceptually. For example, when I react a certain way, or I see that my mother is mad about something, I assume that something that happened long ago probably triggered our reactions.

I definitely think that a Holocaust could happen again. Yes, the world often is stupid. People believe a lot of things they read in newspapers and magazines, without looking into whether these things are actually true or not. But this is not what I worry about. I am more concerned about whether we will have a strong president and how to stop global warming. In the next fifty years we will run out of diesel fuel, for example. These are problems that Adolf Hitler or Grandma Leah could never have fathomed.

35

Rita: Lessons to Be Learned

I open my eyes from sleep. On the floor across the room there is a long, white, blurry bundle. I blink my eyes, not sure what to make of it. Perhaps it is a dense patch of fog. Then it begins moving toward me. It gets closer and closer. I want to run, but I don't. I can't. Just before it reaches me, I wake up in a cold sweat. For fifty years, I have had this recurring nightmare in bits and pieces. I was convinced that it symbolized death crawling toward me. But one night, not long ago, the dream came to me as a vivid, coherent whole. I could see that the white mass actually was in the shape of a mummy, like a body enveloped in sheets. I awakened more petrified than ever. Yet after wrestling with the significance of this nightmare for several days, the fear dissipated. I understood for the first time that the bundle, although wrapped in a white shroud, was not death. It was my mother, trying to connect with me.

By looking at life as a series of lessons to be learned, I forced myself to hang on to a glimmer of hope, even during the darkest moments. I learned from the bad times, trusting that there would be better times ahead. Success is relative. I am proud that I have run a business, raised caring, productive children, and as a loving and dedicated wife helped my husband, Frankie, overcome a catastrophic illness. Feeling joy, being strong, becoming the person I might have been had the war not intervened—that, I decided, would be the best revenge. And an important lesson to pass on to my children, grandchildren, and future generations.

There is no way to cast much of the first half of my life in a positive light. No way for me to wrap it up in a neat bow or to make sense of events that were simply insane. I have faith that whatever happened, happened for some reason, although that reason remains unfathomable. The other day, as I found myself staring at my one surviving baby picture, I felt closer to my past than ever before. I remembered having been an outgoing and sensitive young child, much like my granddaughter, Mikaela. She has a great capacity for joy, but she gets hurt easily, too. Every day I accept more of myself, including that sad, lonely child I became soon after that baby picture was taken. That's why I wanted to tell my story. So people can see that the spirit can be rekindled even after terrible loss.

I never found any shortcuts to healing myself. I had to confront each and every excruciatingly painful episode. I still remember the anger I used to feel at relatives who teased me or didn't comfort me, the way my blood would boil. And what is boiling blood? The high blood pressure I have today. I struggled, working hard to put the pieces of my life together, and in some instances, to re-create parts that were lost entirely. I kept saying to myself, "Don't let go of your dreams. Build on every bit of inspiration."

There are days when I still hear the hurt, deprived little Ruchaleh talking to me. I feel the old ache in my heart, and anger in the pit of my stomach. From deep down in my soul, I become that frightened, neglected, and disappointed child, with no comfort or security. No adult to intervene long enough to say, "This is wrong. This is a child who needs protection." Or at least an explanation. I hear that child inside of me asking, Why? Why is this happening to me? Why am I hiding with a bunch of helpless people who lack the strength to take care of their own children? I think that perhaps there were no answers to those questions. And then I force myself to become the mother of that child who felt abandoned at an age when kids are scared of their own shadows.

With Leslie, I am in awe. I am thrilled that her life has been rich with promises fulfilled, goals brought to fruition, and people cheering her on. I celebrate her inclusive, loving nature, her leadership abilities, and all her many accomplishments. But occasionally, when I'm in a weak moment, I feel stuck being a spectator in her life. At these times, the voids within me ache, and sometimes a smidgen of resentment emerges.

My daughter's success and the differences in our lives make me aware that I never achieved many of my dreams. In high school, I was only able to survive, not to prosper. Before I began a family I wish I had been able to attend a university, to discover more of my talents, to attain some individual success, and to bond with people more similar to the person who I might have become. I would also like to have found the energy, at some point along the way, to make more changes in the world, perhaps helping children. It wouldn't surprise me if someday I overcame these doubting times altogether, since I'm constantly striving to be a better person. In the meantime I remind myself that Leslie is a part of my own self, and once again my heart swells with pride. I experience that deep, binding love that makes me glow inside.

With my seven grandchildren I feel I have won the lottery. Each one has helped me to grow healthier, to put my life in focus. The wonder of love is so amazing. One of my favorite sayings is, "The proof of the pudding is in the eating." For me, I find the validation that I have risen above my past in the way my grandchildren are developing into healthy, loving, and thriving people. I struggle to be the grandmother I would have wanted and to give to my grandchildren the gift of myself, and for the most part I succeed. I have gotten so much love from them. I keep learning and striving for additional wisdom to impart to them. I hope that someday each one of them will remember me with a great deal of love. If they didn't like something I did or some of my admonitions, hopefully they realize that it's because I was concerned about them, perhaps too much so. Mostly, I want them to remember that I loved them.

My path seems less cluttered these days. I have more peaceful moments. I've come to feel freer and more self-confident. I was blessed with the wit and curiosity to make the most of my experiences, and enough love and compassion to do some good for other people. Although I don't spend a lot of time in synagogue, I have always been spiritual. I believe we are all made in the image of God—with a light side and a dark side. Accepting these two sides of myself has helped me to keep my life intact.

I have also come to believe that God meant for me to survive so that I could enjoy a good and full life. I still have more to accomplish. I still talk to God all the time. In fact, I still say good night the way I was taught by my father when I was two years old. Kissing one of the mezuzahs in the house, I say this prayer three times—Shaddai shomreini matzilani michol raim. The prayer may not be precise because I never saw the words in writing. It's the way I remember hearing it as a very young girl, when I had a peaceful home, the highest expectations, and a mother and father who adored me. In its essence, it's a prayer to God to protect me from all harm.

36

The Abyss

MOM STILL POSSESSED a great deal of her youthful beauty. One would never guess from looking at her that she suffered from so many afflictions; she had high blood pressure, high cholesterol, and fibromyalgia, and was often tired or achy. She believed that her muscles had never forgotten those cold, cramped days in the attic and those exhausting, bumpy rides in rickety military trucks, traveling from city to city in search of the next temporary shelter. A visit to her doctor left her worried that her body was "falling apart," but at least her skin was perfect. Neither the doctor, nor anyone else, could have foreseen that Mom would soon lapse into another depression. This one would be even more severe than the two that I had witnessed back in college and law school, over two decades earlier.

Something seemed not quite right in Hawaii, back in April 2006. Mom and Dad came with us as our guests over the kids' spring break. My sister, Gwyn, and her family met us there, too. From the beginning, Mom seemed irritable. She was usually in high spirits on vacations. For all of her worries, she always loved an adventure. Sometimes I marveled at how well she went with the flow, putting up with everyone else's moods. But not this time. Within minutes of arriving at the hotel and being informed that my parents' room would have two double beds rather than the king-size one we had requested, Mom seemed bent out of shape. I felt responsible, since I had planned the trip, and guilty that Cliff and I got a king-size bed in our room. Mom said nothing to assuage my doubts about not offering her our room.

A day or so later, after a morning workout, Gwyn and I wandered into the hotel spa's boutique. Coincidentally, Mom walked in moments later. Seeing us together, she looked hurt. Later, she asked me why we had *excluded* her from our shopping plans. "We didn't make plans, Mom. We just happened to be there," I felt compelled to explain. Another day, after I returned from a beginner's golf lesson, Mom told me that she would have liked to be included. I was frustrated by her disappointment, particularly since she had never before expressed any interest in golfing.

By the end of the trip I was furious. Mom's mood had ruined my week. Wasn't bringing her on our vacation proof enough that I was a loving, good daughter who wanted to be with her? Why did our relationship begin anew every time the sun rose, like Groundhog Day, with no points ever accumulated for my prior efforts? I sensed that any attempt to express my anger would only lead to Mom's feeling hurt. Even more disturbing, I sensed a change in Mom's emotional state, somehow more raw and frail than usual, even though it would be several more months before I or anyone else could put a name to it.

Back in Los Angeles, things returned more or less to normal. But still, I sensed in Mom an amorphous, fragile quality, like an antique piece of fabric that still looked beautiful but could tolerate very little stress. Then, over Labor Day weekend, at Gabriel's bar mitzvah, something again was askew. It was a subtle thing, something only an enmeshed daughter would notice.

Mom smiled and made appropriate comments, but she was distant. Absent was the overwhelming joy I had expected this devoted grandmother and Holocaust survivor to exhibit at her grandson's bar mitzvah. As I greeted guests at the party, I wondered whether I had done something to upset Mom. Dancing with Cliff, I thought about whether Mom felt hurt that she had not had a more prominent role in the ceremony. Unfortunately, our synagogue had strict guidelines concerning family members' involvement. I watched Gabe, gleefully laughing, lifted into the warm night air on his chair during the hora, and noticed that Mom was not in sight. Despite the joyful atmosphere, I couldn't block out the lone cloud that hovered overhead.

Weeks later matters came into focus. Mom's eyes and voice took on that haunting quality reminiscent of her depressions two decades earlier. She sat in my office, trying to describe what she was feeling.

"I have struggled so hard to deal with my father and the loss of my mother. Once we were a family, and now I can't even go to their graves because there's too much pain." Tears rolled down her cheeks as she told me this.

"You can visit your father's grave in Chicago," I said.

"No. I can't. I remember him from when I was a child, and then I feel all of the loss. And the pity I had for him. It's too much." Mom played with her hair, sobbing, then dabbing her nose with a tissue. "I can't believe I'm doing this. I don't want to upset you. I pray to God to let my true self emerge again and get past this temporary setback." She shook her head back and forth, moving her hands expressively. When she referred to herself, or something heartfelt, she lightly tapped her chest with her fist.

"I always thought I had plenty of time to deal with my past and then still enjoy the future. Now suddenly number seventy is coming up, and I have never come to terms with dying."

I had suspected that Mom's big birthday, still several months out, was weighing on her. In the midst of this sorrow, still, she expressed hope. "Maybe you can use your contacts to help me volunteer somewhere," she said, out of the blue.

"Do you realize how many schools and charities would be thrilled to have you volunteer? You don't need my contacts."

"Never mind. I know what I mean. It's different when it comes from you."

Had we not been down this road so many times before, I would simply have agreed to help Mom find a volunteer position. She would have been a tremendous asset to a child in need of emotional or academic support. But inevitably, Mom always changed her mind at the last minute and I was left running interference, explaining her change of heart to some disappointed executive director (and friend). Having to be at a job regularly, particularly for no pay, made Mom feel confined. Soon the issue was moot anyway, at least for the time being.

Mom could barely function. She had stopped driving her car and making social plans, and she barely ate. She left the house only for doctors' appointments and trips to my sister's or my home. Dad was Mom's chauffeur and primary caretaker. Overnight his existence had become a nightmare. He was confined to his home with a stranger, in a melancholy, quiet world. Each day, wearier and more concerned, he looked closer to his seventy-five years. When Mom managed to talk about anything besides her own despair, it usually related to Dad's not taking good care of himself or eating the wrong foods. Not only was Mom worried about turning seventy and her own mortality, but she was also obsessed with losing him.

Mom was in agony. Her psychiatrist struggled to find the right cocktail of medications to compensate for the chemicals that had been depleted from her brain during the course of her traumatic life. "I feel like I'm a shut-in. My whole body is in pain," she told me. Her voice sounded worn out, or dehydrated from shedding so many tears.

Each morning on the phone, my upper stomach tense as a rock, I promised her that she would feel better, just as she used to promise me that the lump on my leg wasn't cancer, or that she would be home after school.

"I hope so," Mom weakly responded on one such morning. "Everything is so hard. Brushing my teeth, taking a shower. I just want to feel joy again."

Blood rushed to my temples, adding to the dull, achy pressure. I had to help her. "Try and force yourself to get out of bed," I pleaded, taking deep breaths to stay calm.

"You don't understand." I hated when she said that. "I would if I could. I just want to feel a spark, and then it will stay with me and I'll make the most of it. But now, I need to be held and cuddled."

Once again, despite all I had learned about depression since my law school days, I found myself blindsided. Mom had been so strong and optimistic in recent years. I had been surprised how even after our interviews she had been able to read through her testimony, over and over again, checking for errors. Now, she sounded like little Ruchel from a half century ago, slipping into an abyss.

Mom had been so young when she was traumatized. Had she been a few years older, she would have had time to develop stronger coping mechanisms. Instead, the damage put her at great risk for depression later in life. I had never seen her so distraught. I feared that her new psychiatrist mistakenly believed that delving deeper into her history was the key to her recovery. Perhaps he didn't realize how much of Mom's past decade had already been dedicated to this endeavor. Just to be sure, I called him.

"What your mother is struggling with is important for her," the doctor told me. "But we are also trying to find the right medication to help that along."

"I just wanted to make sure you knew that my mother is already very aware of her past. She has spent the last seven years telling me about it for the book that we are writing."

"I know. And that opened up some old wounds. Ultimately it will be a good thing, I think, but for now it's very painful."

I got a sudden pang in my chest. Had I caused this? Was writing the book a mistake? It had seemed the best way to immortalize Mom's life, to ensure that her voice would be heard. But what if, in an ironic twist of fate, it destroyed her instead? By adding dialogue to Mom's recollections, putting words back into the mouths of Grandma Leah and other deceased relatives, had I made those memories too real? Perhaps Dad had been the most perceptive of all of us when he chose not to ask Mom about her past.

Just in case I had not been clear, I told the psychiatrist, "I need you to understand that Mom will never dig deeply enough to make sense out of what happened, because it was senseless. I only hope that you find the right medication or treatment so that she can enjoy her future."

"That is exactly what I am trying to do," he told me. "But these things take time."

Over the next few days, I continued to wonder whether the book had been a mistake. Even if my conversations with Mom had not *induced* her depression, she was certainly not in any state to continue working with me. The window that Mom had opened wide into her past had suddenly slammed tight. But then Mom's condition grew so precarious that my thoughts shifted entirely to bringing her back to life.

Mom was not responding to antidepressants as she had in the past. She was barely communicating, and her weight was down to ninety-seven pounds, from one hundred and forty or so the year before. I had read that Holocaust survivors suffered disproportionately from depression and premature senility. The cerebral tissue, which holds keys to depression and memory, is fragile and easily damaged by childhood trauma. Yet nothing I had learned had prepared me for this sudden, dramatic downward spiral.

My sister and I consulted psychiatrists around the country. Mom, unable to endure much more despair with no foreseeable hope on the horizon, was open to trying anything. Dad, nearing the end of his own rope, remained cautious, resisting any risky options. Eventually, however, he was outvoted. Mom underwent electroconvulsive therapy, also known as electroshock therapy, or ECT. This somewhat controversial procedure, in which small seizures are carefully induced in the brain with electricity, had been found to be successful in some severely depressed patients.

Dad, my brother, David, and I sat with Mom in the light blue, futuristic-looking hospital waiting room. My sister, Gwyn, was in another hospital room across town, having given birth to her second daughter, Noa, the day before. It had been upsetting to watch Mom passively witness her granddaughter's arrival, virtually devoid of emotion. She was a different woman entirely from the kvelling, eager new grandmother of fourteen years earlier, who couldn't stop smiling as she rocked my infant son, Gabriel, in her arms, mesmerized by his love for her.

David had come down from San Francisco with his family for this birth of his niece and to support Mom. At forty-one, he was a husband, father of a young son, Elijah, and a teenage stepdaughter, Zoë, and working as the principal of a special education school. Like Mom and me, he was a protector of children. He was still slim and youthful in appearance, with large, dark brown eyes, a chiseled nose, and prominent cheekbones. He wore wire-rimmed glasses that emphasized his serious, scholarly demeanor, and his dark hair was shorter than usual. For the first time, I noticed strands of gray in his temples. Mom sat between David and me and sadly put her head on my brother's shoulder. He held her hand.

My cell phone kept ringing. David looked annoyed each time I answered. *I'm always around Mom,* I wanted to remind him. *I can take all the phone calls I want.* A nurse came and summoned Mom for her treatment. We hugged her good-bye, watching her disappear with an orderly behind steel double doors. *Please let her come out physically and mentally intact,* I said to myself. What if Dad was right, and we had rushed to a dangerous decision? Would he ever forgive us?

"I'm going downstairs to get a snack. Want to take a walk?" Dad asked David.

"That's okay, I'll wait here."

I was impressed by David's concern. I had spent so much time being disappointed in him in recent years that I had almost forgotten what an empathetic and kind person he was. Our relationship was not as effortless as it had been in childhood. David could not "get his arms around the idea" that I seemed to travel everywhere except to northern California, where he lived. And I could not understand why he did not come down more often to see all of us, particularly Mom and Dad, since he was the one who had chosen to move away. As I saw it, he had fled the city and assumed that my sister and I would cover for him.

That morning, David seemed sad. Probably not coincidentally, he had married a woman not unlike Mom. His wife was strong and bright, yet wounded, carrying around sorrow of her own. He and I were the only ones in the waiting room. I snatched the opportunity and asked David why he was feeling down.

After gathering his thoughts, he admitted that he wasn't sure what the matter was, exactly, but he knew that his periodic bouts of depression were attributable to growing up with Mom's. "I think I actually absorbed it by osmosis. Just by looking at me, Mom conveyed her need for me to make her happier," he said. As a result, he developed a desire to please and a need to be there for others, even to his own sacrifice.

It occurred to me that David, like me, had probably wanted to be "good" for Mom's benefit. Although he had a rebellious spirit, I never once remembered him saying anything mean or getting into trouble. Now I felt bad that this goodness had not shielded him from struggling with depression as an adult, just as in all likelihood it had never served to buffer any individual from suffering any other disease.

As David and I continued to reflect in the waiting room, he told me how proud he was of the way Mom had made a positive life for herself and for our family. His biggest frustration was with himself. He wished he could enjoy his life more.

Our conversation reminded me of a similar one I had had with Gwyn when she was pregnant with her older daughter, Sydney, and feeling down. I had sat on her bed in an attempt to cheer her up, all the while working on a crossword puzzle.

"I can't talk to you while you're doing a puzzle," Gwyn had said. She had never liked my habit of multitasking.

"Then let's go for a walk. If I sit here, I have to finish it."

On our walk through her Santa Monica neighborhood, with its refreshing ocean air, wide, tree-lined sidewalks, and homes alternating between stuccoed Mediterranean-style mansions, Craftsman gems, and original early-twentieth-century bungalows, my sister revealed that she, too, connected the sadness she carried with her more to Mom's past than to her own. "None of us earned the darkness we feel," Gwyn had said. "Do you ever stop to think how strange it is? Here we are not even trusting the next moment, and yet our family won the lottery." Mom had survived, after all, defying all odds.

Back in the waiting room I thought about the three of us. My sister, my brother, and I were strong and accomplished. In our own ways we led rather than followed, created rather than imitated, and sought to improve rather than merely critique our worlds. Among us, we had traveled widely. Still, when we came together, we were children again, and Mom was a central theme in our conversations.

Long ago, perhaps in the womb, we each had been exposed to Mom's wounds. It probably had never occurred to her that her tainted blood could seep through to our immature emotional systems, and that we would be in the process of healing for most of our lives. None of us was as sad or fragile as Mom. Hopefully, none of our children would be as traumatized as we were. Each generation would be further removed from the shock and devastation of the original event. My siblings and I were doing what we could to make the world not seem like a fearful place for our children. And yet we wanted our children and grandchildren to have an awareness of Mom's past. Her status as a survivor seemed integral to the values and strength they would develop.

Mom was wheeled out from her treatment. She was groggy but otherwise intact. It would still be two or three weeks and several more sessions before we would notice a difference. Even as she regained her spirit, things were not quite the same. When I looked at her now, I was always aware of the sorrow somewhere just beneath her stoic veneer. My illusion that Mom would ever be entirely at peace, able to truly enjoy the dawn she always hoped to greet once she made her way through the darkness, was shattered. All of the love and pearls and vacations I could ever hope to provide would never make up for what she had lost.

37

Legacy

AT MY ANNUAL physical, my doctor, who also happened to be Mom's doctor, asked where I got my athletic ability. When I told him that neither of my parents was especially athletic, he suggested that Mom would have been, given a different childhood. Later, when I relayed this to Mom, she was delighted. I liked the idea, too.

Mom and I played numerous games of Scrabble while we were putting the finishing touches on this book. I looked forward to taking breaks, when we would squeeze in a game. I loved the way she hunched over the board, calculating her next move. She never mastered keeping score or how to spell certain words. Perhaps she just wished some words were spelled differently. Sometimes Mom had a childlike belief that she could will good outcomes. Did she really not know that *FUZZ* had two *Z*'s, for example, or was she just hoping that by some miracle, it didn't? I loved her determination. Sometimes Mikaela, Gabe, and Chris played, too, three generations of word freaks putting the pieces together.

"We have to open a window," Mom said as she walked into my office one day. "It is twenty degrees hotter here than when we left Malibu."

"Hang on. I'll be finished with these last pages of the book in a few minutes," I told her as I kept typing. "It's done."

"Done? Really?"

I turned to her. She didn't look nearly as excited as I had anticipated, not nearly as excited as I was. By this point our endeavor had taken its toll on my entire family. Year after year, weekend after weekend, I had continued to conduct interviews, write, and finally revise a manuscript on a topic that would be difficult for any child to hear about even in passing, obsessively searching for some sort of order or logic that would never arrive. Now the process was finally coming to an end, and Mom's story was moving toward the light of day. But you wouldn't know it by looking at her.

"You seem disappointed," I said.

She shrugged. "It's another ending."

She was right. An ending to the long stretches of time we had spent together. An ending to the intense gaze I had focused on her—as an adult, this time. I have been told that religious Jews say kaddish, the mourner's prayer, when they finish writing a book. The completion is viewed as a death of sorts. We did not say kaddish. I followed my own tradition of putting things in the most positive light for Mom.

"Just think, you'll never have to dwell on your past again. All of your sad memories are now safely bound together in one manuscript."

Mom forced a smile. It was hard for me to remember her real smile, her easy one, which used to appear so many times each day. I walked over to give her a hug. She stood gingerly to protect her aching back, and wrapped her arms tightly around me. She felt thin and frail in my arms. She didn't seem to want to let go. And this time, that was fine with me.

My thoughts returned to that afternoon in 1987, in Poland, when my cousins, my sister, and I sat shivering in the Grajolskis' attic. Afterward, in their garden, we attempted to fulfill Mom's one request that we locate Grandma Leah's and young Nachum's burial sites. The tranquil mid-summer garden was a dramatic shade of jade, sandwiched in between the pine green farmhouse on one side and dramatic fields on the other. As a pair of gobbling turkeys strutted back and forth, we searched each

Poland, 1987. Gwyn and Leslie Lurie bury a letter to their grandmother, Leah Gamss.

tree and patch of grass for some secret sign Mom's uncles may have left. But we could not find one. Even Maria Grajolski could not help us. She said that toward the end of the war her nerves were shot, and her family didn't tell her very much.

Undaunted, my sister and I devised a contingency plan. With a pen and sheets of paper we settled down in the grass, under a leafy green apple tree. Quietly, we talked about how proud our grandmother would have been of both of her daughters, Mom and Auntie Sandra, and of her five now-grown grandchildren. After a time, Gwyn and I began composing the only letter we would ever write to our maternal grandmother. Our voices merged into one, as did our tears, staining the paper as we scribbled the words.

Dear Grandma,

Mom couldn't be here. She wanted to be. But it was too difficult for her. We have such a hard time trying to express for our family, especially Ruchel, how very much you have been missed. She wants you to know that she loves you very much—that she hopes you are resting in peace, even though peace had nothing to do with the way you died. Most importantly, though, we think she wants you to know that she doesn't blame you for leaving her, that she knows you gave all you had, much of which she still carries with her every day. It's strange to be writing this letter to you. You never even knew us. But we know you.

Our mom has been shaped by so many experiences. But still, much of who she is must have had a great deal to do with you. She is a magical person with an inexhaustible capacity to love and to nurture. We only wished you lived long enough to share more of this with her. But you didn't, and so we all lost—every life you could have and would have touched.

There is solace in all of this, though. Your life, no matter how short, and Grandpa's life, no matter how difficult, left a legacy of immeasurable value. . . . There are so many children who've been born to members of the family and have grown up to tell the story of your struggle to survive and how you died in your attempt to save the lives of your family during the war. We have come to find you and to somehow let you know we love you—through our mother, whom we love with all our hearts.

All our Love,

L and G

Gwyn and I also wrote a short note to our young Uncle Nachum, letting him know that we loved him and would never forget him. Afterward our cousins joined us in an impromptu kaddish. The memorial was consoling. As we buried our written notes in the cold dirt, under the vibrant apple tree, I felt some closure, albeit for a tragedy I had experienced only indirectly. In the garden of good and evil in Poland, we were healing ourselves, and hopefully Mom. At the time I believed that if Mom had been there, somewhere in the vicinity of Grandma Leah's final resting place, she might have felt some closure, too. But now, nearly two decades later, I was less sure.

Mikaela walked into my office to join Mom and me. She had recently begun to wear makeup, just for fun, around the house. She did not clumsily apply thick eyeliner and gobs of shadow the way so many other twelve-year-old girls did. Instead, she subtly blended them onto her eyelids and cheeks, as Grandma Rita had taught her. "What's going on in here?" she asked.

New York, 2008. Rita Lurie and Mikaela and Leslie Gilbert-Lurie.

"It's a mother-daughter hug," Mom said.

"I want to be part of the sandwich," Mikaela announced, squeezing between Mom and me to get in the center. The love I was feeling for Mom flowed through to my daughter. She was still small for her age, at four foot eight coming up just to my chin. Her petite, heart-shaped face tilted up, fixing on me with large, almond-shaped brown eyes. I knew those eyes. They were mine, and Mom's, and Grandpa Isaac's. They were wise. They were funny. They were happy and sad. They were endlessly deep, dark pools surrounded by flawless skin. But where Mom's skin was alabaster, Mikaela's was gold. Mikaela, after all, had been blessed by the gift of spending her childhood outdoors whenever she chose to. Even better, she was grateful for that blessing, and for the grandmother who made it possible. Gratitude, was my portion, too, for the opportunity to pass on the best of my family's legacy, so that my son and my daughter and their children and grandchildren could work to better the world, to hope and to dream, to both acknowledge and leave behind a time when their forebears lived in darkness, hiding from monsters who ruled the land, and to enjoy ever more deeply the life-giving warmth and energy of the sun.

Acknowledgments

I HAVE BEEN overwhelmed by the generosity of many individuals who have poured out their hearts, wracked their brains, guided and encouraged me through every phase of my decade-long obsession.

It all begins with Rita (Mom), the protagonist in our story. I am so grateful not only to be her daughter, but in this endeavor, to have been her partner. The depth of detail she was able to recall, the courage that she demonstrated as she dredged up painful memories, and her dedication to this book, were awe-inspiring.

I also owe a huge debt of gratitude to many family members who generously and patiently offered supplemental stories and impressions, and answered my endless questions, even when doing so meant rehashing their own upsetting pasts. Sandra Weiss (Auntie Sandra) spent teary mornings with me in her kitchen, lovingly sharing her recollections, and helping me to evaluate the accuracy of my mother's earliest memories. Sally Frishberg patiently responded to more inquiries from me than I can recall. This could not have been easy for her given the subject matter and the fact that she hates talking on the telephone. Along with her husband, Kenny, Sally also brought our larger family together for one of the most memorable evenings of my life.

Arthur Gamss, Benny Gamss, Brad Gamss, Clara Gamss, Felicia Gamss, Helen Gamss, Jeffrey and Tova Gamss, Sam Gamss, Lola Goodstein, David Seitelbach, Miriam Silver, Marilyn Weisberg (Mom's best high school friend), and Chana and Henry (Avraham Haim) Weltz each made this book richer and more authentic. Their impressions and stories, shared with love and generosity, meant so much to me. The late Sonia and Max (Mordche) Gamss filled in more of the missing puzzle pieces than anyone else. I relished each moment I spent talking with them, and deeply regret having come to know them so late in their lives. I also want to thank my New York cousins, Barbara Goodstein, Debbie Goodstein, and Leslie Wolfowitz, for their unwavering support of me to tell my mother's story as she knew it to be. My Los Angeles cousins, Lauren Schneider and Karen Weiss, also encouraged me from the very start. I am deeply appreciative of their lifelong love and friendship, the stories that they shared, and the relevant research that Lauren passed on to me along the way.

I am so grateful to my siblings, Gwyn and David. Their recollections and stories were enormously helpful, and their love and encouragement, in every challenge I've ever undertaken, is one of the great foundations of my life. Gwyn also read several drafts of this manuscript, and offered brilliant insights. And I am eternally grateful to Franklin Lurie, my father. His patience, support, and concern for my mother throughout the course of this project, and the love and pride he has shown me every day of my life, made completing this book possible. Christopher Gilbert, my stepson, proofread my manuscript from beginning to end, not once but twice, each time giving me the confidence to hit the "send" key on my computer, and deliver the manuscript. He also beautifully edited the cover photograph and managed to fit as many names as possible on our family tree. Where words about him may be sparse in this memoir, his importance in my life is immeasurable. I also cannot express the magnitude of my gratitude to the lights of my life, my children, Gabriel and Mikaela, for their patience, interest, and unwavering love, as year bled into year on this manuscript. Leaving them a legacy of answers and a model of resilience against all odds is what kept me at work on this long after others might have said "good enough."

To no one do I owe more thanks than to Cliff, the love of my life. Over countless weekends, he kept our household afloat while I sat holed up in my office, writing and rewriting. Then he spent treasured days on our vacations editing these chapters that dealt with neither wine, stamps, nor astronomy. Cliff encouraged me to keep going and never doubted (at least when I was within earshot) that this book would see the light of day.

I am eternally grateful to my great friends, Paul Cummins, Rabbi Laura Geller, Amy Gordon, Yadin Kaufmann, Leslye Louie, Rick Tuttle, Rabbi Stewart Vogel, and Dick Wolf, each of whom gave me detailed, insightful, and brutally honest notes which made their way into the book. Amy Gordon also took the beautiful photograph which became the book's cover. Thank you also to Donna Bojarsky, Susan Derwin, Les Firestein, Gayle Gilbert-Hammerling, Ann Hollister, Leila Lurie, Eric Myers, Debbie Porter, Barbara Riegelhaupt, Dov Seidman, Shelley Eisinger Stark, Lynne Wahl, and Zev and Barbara Yaroslavsky for your encouragement and support at critical times in this project. And finally, I am deeply appreciative to two newer friends, Lyle Hurst and Dr. Frank Dines, who were also extremely helpful to me in this endeavor. Neither of them knew me when I began this project. Out of sheer kindness and generosity, and with a great deal of insight, each played a critical role in helping me to shape my thoughts and ideas. And I also want to thank Tim Bergstrom and Molly Messmer, for the many ways you graciously assisted me along the way.

Several literary experts helped me to shape the memoir that unfolded from the stories told to me. Mark Rosin was the first to convince me that we had a powerful story, and that there was an end in sight. The encouragement and direction early on from the esteemed agent Sylvie Rabineau was also pivotal. And I owe a tremendous thank-you to Beth Lieberman, who relentlessly urged me to be more forthcoming, and to not settle for anything short of excellence in any portion of the book. Not only was her editorial advice generous and superb, but she introduced me to the best agent I could have hoped to have, Larry Kirshbaum.

I cannot thank Larry Kirshbaum enough for taking a chance on representing a first-time author with a Holocaust-themed story. His advice through every step of the process was critical. His breadth of experience in the publishing world, and the passion, wisdom, and dedication he brings to his work remains an inspiration. The warmth and friendship Larry extended to my entire family, is a gift for which I am deeply grateful.

Another huge thank-you goes to Pam Golum, who lovingly guided me in matters of publicity from the sidelines, before there was even a publisher or a completed manuscript. And then to Sandi Mendelson and Judy Hilsinger and Fauzia and John Burke, thank you for all of your superb guidance. I also want to thank Peter Guzzardi, who got me to say all I wanted in far fewer words. Not only did I learn so much from working with him, but hearing his warm, calm, and upbeat voice on the other end of the phone line was something to which I very much came to look forward.

Finally, I am deeply grateful to Claire Wachtel, my editor at Harper-Collins. I am so thankful that she recognized the uniqueness of Mom's experience and the potential for inspiration in our multi-generational story. Claire not only believed in our book and offered encouragement and the sagest of advice all along the way, but she also always made me feel that I had the enthusiasm and support of all of HarperCollins. For that support, from Tina Andreadis, Rachel Elinsky, Julia Novitch, and particularly from Jonathan Burnham, I offer my final and most humble thank-you.

Rita's Acknowledgements

Thank you to my daughter Leslie (my partner in this endeavor), without whose constant encouragement and love I could not have hung in there.

To my husband, Frank, my life partner, lover, and constant source of support, thank you for being there through every day of this journey.

To my daughter, Gwyn, thank you for your love and companionship and to my son, David, even though you live farther away, I always feel your love in my heart.

To my sister, Sandra, I am grateful to have you as my big sister, and for the time we get to spend together. To my cousins, Sally, Miriam, and Lola, thank you for your generosity and assistance to us in writing this book. I am so glad to have you in my life. To my brothers Brad and Sam, thank you for participating in this book, even when you knew that we would see some things differently. Although we have not spent enough time together, I always love you.

Thank you to my wonderful sons-in-law, Cliff and Les. Cliff's warmth and love of life were a source of comfort all along the way, and Les's sense of humor, well that's another story.

To all of my grandchildren, Noa, Sydney, Elijah, Zoe, Mikaela, Gabriel, and Chris, I love each and every one of you and life would sure be dull without you.